Thinking Critically About

CHILD
DEVELOPMENT

Third Edition

To the memory of the great developmental scientist Gilbert Gottlieb (1929–2006) and for Andrew, Sean, Jack, and Teagan (the little rosebud)

Thinking Critically About

CHILD

DEVELOPMENT

Examining Myths and Misunderstandings

Third Edition

JEAN MERCER
Stockton University

Los Angeles | London | New Delhi
Singapore | Washington DC

Los Angeles | London | New Delhi
Singapore | Washington DC

FOR INFORMATION:

SAGE Publications, Inc.
2455 Teller Road
Thousand Oaks, California 91320
E-mail: order@sagepub.com

SAGE Publications Ltd.
1 Oliver's Yard
55 City Road
London, EC1Y 1SP
United Kingdom

SAGE Publications India Pvt. Ltd.
B 1/I 1 Mohan Cooperative Industrial Area
Mathura Road, New Delhi 110 044
India

SAGE Publications Asia-Pacific Pte. Ltd.
3 Church Street
#10-04 Samsung Hub
Singapore 049483

Acquisitions Editor: Lara Parra
Editorial Assistant: Morgan McCardell
Associate Editor: Nathan Davidson
Production Editor: Kelly DeRosa
Copy Editor: Diana Breti
Typesetter: Hurix Systems Pvt. Ltd.
Proofreader: Ellen Brink
Indexer: Mary Mortensen
Cover Designer: Gail Buschman
Marketing Manager: Shari Countryman

Printed in the United States of America

*Library of Congress Cataloging-in-Publication
Data Mercer, Jean.*

[Child development.]

Critical thinking in child development : myths,
mistakes, and misunderstandings / Jean Mercer,
The Richard Stockton College of New Jersey.—
Third Edition.

pages cm

Includes bibliographical references and index.

ISBN 978-1-4833-7009-5 (pbk. : alk. paper)
1. Child development. I. Mercer, Jean. Child
development. II. Title.

HQ771.M47 2015

305.231—dc23   2015012472

This book is printed on acid-free paper.

15 16 17 18 19 10 9 8 7 6 5 4 3 2 1

Contents

Part V: Adolescents 255

Acknowledgments

The author and SAGE Publications gratefully acknowledge the contributions of the following reviewers:

Mary Beth Ahlum, *Nebraska Wesleyan University*

Margaret Hayes Annunziata, *Davidson County Community College*

Christia Spears Brown, *University of Kentucky*

Catherine L. Caldwell-Harris, *Boston University*

Maria A. James, PhD, *South Carolina State University*

Jeffrey Liew, *Texas A&M University*

Patty O'Grady, PhD, *University of Tampa*

Ariane K. Schratter, *Maryville College*

LaShorage Shaffer, *University of Michigan-Dearborn*

Jennifer M. Zosh, *Pennsylvania State University, Brandywine*

About the Author

Jean Mercer (PhD, Psychology, Brandeis University), professor emerita of Psychology at Stockton University, has taught undergraduate courses on developmental psychology, infant development, statistics, and research methods for 30 years. A past president of the New Jersey Association for Infant Mental Health and a fellow of the Commission for Scientific Medicine and Mental Health, she has written a general interest book about early emotional development, *Understanding Attachment* (Praeger, 2006), and a textbook, *Infant Development: A Multidisciplinary Introduction* (Brooks/Cole, 1998). Her most recent publication is *Alternative Psychotherapies: Evaluating Unconventional Mental Health Treatments* (Rowman & Littlefield, 2014), an exploration of "crazy therapies" for both adults and children. She served as an expert witness in the trial of a mother who kept her adopted children in cages and claimed she had a book advising this—a good example of failure to think straight about child development. A member of APA Division 37 (Society for Child and Family Policy and Practice), she writes a blog, "Childmyths," at http://childmyths.blogspot.com.

SAGE was founded in 1965 by Sara Miller McCune to support the dissemination of usable knowledge by publishing innovative and high-quality research and teaching content. Today, we publish more than 850 journals, including those of more than 300 learned societies, more than 800 new books per year, and a growing range of library products including archives, data, case studies, reports, and video. SAGE remains majority-owned by our founder, and after Sara's lifetime will become owned by a charitable trust that secures our continued independence.

Los Angeles | London | New Delhi | Singapore | Washington DC

Introduction

Although this book contains a lot of information about child development, it is not a textbook that provides a thorough overview of the field. Instead, it is written as a supplementary text, with the assumption that readers have access to a standard textbook or to other sources of information about children and adolescents. The purpose of the book is to guide students to use critical thinking about child development issues. To that end, the book provides a variety of essays discussing common mistaken beliefs and confusions about development, each one followed by a series of questions that require not only knowledge of facts but also critical thinking skills.

This Introduction will discuss common critical thinking issues that crop up when people talk about child development. To answer some of the questions about the essays, readers will need to understand some components of critical thinking as they will be described here (so it is not a good idea to skip the Introduction as people often do!). In addition, the Introduction will address some of the reasons why the study of child development can be especially fraught with critical thinking problems and why students of this topic—prospective teachers, psychologists, social workers, or just plain parents—need to have excellent critical thinking skills.

Critical Thinking

Students may well yawn when the idea of critical thinking is pressed upon them. Many readers of this book have been asked to do "critical thinking" exercises as far back as elementary school, but on the whole their experiences have simply been of exercises that asked them to go beyond the information they already had, not necessarily in a logical or critical way. Unfortunately, when we look at common secondary school experiences of the last couple of decades, we see that some of these may diminish rather than foster critical thinking abilities.

1

Some years ago, the novelist Francine Prose (1999) examined efforts toward critical thinking used in high school English textbooks. In her article, aptly named "I Know Why the Caged Bird Cannot Read," she noted a failure to require close, line-by-line reading and a tendency to ask questions about social or moral implications rather than about the actual content of the novel. Prose referred to one teacher's manual that asked students reading *Huckleberry Finn* to count the ways in which Mark Twain negated the humanity of the slave character, Jim, rather than asking them to compare the number of such incidents with the number in which his humanity was witnessed. Prose also noted the frequency of assignments in which questions asked were only peripherally relevant to the information available to the student. For example, students might be asked questions whose answers they would be unlikely to know, such as a question about the mental health prognosis of the heroine of *The Bell Jar*. Assignments of these types discourage a focus on recognizing relevant, available information and encourage the view that all possible answers (if long enough) are acceptable. College students who have experienced high school assignments of the kind Prose described are likely to feel comfortable with irrelevancies, low levels of abstraction, and assignments that provide insufficient information, and even to believe that they are excellent critical thinkers because of their handling of such matters.

What Is Critical Thinking?

If the critical thinking assignments you did in high school, or even in some college courses, did not actually involve critical thinking, what in the world *is* the critical thinking that this book will ask you to do? One definition, offered by a group that exists to encourage critical thinking as part of education, is as follows: "Critical thinking is the intellectually disciplined process of actively and skillfully conceptualizing, applying, analyzing, synthesizing, and/or evaluating information . . . . It is based on universal intellectual values that transcend subject matter divisions: clarity, accuracy, precision, consistency, relevance, sound evidence, good reasons, depth, breadth, and fairness" ("Defining Critical Thinking," 2013).

This sounds like a great deal to ask of any student, so let's look at some of the factors that may seem more doable. Critical thinking is *active*; it's not just a matter of absorbing and reflecting back pieces of information, so it can take time and energy. Critical thinking is *evaluative*; it involves assessing the evidence for claimed facts and the reasoning by which they are related to each other and to conclusions. Critical thinking examines the *relevance* of information to conclusions and rejects conclusions based on facts that may be correct but have nothing to do with the issue.

How Do You Think Critically?

Achievement of critical thinking skills is a lifetime's work. No one succeeds in applying good critical thinking skills to every problem, every day. But we can learn how to do this important job by dealing with two issues.

First, in order to do a good job of critical thinking, we have to be as sure as possible that we are thinking about valid information. Without trustworthy facts, our application of thinking skills is not worth much. This is why *evaluation* is an important part of critical thinking. Students of child development need to learn some specialized skills for assessment of information, and those skills will be discussed later in this Introduction.

Second, if we want to think critically, we need to recognize some common *fallacies*, or errors of reasoning. We need to be able to see when other people are reasoning fallaciously, but it's even more important to be able to check our own reasoning for fallacies. Many authors have created lists of fallacies to watch out for, and the study of fallacies has become a topic of its own. Fortunately, not all of these fallacies are common in the study of child development, so we can limit the useful fallacy list to a relatively small number.

Fallacies to Watch for When Studying Child Development

Analogies and Metaphors

Analogies and metaphors are useful thinking techniques that compare two different things by showing the ways in which they are similar. These techniques are helpful in teaching about development, as many developmental events are difficult to observe directly or occur over long periods of time. The problem with analogies and metaphors is that although they may be used to convey ideas, they cannot in themselves establish an argument or support an inference. One problem is that they fail to note how the two things are different. Analogies can be abused as well as used, and such abuse leads to fallacious conclusions.

Common analogies. Here are some common analogies and metaphors used in the study of development: (1) "stages" or "milestones" of development; (2) the term *attachment* or *bond* to describe an attitude toward another person; (3) brain/cortical/hand/gene "dominance" (use of this metaphor may be one reason why it is so difficult for students to define dominant and recessive genes); (4) "regression" (not the statistical kind); (5) the term "sexual" in the description of psychosexual stages of development. These comparisons may be extremely valuable for teaching purposes, but their downside is the fallacious assumption that phenomena with some things in common will have everything in common.

Easily abused analogies. In the study of development, one common instance of abuse of analogies involves fallacious reasoning from aspects of nonhuman development to aspects of human development. For example, John Bowlby's application of ethological concepts of imprinting in birds to human attachment abused an analogy, and fortunately it was rejected after some consideration by developmental scientists. But this type of critical thinking error is still with us, and not in textbooks alone. For example, an article in the APA *Monitor on Psychology* (Price, 2009) titled "Programmed for Life?" has a subhead stating that "your developmental environment can undercut your memory, give it a boost, or possibly even predict how you'll treat your children," but the reported study deals with factors influencing how much mice lick and groom their pups.

Affirming the Consequent and Other Forms of Transductive Reasoning

If you have not already read about Piaget's work on early cognitive development, you are bound to meet this topic as you study children and adolescents. Piaget's discussion of early childhood cognition included a description of *transductive* reasoning, a form of primitive logic in which a child assumes that when two events share some characteristics, they are likely to share others, including a cause-and-effect relationship that may work in either direction. Piaget's famous example of this was a situation in which his daughter, given a cup of orange-colored chamomile tea, insisted that a green orange she wanted must have become ripe and attained the color that meant she could eat it. Unfortunately, we adults are not entirely immune to transductive reasoning, and when we use it, our reasoning can also involve fallacies.

Affirming the consequent. This fallacy or error in critical thinking involves the practice of assuming that the converse, or reverse order, of a claimed condition is true. For example, let's take the following statement:

> If a child has Reactive Attachment Disorder, she has lived in an orphanage or under similar conditions. [This is true, as the list of criteria for the Reactive

Attachment Disorder diagnosis includes the experiences that seem to have caused the disorder.]

The converse of the statement is the following:

If a child has lived in an orphanage (or under similar conditions), she has Reactive Attachment Disorder. [This claim is made on a number of Internet sites.]

To assume that this converse statement is true—without requiring other evidence—is to *affirm the consequent*.

Denying the antecedent. This critical thinking error involves the assumption that if a positively stated claim is true, a negative statement (the obverse) can also be assumed to be true, without further evidence. For example, here is a common (although questionable) claim:

If a toddler carries a blanket around, it means he feels insecure without it.

Here is the obverse of the claim:

A toddler does not feel insecure [without a blanket] if he does not carry a blanket around (and therefore, taking the blanket away is a cure for insecurity).

Other Fallacies in Discussions of Child Development

Although fallacies that involve analogies are a real problem for critical thinking about child development, they are not the only fallacies students need to be able to identify. Here is a list of other problems you need to watch out for:

1. The fundamental attribution error: Although this mistake is not often listed as a fallacy, students of all aspects of psychology are warned against the error of assuming without good evidence that a person's behavior is caused entirely by his or her own individual characteristics, rather than being influenced by past or present situational factors that can range from number of brothers and sisters to being in a frightening physical environment. Of course, it is possible that some problems are entirely the result of personal characteristics, but it is a mistake to think this without good evidence. The fundamental attribution error can include the idea that behaviors occur because an individual wants their outcomes, at either a conscious or an unconscious level, even though he or she seems unhappy with the result.

2. The irrelevant conclusion: When the information used to draw a conclusion has nothing to do with the conclusion, fallacious thinking is at work. For example, it may be a mistake to assume that because parents of a delinquent adolescent claim membership in a strict religious organization, their parenting behavior is therefore not a factor in their child's situation.

3. *Post hoc, ergo propter hoc* fallacy: This common error is a matter of assuming that if Event B occurred after Event A, B must have been caused by A, rather than by one or all other earlier events. The post hoc fallacy is important to the study of child development because so many developmental issues involve questions about early causes and possible confusions between the effects of experiences and of biologically based maturational changes.

4. *Argumentum ad hominem*: In this fallacy, weaknesses of an individual or of his or her work are used to evaluate entire systems. For example, a discussion of economics on National Public Radio began with some of the less attractive personal characteristics of the economist John Maynard Keynes, and one discussant expressed surprise that the country was turning to such a person for solution of its economic difficulties. In psychology, Piaget's observations of his own children are sometimes presented as a reason to dismiss his entire theory of cognitive development; J. B. Watson's questionable treatment of "little Albert" and his ill-judged advice about parenting are seen as arguments against behaviorism; Lawrence Kohlberg's suicide is taken to mean that his work on moral development is worthless. In popular discussions, personal experiences may be taken to be supportive evidence for claims—for example, in Internet discussions of adoption, statements by nonadopted persons may be dismissed as meaningless.

5. Overgeneralization: This fallacy involves assuming without evidence that experiences or characteristics of one group must be very similar to those of another group. For example, adults may think that because they would dislike the experience a baby has during birth, the baby must also dislike it. Or, they may assume that because a toddler cries and is frightened when separated from her mother, a newborn baby will have the same feelings.

This list of fallacies that interfere with critical thinking is an incomplete one, but it provides student readers with names for some basic problems that contribute to the misunderstandings of child development that are a focus of this book.

Claims About Child Development

Everyone has some knowledge about children because everyone has been a child. Most people have also observed other children and have heard adults talking about children. As a result, students arrive in a child development course with a lot of background knowledge, not as the "blank slates" they would be for a course in Russian, introductory physics, or the Victorian novel.

Students entering a child development or developmental psychology course bring more than observed facts with them. All of us have *theories* of child development based on our observations, the connections among these observations, and the ideas we have picked up in school or social settings. For example, almost every person has a way to explain juvenile delinquency—and chooses either genetics or family experiences as the cause. These explanations come from individuals' theories about child development. Very few people can state their theories in words, but the theories are there, and they exert a strong influence on expectations about development.

So far, this sounds like a good arrangement. Students come to study child development, not "from scratch" but with some knowledge and thoughts already in place. How can this not be good? The answer is this: Not all past observations are completely accurate, and not all theories are good descriptions of the rules of development. In other words, people can "know" a great deal that cannot be substantiated by systematic research. As is often the case, the problem is not what students don't know but what they know that isn't true. Most people who study developmental psychology find that they need to examine their own beliefs and assumptions, throw out some of what they've always thought, and make way for information supported by good evidence. If your old assumptions are in conflict with new information, you may not thoroughly understand or remember the new information.

Surprisingly, people who have their own children already do not necessarily have more accurate information than beginning students do. A survey of parents conducted by one of the premier associations for education about early development, Zero to Three, showed that parents performed especially poorly on understanding of social and emotional development (DYG, Inc., 2000). The power of old, inaccurate information is a real problem for everyone who needs to know about child development.

This book consists of a series of essays on common but inaccurate claims and beliefs about childhood growth and development. These essays serve to call students' attention to the assumptions they bring to a child development or developmental psychology course. Careful examination of your own assumptions—the "facts" that everybody knows but that may not be true—is an exercise that can help prepare you to understand some important issues in the study of development. You will find that the examination process is important because of the complexity of the modern view of developmental change. As is frequently noted among developmentalists, developmental psychology isn't rocket science; it's a lot more complicated than that. When material is complicated, one has to be especially careful to resist falling back on "what everybody knows."

Types of Mistaken Claims

Naturally, not all incorrect claims about child development are of the same type. A range of inaccuracies exists, from completely invalid ideas to incorrect conclusions drawn from correct information.

Some beliefs about development are so far off base that one can call them *myths*—ideas that are so far from what research evidence shows that they are essentially superstitions. To use an example from another topic, most cultures have creation myths, which are old stories that explain the origin of the world. Although the stories are interesting and enjoyable to hear, they do not stand up well to close examination. One story tells of an anthropologist who questioned a person who believed the world rested on the back of a giant turtle. The anthropologist asked, "And what's under that?" The person replied, "Another turtle." The anthropologist repeated the question and received the same reply. After the anthropologist's repeated questioning, the exasperated informant declared, "It's turtles, turtles, turtles, all the way down!" Myths about child development do not stand up to examination any better than the "turtles, turtles, turtles" explanation, but nevertheless these myths are so deeply entrenched in U.S. culture that they are not easily dismissed. For example, the belief that children learn moral values by experiencing punishment for mistakes is generally accepted, but it is probably not correct, nor is the idea that learning right from wrong is a simple matter.

Some erroneous beliefs about child development are *mistakes*, which are based on errors in research design or conclusions, leading to much-publicized statements that are difficult to correct. For example, in the early days of crack cocaine use, statements about the terrible problems of "crack babies" were common, but later work showed that good environments and early intervention corrected many of the difficulties the babies might have had as a result of prenatal drug exposure.

Some erroneous claims are based on a *misunderstanding* of complex issues and are often related to mistakes in the definition of words. Ideas involving the use of the terms *bonding* and *attachment* are often good examples of such beliefs. As an essay in this book shows, people who make claims about bonding and attachment often assume meanings for these terms that are different from their technical use. These claimants also often believe measurement of these behaviors is easy and the discovery of all of the factors involved in emotional development is uncomplicated.

Some erroneous beliefs are related to *missing information.* Strange though it may seem, researchers are still very far from having all of the basic data that will show people how development proceeds. For example, it is common to hear explanations for child behavior couched in the term *brain development,* but in fact there is very little information about normal brain development or how it relates to behavioral and cognitive change. At the time of this writing, research related to this concept of brain development is being conducted by studying developmental changes in 500 typical children (Waber et al., 2007). Also, though we may hear "it's genetic" or "it's in the DNA" as explanations for children's behavior and cognition, we need to remember that there are many questions to answer about the role of genetics in development.

"Seductive Ideas"

In the late 1990s, a leading developmental psychologist, Jerome Kagan, published a book with the intriguing title *Three Seductive Ideas.* Although Kagan's book is not quite as juicy as its title suggests—these ideas would not be much help if you wanted to seduce someone—*Three Seductive Ideas* addresses some important issues for our consideration of child development claims. Seductive ideas, according to Kagan, are assumptions that are so attractive to people that they quickly give the ideas credence and fail to give them the examination they require. They are ideas that people respond to with an immediate "yes, of course" and can confuse an examination of claims about child development. Kagan referred to one of his seductive ideas as the love of abstraction. *Abstraction* is a necessary tool for forging an understandable conclusion out of many pieces of information, but it can prove dangerous when people abstract excessive simplicity out of complication and are thus unable to tell the difference between two events. Humans care for their offspring, and ducks care for their ducklings: People can abstract from these facts a simplified statement about maternal care. But how important are the details that were lost? Can people make conclusions about human caregiving by studying ducks with their ducklings? In examining claims about child development, people need to notice whether supportive material comes from studies of another species and decide whether a claim is acceptable. Our tendency to pursue abstraction can make this difficult to do.

A second seductive idea discussed by Kagan is one of enormous importance for the study of child development: *infant determinism,* which is the assumption that experiences in the first few years of life are of overwhelming importance and cannot easily have their impact altered or corrected by later events. It is possible that this idea is true, but it is presently a seductive idea rather than a well-supported principle. Again, examination of claims about development should check for the presence of the assumption of infant determinism and consider that conclusions drawn directly from this assumption may not have a solid basis in fact.

Adults may also find their thinking "seduced" by the assumption of *adultomorphism*, a made-up word based on *anthropomorphism*, or the assumption that animals think and feel as humans do. *Adultomorphism* is the assumption that infants, children, and adolescents share the motives and abilities of adults. Adults holding this assumption feel they are able to understand child development issues on the basis of their own experiences, without examining the facts of child development. At best, adultomorphism confuses students; at worst, of course, it can lead to child abuse by adults who assume that a child is able to obey any adult command and refuses to do so only out of malicious opposition. Professional research reports rarely involve adultomorphic thinking, but claims made by nonprofessional life coaches and parent educators may be based on adultomorphism.

Why Is It All So Complicated?

Intuitively, people expect young children's lives to be explained by simple factors and uncomplicated connections and expect only a bit more complexity for adolescents. (At the same time, adults think their own lives are so full of complications that no one can appreciate them.) This expectation is a mistake, of course. If anything, children's lives are governed by more complex rules than those of adults because the rapid physical and mental changes of childhood are factors in themselves, beyond the experiences and hereditary factors that are more obvious. In this section, I comment on some other issues that contribute to the complexity of child development and can slow students' understanding.

Understanding Basic Facts

As I pointed out earlier in this introduction, critical thinking skills are not much help unless they have valid information to work on. Before you can evaluate statements about child development, you must have some understanding of developmental facts. Those facts may be quite different about one aspect of development than they are about another; for example, development of speech will proceed along different lines from development of moral judgment. This means that we can't just "study development" but must study with care the aspects of development that are most related to the problem we are dealing with. This needs to be done systematically, with the attention to detail and line-by-line reading essential to critical thinking. One useful systematic approach, suggested years ago by Everett Waters (Waters, Kondo-Ikemura, Posada, & Richters, 1991), but rarely mentioned in a teaching context, involves a set of five questions that can be applied to any developmental topic and that help to organize thinking and to stress "what's important." The helpful organizing questions are these:

1. *What develops?* That is, what aspect of the phenomenon under consideration actually changes with age, and in what way does it change?

2. *What are the rate and pattern of development?* How quickly or slowly does change occur? Is change gradual and continuous, or are there periods of rapid change and other periods with little or no change in this particular phenomenon?

3. *What are the mechanisms of development?* What actually causes these specific developmental changes to occur? Does it depend on genetic characteristics of the individual or species? Does the environment directly cause change? Or is there some interaction between the two, as when the environment guides the direction of developmental change that is caused genetically? Does the environment have an effect only at certain periods in development?

4. *Are there normal individual differences in this aspect of development?* Is it to be expected that there will be variation on this factor among a large group of healthy individuals, or does atypicality indicate that an individual is at risk for developmental problems?

5. *Are there predictable population differences in this aspect of development?* Are there differences between populations (e.g., boys and girls) in the amount of developmental change, its speed or pattern, its variability, or its causes?

If you can answer these questions accurately about some aspect of development—whether it's physical growth or gender identity—the chances are that you understand the facts well enough to go ahead and apply critical thinking methods to a related question.

Values and Political Goals

An important complicating problem in the understanding of child development is that some of our beliefs are guided by *values* and others by *political goals*. As is the case in many areas of life, our thoughts about child development are affected as much by how we want things to be as by what they actually are.

The values connected with child development issues are powerful. They include the status and obligations of men and women, the importance of obedience and independence, and the relative values of the immediate family and the community. The duties and entitlements of boys versus those of girls, as well as the duties and entitlements assigned to minority versus majority populations, are part of our value system. With respect to infants and sick or injured older children, important values include the importance of quality of life versus life itself. Unfortunately, in the universal situation of limited resources, the needs of children are often compared to the needs of the elderly, and values help people determine which group is given more. Further, beliefs about how life should be—equity as a measure of fairness, for instance—may help to determine expectations about similarities or differences between groups of people (boys and girls, perhaps). An individual's commitment to any of these values helps to determine the questions he or she asks and the answers he or she accepts about aspects of development.

Although values play a strong role in guiding individual thoughts, it is important to remember that groups of people share values that help determine their political goals, which in turn help to determine the group's actions regarding children, such as a vote on school funding. Values also make it likely that the group will emphasize beliefs about children that are congruent with their goals. Political organizations may feel little need to present all relevant information when making a decision affecting children but instead may choose to work with myths, misunderstandings, or partial truths that predispose others to agree with them. The existence of political goals can influence discussion of research evidence, as was seen some years ago in the books *The Bell Curve* (Herrnstein & Murray, 1994) and *The Myth of the First Three Years* (Bruer, 2002). These popular books discussed the effects of genetics versus early childhood experience on children's school performance and contributed to arguments about the appropriateness of funding for early childhood and other school programs.

The study of child development has probably never been a "pure" science. For example, developmentalists may be interested in certain issues because the issues are related to programs to improve children's physical and mental health. In fact, value-based decisions are a major way of deciding what is an improvement and what is not. The book *Science in the Service of Children* (Smuts, 2006) describes how the developmental sciences came out of a combination of ideals, scientific and otherwise. Does this mean that the study of child development is vague and subjective in nature? Is it an immature science or one with inadequate methods (Cahan, 2007)? No, but the role played by values in the study of child development is so strong that one must be careful to evaluate what is really so and what is simply how people think things should be.

Variations on the Developmental Theme

Individual Differences

The complexity that must be faced before one understands child development is only partly a matter of values and politics. The facts about development are complicated. The common term *average child* is confusing shorthand that means that any group of children will contain individuals who are quite different from each other. People can accurately say they know a child whose measurable characteristics are equivalent to the mathematical average of the measurements of all children in a group, but in fact we can average only numbers, not children. Paradoxically, a group may not include any child whose measured characteristics are exactly the same as the average child, that hypothetical person who has measurements equivalent to the average taken from every child's measurements.

In child development, perhaps even more than in adult life, individual differences are key, and understanding the extent of those differences is vital in understanding how development progresses. The term that describes the extent of individual differences is *variability*. (This word applies to other kinds of difference, too, but those are discussed later.) Without getting too deeply into statistics, there are quantitative measures of variability, such as standard deviation or variance. These statistics are ways of stating the amount of variability in a group, just as the average or mean is a way of stating the number that best describes the whole group.

Information about children often states the average measurement (e.g., IQ) in a group but less frequently gives a measurement of variability. However, knowledge of variability provides greater insight into the nature of a group and helps in making good decisions. Take, for example, a decision about giving resources to two groups of needy babies, if you can give money to one group only. The average weight of both groups is six pounds, which is within the normal range. But what if one group had very low variability in weight, with all of the babies weighing about the same? And what if the other group had very high variability, with half of the babies weighing only three pounds and the other half weighing about nine pounds? When you have this information about variability, it's easy to see that the group with the very small babies needs more help, even though both groups have the same average weight.

Individual differences may be brought about by different events in the environment, by hereditary factors, or by a combination of the two. In the highly variable group of babies described previously, the small babies may have had small parents, they may have been born prematurely, or a combination of factors, such as a small mother receiving poor nutrition during pregnancy, may have affected the birth weights. The description of individual differences identifies only the variation, not why it occurs, although the "why" is also an important issue.

The existence of a great deal of variability and individual differences in children's development is one of the reasons our casual observations cannot give us a very good idea of what children are all about. Especially in today's small families, people have limited opportunities to observe anyone's development except their own. As it happens, a small sample of people chosen out of a large population (all children in the world) may not resemble the large population at all closely. In fact, in choosing a small sample, we may accidentally come up with a group of people who are dramatically different from others. Our own observations may be helpful in providing us with vivid stories and examples, but they will not necessarily help us avoid myths and other mistakes.

Population Differences and Diversity

The issue of diversity is another aspect of variability. The term *diversity* means variation, really, but today the term is used primarily to refer to the importance of considering ethnic differences. Discussion of diversity often focuses on the consideration of everyone's needs and tolerance and encouragement of ethnic differences, such as those of speech, dress, or religious practice. In terms of the study of child development, however, the concept of diversity should also mean that people base their understanding on information from many different types of human beings, rather than assuming that one group can represent the world's total population. Although it may seem to some students politically incorrect to suggest that developmental events can be different for different ethnic groups, this is the case, and to ignore the fact is to risk unfair and inappropriate treatment of some groups of children. Diversity and its implications involve a form of variability based on population (group) differences, not on individual differences. Such variability may be based on genetic differences between groups or on experiential factors, such as diet or health care, or, in some cases, on a combination of both. Once again, describing variations does not immediately explain them.

Age Differences

The concept of variability is a useful way to think about the most-studied aspect of childhood: developmental change. Whether considering physical growth, sexual maturation, cognitive advancement, or emotional change, when talking about development, people are talking about variation among age groups. Older children as a group are taller than younger children, and younger children as a group are more emotional than older children. We designate a course as a child development, developmental psychology, or developmental science course because its basic focus is on variations that go along with age. Developmental change may be caused by genetic factors, by experience, or by a combination of the two, but it accompanies changes in chronological age. Note that this last sentence does not say development is *caused* by age; age cannot cause anything except perhaps permission to get a driver's license. Factors such as experience and maturation (the result of genetic commands) cause developmental change. Because these factors accompany age changes, it is easy to forget that they are separate from chronological age.

Examining the Evidence: Recognizing That a Belief May Be Mistaken

Most questions about child development involve one of the forms of variability just discussed and may include considerations about why variability occurs and the form it takes. These questions may be answered by references to myths, misunderstandings, or seductive ideas, or the answers may be derived from systematic research. The assumption of this book is that a better understanding of child development comes from systematic investigations of the facts rather than myths or unexamined ways of thinking. But how do we examine beliefs about child development? How can we decide whether a statement about development deserves our confidence or not? Myths and misunderstandings do not come neatly labeled and, where these beliefs are widespread, the situation may be very confusing.

Defining Terms

Of all of the steps necessary to examine a statement about child development, the first is probably the simple matter of defining terms. Many terms used in discussing development lead people to say "I can't define it, but I know it when I see it." Unfortunately, this is not good enough, because vague definitions or guesses make it impossible for people to use words to communicate information. In addition, many words used to describe children's characteristics, such as *aggression, autism,* or *independence,* carry their own value messages that may be interpreted differently by different listeners. The meaning assigned to some terms may be influenced by movies or other media presentations—an example is the movie *Rain Man,* which has a near monopoly on most people's definition of autism. Words with strong value and emotional implications, such as *bonding* and *attachment,* are not often used with their technical definitions in general conversation or in media presentations.

Care in using words about child development is essential to communication and has significance for practical decision making. A jury that makes a decision about *attachment* should know what the word means or their deliberations may not be at all to the point. Children and families can be affected for good or ill by accurate or inaccurate use of words. As stated in one discussion of this issue, "If our careless, underspecified choice of words inadvertently does damage to future generations of children, we cannot turn with innocent outrage to the judge and say, 'But your honor, I didn't realize the word was loaded'" (Elman et al., 1998, p. 391).

One way to examine a statement about child development is to check the definitions of the words used. Do the stated or implied definitions match the way other sources define the terms? Do the authors at least discuss the issue, perhaps saying that they intend to use a term with a slightly different meaning than is common? If there is no discussion, and if the meanings do not seem to jibe with the technical definitions typically used in professional materials, it would be wise to question the reasoning involved. Particular caution should be used when a condition or characteristic is frequently referred to by an abbreviation, such as ADHD (attention deficit hyperactivity disorder) or RAD (reactive attachment disorder). Using these abbreviated forms saves time, but it can also lead both speaker and listener to assign to the condition some qualities that the condition is not usually considered to have. This *criterion creep,* or slow change in definitions, results in conclusions that are not necessarily justified by the evidence.

Developmentally Appropriate Practice

The term *developmentally appropriate practice* refers primarily to the use of procedures that are beneficial to a particular age group of children. For example, caregivers should frequently pick up and carry infants. A 6-year-old, on the other hand, does not need this type of care and would probably be very annoyed if subjected to it. For our purposes in this book, the concept of *developmentally appropriate practice* is a reminder that information collected from one age group may or may not explain anything about the characteristics of other age groups. A belief formed from information about adolescents and generalized to preschoolers, or vice versa, may be legitimate, but caution should be used. One must examine the information carefully and decide, on a case-by-case basis, the appropriateness of the generalization. For example, people often speak of dementia in the elderly as a "second childhood," but in reality the cognitive losses of dementia do not cause the individual to think as a young child does. Such comparisons and confusions may lead to inappropriate conclusions, as when a frustrated and distressed school-age child is regarded as "a big baby."

Where Did the Information Come From?

Definitions and developmental concepts can be clues to mistaken conclusions about child development, but the most significant question relates to the way information was collected and analyzed—the research design. Systematic investigations of child development can lead to reliable information and permit valid conclusions. What conclusions are permitted depends on the research design, so examination of a claim needs to include examination of the sources of the information. The lengthy, detailed research reports one finds in professional journals are lengthy and detailed for precisely this reason: They allow readers to examine the background of the information that led to a conclusion.

Understanding how a study was carried out is essential for most questions about child development, but in no case is it more important than for studies of interventions, which are defined as any procedure or treatment used to assist or improve development. Interventions for children may include psychotherapy; educational programs, such as specialized reading approaches; dietary improvements, such as the sale of fruit instead of candy in school lunchrooms; or sex education programs, whether abstinence focused or otherwise. Conclusions about the effectiveness of interventions have enormous practical significance, both in terms of the children helped and in terms of the allocation of resources to programs or localities. Understanding the systematic research used to test an intervention is an essential step toward concluding whether the intervention is, or is not, effective. Concern about the evidentiary basis of treatments is of great importance in clinical psychology today, and authors commenting about clinical issues have provided important ways to think about various childhood interventions.

Anecdotes and Testimonials

Statements about child development that are based on personal experience should be taken for exactly what they are—a description of a single experience—and should not be generalized to other children. A story about a specific child is interesting and valuable as a story about an individual. However, it is impossible to determine how typical the child is of children in general—or to judge the uniqueness of the child compared with other children—from reading an anecdote or a testimonial. Unfortunately, readers can be easily distracted by the vivid details of a personal story and assume that there is more meaning in the anecdote than there is in "dry" statistics, but the truth is the opposite (Stanovich, 2003). Stories can be valuable ways for students to imagine some flesh on the bare bones of academic description, but conclusions drawn from them must be examined with care.

Testimonials are a special type of anecdote. A testimonial is a statement given by a person who has received an intervention and feels that he or she has benefited from the treatment or program. (You will notice that testimonials never say the person thought the treatment was a waste of time.) Again, even if one assumes that the testimonial is an accurate description, it is not appropriate to conclude that everyone would have the same response to the treatment. In fact, dozens of other people may not have been helped or even may have been harmed by the intervention. Testimonials should never be taken as reliable evidence for a statement about child development, and if they are offered, other aspects of the claim should be examined carefully. The ethics codes of some professions, such as clinical social work, prohibit professionals from asking for testimonials.

What if the testimonial is your own? Is your own experience to be weighed more heavily than data gathered from a large number of other people? Are you unique, so it's not surprising that research does not seem to apply to you? Or do your contradictory experiences (if any) invalidate reports of research on other people? These are all difficult questions because there is no doubt that people intuitively feel their own experiences are the most important of all sources of information. Looking at the matter objectively and honestly, however, people need to be aware that, if a testimonial about another individual is untrustworthy, so are one's own personal stories. Like every other individual, you have much in common with the average person's experience, but you also share in the variability of the group and are thus different from the average. Research reports based on participants who are like you speak to some aspects of yourself but do not reflect every detail of individual difference. Unusual individual characteristics or experiences deserve careful study but do not usually mean that information based on a large group can be dismissed as wrong.

Systematic Investigations

Anecdotes and testimonials are based on information collected without any particular plan or design. Acceptable statements about child development need to be supported by investigating ideas systematically, following established rules, and drawing conclusions on the basis of those rules. However, there is more than one kind of systematic investigation into child development, and more than one kind of conclusion that can be drawn. An important step in examining a statement about child development is to examine the type of investigation performed and the appropriateness of the suggested conclusion.

Experimental research and randomized designs. In considering experimental designs, one needs to begin with the definition issue. Although in everyday speech people often use the word *experiment* interchangeably with *research* or *study* or *investigation,* the term *experiment* is a technical term with a specific meaning. In an experiment, a researcher can determine whether participants have one set of experiences or another and thus can compare people who have had one treatment to those who have had a different treatment, but who are similar in all other ways. (*Treatment* in this case could mean an intervention, a learning condition, a book to read, a food to eat, or any other experience.)

The researcher assigns participants *randomly* to one treatment or another. This does not mean that the researcher assigns participants on impulse; rather, random assignment involves a repeatable randomization procedure, perhaps using a random number list, and assignment to a treatment without consideration of participant characteristics or the whim of the researcher. The assumption is that there will be nothing about a participant that will make him or her more likely to get one treatment or the other, so any differences in outcome are the result of the treatments, not of preexisting characteristics of the participants. Studies of interventions that follow this pattern are sometimes called randomized controlled trials (RCTs).

Randomized designs are considered the gold standard for investigation. Because existing characteristics of participants are randomly distributed across the two groups, any differences in results (e.g., children perform better with one reading program than another) may be said to have been *caused* by the treatment, provided that the statistical differences in results are big enough. If a statement about a child development issue claims that a treatment has caused the outcome, but the design is not randomized, the reader should seriously question the conclusion. A number of the essays later in this book address this issue.

The purpose of randomization is to allow researchers to *isolate* variables and study the effects of each one independently of the others. When only one variable is being considered, participants can be randomized to two groups, each experiencing a particular level of the variable (including its presence or absence). If there are two or more variables at work, though, randomization has to be to more than two groups, each with its own combination of variables and levels. For instance, randomization of children to a group in a low-quality orphanage and a group in high-quality foster care does not isolate the variables of care method and of quality but leaves them confused with each other.

Randomized designs sound like a desirable approach to investigation, and they are—when they can be carried out. But studies of child development cannot always employ randomized designs, for several reasons. For one, some of the treatments or conditions under study are of interest precisely because they are potentially harmful. Ethical considerations prevent intentional exposure of children to harmful situations, so no matter how useful it would be to know about certain outcomes, researchers cannot find out about them in an experimental way. Second, many of the factors researchers would like to study are not under their control, and thus children cannot be randomly assigned to one group or another. For example, researchers would like to know about the effects of gender or ethnicity on a number of developmental outcomes, but boys cannot be transformed into girls or children of one ethnicity changed to another ethnicity. And, of course, the central question about child development relates to change with age, and researchers can only wait for a child's age to change, not control what age a child is.

Even where a randomized design is possible, it may not be very clear what to randomize. For example, a burning issue in schools involves bullying: Is it possible to establish effective antibullying programs? How do we find out whether or not a program is effective? Assigning individuals to treatments does not make much sense because this would mean that different children in a classroom receive different treatments, but the children affect each other, so researchers cannot know for sure whether one treatment or another was effective. What if researchers assign classrooms randomly to different treatments? These children still meet on the playground or in the neighborhood, and the treatment one group received can indirectly affect the others. What if researchers randomly assigned entire schools to treatments? This would be better in terms of conclusions but would require a large number of schools and children. The simple term *randomized design* does not seem so simple when considering specific applications. Examining these issues is essential as one tries to assess claims about child development.

Why is there such emphasis on control groups—perhaps better termed *comparison groups?* Why not just see how a group of children is doing at the beginning of the school year, make sure they receive an important educational program, and then test them again at the end of the year? This can be a reasonable approach for adults, but it is not acceptable for children, and researchers who take this approach should be questioned about their conclusions. Children continue to develop in all ways even though their experiences are limited. The process of *maturation*, or change with age caused by genetic factors, is always operating, even in severely handicapped children. Children change in the course of a school year, whether they are in a wonderful or a mediocre school, whether they spend their time herding goats or whether they are bedridden for serious medical treatment. The question is not whether children change during a treatment; children do change. The question one should ask is *how much* of the change is caused by the treatment and how much by maturation. The more rapidly change occurs at a particular point in development, the more important it is that a comparison group's progress be charted and compared to the development of a group receiving a treatment. Without such a comparison, it is all too easy to assume that any change was caused by the treatment, and without a comparison, one cannot know whether a treatment actually did harm rather than good.

Nonrandomized designs. When investigating aspects of child development, researchers can easily find themselves dealing with factors that cannot be randomized, or problems where it is not clear how to do the job of randomization. In these cases, researchers turn to *nonrandomized* approaches in which there is much less control over the many factors that can influence an outcome. This is perfectly acceptable—there is little choice in the matter, in fact—but it means that readers must be especially alert in their assessments of conclusions from the investigation.

When a randomized design is used, it is assumed that characteristics of the children are similarly organized in the two groups being compared. These characteristics (called *variables* because they can vary from person to person or over time) are not exactly the same for all participants, but one expects randomization to mean, for instance, that redheads or hockey fans are equally likely to be in either group. The only consistent difference between the groups is initially the *treatment variable*, or the condition they experience. (This is a variable because it varies from one group to the other.) If the two groups are different on the *outcome variable*, the characteristic measured (e.g., school success), and there were no other consistent differences between the groups that could have caused their outcomes to be different, then one can say that the treatment caused the outcome.

In a nonrandomized design, however, one cannot be sure that the treatments are the only differences between the groups. Therefore, it is not possible to draw a clear conclusion that a treatment caused an outcome. To make this assessment, one needs to decide whether the design was randomized or nonrandomized. If the design was nonrandomized, caution in drawing conclusions is essential. Many of the essays in this book repeat this caution.

One common nonrandomized design is a *quasi-experiment.* This term is misleading, causing some students to assume that a quasi-experiment is a type of experiment. It is not, by definition, because experiments always involve a type of randomization or a similar approach that ensures that treatment variables are not mixed with other variables. Quasi-experiments are studies in which a researcher compares outcomes for people who were nonrandomly assigned to groups. This nonrandomized assignment might mean that people assigned themselves, for instance by seeking out a certain kind of psychotherapy. Or participants may have been placed into a group by another person. For example, a mother might have decided that her shy child would benefit from camp or karate lessons, or a teacher may have wanted all the bullies in her class to be in the program she personally believed in. These are situations where characteristics of the child had an effect on the treatment received.

When a child's characteristics contribute to the choice of treatment, there is no way to know whether the outcome results from the treatment or from something directly related to the children. The two treatment groups are different on more than one variable, but there is little information about anything but the treatment variable. A poorly understood characteristic of each child is accompanying the child's treatment, and the variables cannot be separated from each other. When two variables go together in this way, they are said to be *confounded,* although *confused* and *confusing* might be better words. Confounded variables make it difficult to draw a clear conclusion, as many of the essays in this book attest.

Studies of Age Differences

Nonrandomized studies are used to investigate age differences because, of course, researchers cannot assign children to ages or make them older or younger than they actually are. As children age, they have varied experiences to learn from, different diets or disease exposures to affect their development, and so on. Children of different age groups are different in ways that are associated with their chronological ages but are not necessarily caused by the genetic factors that guided their maturation. This means that comparison of age groups can be confounded with accidental differences between the groups.

Although some complex designs have been brought to bear on the investigation of age differences, two fairly simple types of design are common and need to be understood. One is a *longitudinal* design, in which one group of children is tested or measured repeatedly over a period of time to discover changes that occur with age. When the data are analyzed, each child is compared to him- or herself at different ages, rather than to other children. In this way, individual experiences, such as cultural differences, are ruled out of the discussion, and the focus is on the basic changes over time. This approach is in many ways ideal, but it can take a long time (depending on the period of life being studied) and requires a lot of clerical work to keep track of participants. If families move away or lose interest, the work already done on those children may be lost.

A second fairly simple design for studying age differences is the *cross-sectional* approach, which studies groups of children of different ages but tests each child once. The results from each age group are then compared to the other age groups. This seems like a short, sweet, sensible way to do things, but there is a problem: What if there were something unusual about one of the groups? For instance, what if an epidemic during the gestation of one group caused a developmental problem that was not obvious? The development of members of that group could be slowed, causing the researchers to assume that development was slow during a certain age period, then sped up rapidly (this would appear to be the case when looking at the normally developing, slightly older group). If the groups are close together in age, medical problems would probably be the primary source of confusion, but if younger and much older children were compared, social changes such as new methods of teaching reading or reductions in school athletic activity could become confused with age differences.

Correlation: A different nonrandomized approach. Another type of nonrandomized design involves a *correlational study*. In this type of design, there is no comparison of groups or treatments. Instead, each member of a large group of children is examined on two or more measurable characteristics. For example, a researcher might look at skeletal age (the development of the bones toward their mature form) and at measures of reproductive maturity, such as breast development. For each child tested, two measures would be labeled so that researchers would know which skeletal age measure went with which breast assessment. All of these paired measures would be analyzed by means of a statistical test for correlation, and the results would tell whether one measure predicted the other—that is, do girls with less-mature skeletal development also have less-developed breasts, and do those with more advanced development in one area also show advancement in the other area? If the numbers are related in the way just described, skeletal age and breast development would be said to be positively correlated.

Correlational studies can be very informative and good guides to further work on a topic. However, conclusions drawn from correlations must be carefully stated. Correlational studies are not good enough to support the claim that one factor *causes* the other. Both may be caused by one or many other variables. Unfortunately, writers of headlines and speakers of television sound bites regularly ignore this fact and confidently declare correlations to be evidence of causality. Many studies of child development use a correlational approach, especially if they are dealing with an important issue where variables cannot easily be controlled, such as education, delinquent behavior, or adolescent sexual activity. Caution is needed when claims are made about causality based on the outcomes of correlational studies.

Sources of Information: Safe or Sorry?

So far, our discussion of ways to examine child development claims and beliefs has focused on assumptions and ways of investigating issues. Consideration of these points is indeed the best way to examine claims and reject myths or mistakes. Some claims are perfectly adequate in these ways but nevertheless should be rejected or given limited acceptance. These claims fail to take into account other existing evidence, either because the author missed its existence or failed to understand it completely. (Isn't there enough trouble for students without this? Yes, published authors can and do make mistakes.) Unfortunately, some authors practice cherry-picking and include only material that supports their own conclusion; this is an unethical practice and not likely to be found in work published in professional journals, but it has been known to occur.

How can you find further evidence about a claim or belief about child development? Often students become frustrated by electronic searches and cannot figure out a suitable keyword. It may be easier and more effective to start with the publication in which the claim was made. Whether reading a book, a professional publication, or a popular magazine, you will find a bibliography or reading list at the end of the article or book that provides a good starting place for your search—and in many cases it will be all you need. Reading the listed materials provides an idea of whether the author of the original publication was correct in citing those sources as supporting his or her conclusion. Don't forget that each listed reference is also likely to have its own bibliography, and if you follow up on those lists you will soon have a great deal of information to examine.

Textbooks also are an important source. Although textbooks may not have much to say on a particular topic, a textbook's bibliography provides relevant references. Follow these leads for further information.

Two outstanding professional journals provide excellent research reports on child development issues: *Child Development* and *Developmental Psychology*. Unfortunately, the growth of child development studies and the shortage of journal space have made some articles in these publications so concise and complex that they can be quite difficult for beginning students to follow. Even so, if a given article is overwhelming, reading the abstract, introduction, and discussion sections can be very informative.

Parenting magazines and similar popular publications can provide articles with useful overviews, but generally these articles do not provide references to background material, making it difficult to follow up on the evidence or rationale for claims. If you want to follow up on an unusual topic in such a magazine, searching for other work by the same author may provide helpful background. Magazine materials intended for life coaches or parent educators should be considered with caution; they may be excellent, or they may simply repeat common myths and mistakes. Internet sources on child development range from brilliant to dangerously deceptive. A Google search can be a wonderful way to find statements of common beliefs that may be myths or mistakes. A keyword search using *child discipline* can bring up thousands of websites for advocacy organizations, support groups, and concerned individuals, providing a picture of popular positions on this topic. Such a search shows whether a mistaken claim is just an unusual error or whether it is part of a popular belief system. Inspection of these websites reveals whether proponents of a position refer to serious systematic evidence for their stance or whether they operate at the level of anecdotes or testimonials. Inspection can also reveal whether the site is run by a commercial organization with a primary interest in sales of products and services rather than in the sharing of information.

In some cases, a Google search can show research evidence itself, but this depends on whether authors have posted published material on websites. Many professional journals place an embargo on publications for some months after they are issued, and of course many authors do not choose to put material on the Internet when it is available in print. But searching the Internet for specific research material is worthwhile. Students should keep in mind that a publication that appears only online may not be as well managed or edited as one that has a print version, although some online publications are excellent. When an Internet search yields references to journal articles that must be paid for, students should be sure to check their own college or university library to see whether the publication is available there in print or electronic form.

Some excellent websites specialize in guiding readers to reliable child development material. One of these, www.cfw.tufts.edu, has existed for some years and provides links to other websites that provide good information about children and families. Links on this site are presented by topic and by age group, so it is easy to use. The Society for Research in Child Development (SRCD), the organization that publishes *Child Development*, has an informative website that includes material about children of all ages. For information about the infant and preschool periods, a very helpful website is that of the organization Zero to Three.

The study of child development has an important characteristic that makes it different from, for instance, the study of psychological testing. Child development studies involve a *multidisciplinary* approach. Children develop in an environment shaped by family, school, community, national, and world events, all of which can affect developmental change. Information relevant to child development can come from psychology, social work, nursing, pediatrics, public health, epidemiology, psychiatry, occupational therapy, physical therapy, education, and many other sources. Students who are searching for supporting and challenging information related to a claim should remember this and look to more than one discipline for evidence.

The Work Ahead

The main part of this book involves a series of essays on child development claims that may be myths, mistakes, or misunderstandings. These essays are marked according to age group and topic, so they can be used in conjunction with textbooks that are organized either chronologically or topically. The essays discuss the claims and consider them with respect to appropriate issues of research design, internal logic, and supporting or opposing evidence from other sources. Because the goal of this book is to encourage critical thinking and thorough consideration of claims about child development, each essay is followed by a short reading list and a set of questions for active student involvement. Referring to this introductory section may be helpful if you have trouble answering a question, especially if you forget the names or descriptions of critical thinking problems.

The ability to analyze and evaluate claims comes only with practice. No amount of reading or instruction can provide you with assessment skills that must be honed through active involvement with relevant questions and answers. Such active involvement can be fun but can also be a painful struggle at times when your favored mantra is "just tell me the answer." Unsupported claims do just tell the answer, which is why they are so attractive to readers. But unsupported claims, accepted when they should not be, can cause problems for children, families, communities, and schools if no one attempts to evaluate them. In the long run, adults who are able to evaluate child development claims can provide the best environment for children and the best future for all of us.

What Difference Does It Make If You Can or Can't Think Critically About Child Development?

What will happen when you master ways of assessing claims about child development? Will you be able to win arguments at holiday dinners and in bars? Regrettably, no such short-term benefit can be predicted. It's more likely that your dissection of a mistaken claim will get the response "Well, I believe it, anyway." Just like children, adults are more likely to depend on the statements of sources they trust than to try to examine evidence. Where values are concerned (as is the case with child development), this tendency is even stronger (Bloom & Weisberg, 2007). But even though you will still lose arguments, the task of evaluating evidence is well worth doing, for yourself and for others, and once you have mastered these skills you will know that you have learned something important.

If you always think uncritically about child development, you may well make a great many mistakes in real life as well as in your coursework. You may be persuaded to buy or use methods that claim research support but do not actually have any. As a teacher or school board member, you might decide to use tests or teaching methods that are not what they claimed to be. As a parent, you might seek lessons or treatments for your children that turn out to be potentially harmful as well as ineffective. As a mental health professional working with children, you might accept practices as effective when in fact they are not. There is no Food and Drug Administration to protect adults and children from mistakes made through uncritical thinking about child development! Critical thinking and correct conclusions about children's lives are up to you, and the purpose of this book is to help you protect yourself and others against mistakes that can have serious outcomes.

References

Bloom, P., & Weisberg, D. S. (2007). Childhood origins of adult resistance to science. *Science, 316,* 996–997.

Bruer, J. T. (2002). *The myth of the first three years.* New York: Free Press.

Cahan, E. D. (2007). The child as scientific object. *Science, 316,* 835.

"Defining critical thinking" (2013). Available at www.criticalthinking.org/pages/defining-critical-thinking.htm.

DYG, Inc. (2000). *What grown-ups understand about child development: A national benchmark study*. Washington, DC: Zero to Three.

Elman, J. L., Bates, E. A., Johnson, M. H., Karmiloff-Smith, A., Parisi, D., & Plunkett, K. (1998). *Rethinking innateness*. Cambridge, MA: MIT Press.

Herrnstein, R., & Murray, C. (1994). *The bell curve: Intelligence and class structure in American life*. New York: Free Press.

Kagan, J. (1998). *Three seductive ideas*. Cambridge, MA: Harvard University Press.

Price, M. (2009). Programmed for life? *Monitor on Psychology, 40*(2), 28.

Prose, F. (1999, September). I know why the caged bird cannot read. *Harper's Magazine*, 76–84.

Smuts, A. B. (2006). *Science in the service of children, 1893–1935*. New Haven, CT: Yale University Press.

Stanovich, K. (2003). *How to think straight about psychology*. New York: Allyn & Bacon.

Waber, D. P., de Moor, C., Forbes, P., Almli, C. R., Botteron, K., Leonard, G., . . . Brain Development Cooperative Group. (2007). The NIH MRI study of normal brain development performance of a population based sample of healthy children aged 6 to 18 years on a neurophysiological battery. *Journal of the International Neuropsychological Society, 13*, 1–18.

Waters, E., Kondo-Ikemura, K., Posada, G., & Richters, J. E. (1991). Learning to love: Milestones and mechanisms. In M. Gunner & L. A. Sroufe (Eds.), *Minnesota Symposia on Child Psychology* (Vol. 23, pp. 217–255). Hillsdale, NJ: Erlbaum.

Part I
Genetics and Prenatal Life

Claim 1

Genetic factors play such a strong role in human development that genes alone can determine certain human behavioral characteristics.

Susan likes coffee a lot and often has some when out with friends. But she'd rather have it at home because there it's easier to fix it the way she wants. Susan likes to put the cream in the cup and then add the coffee to it, rather than the other way around. "That's weird," say her friends. "How come you do it like that?" "I don't know," replies Susan. "My dad does the same thing, and so does Grandma. I guess it must be genetic. People say I smile just like the two of them, too. But, you know, my adopted sister fixes her coffee the way I do."

Could Susan's coffee habits be genetic in origin?

The connection between genetic factors and behavior is sometimes obvious in animals. For example, some dog breeds tend to be very calm and friendly, and others are quite aggressive. Some cattle are much less aggressive than others, which is important because no matter how much milk a cow can give, if you can't get close to her, you won't get milk. Other animal behaviors may be affected by both genetic factors and experience—for instance, some dogs have the potential to become excellent retrievers, but unless they have a chance to be trained in this skill, they will not master the retrieving task.

Some human characteristics are strongly determined by genetic factors, and a specific genetic difference may govern many aspects of development (Kaplan, Wang, & Francke, 2001). On the other hand, some developmental changes appear not to be genetically governed but instead are influenced by experience only (Roisman & Fraley, 2006).

It is often quite difficult to figure out the connection between human genetics and behavior. Human beings select their own mates; they are not deliberately bred for certain behaviors as dogs may be. The belief that genes are directly responsible for a person's habits and actions is probably based on dramatic claims derived from some studies of twins. Popular reports about twins who were separated at birth and later reunited contain startling similarities. Some twin pairs who were raised apart from each other are reported to have given their dogs the same name and to have displayed identical idiosyncratic behaviors, such as flushing a toilet both before and after using it.

Can such reports provide strong evidence about the connection between genes and specific behaviors? A number of problems arise when making too much of this kind of evidence. One problem has to do with possible differences between volunteers and people who are reluctant to participate in research. Studies of reunited twins depend on twins responding to advertised studies or seeking out ongoing research programs. In these cases, the reports may represent only the twin pairs who discover, to their surprise, that they resemble each other greatly, rather than those who discover that they are not at all alike. And, of course, twin pairs who were not reunited—or people who never even knew they had a twin sibling—would not be included in this study. It's possible that twins who resemble each other are more likely to go to the same places, do the same things, and discover each other than are twins who are quite different.

Another issue has to do with the small number of separated and reunited twins compared with the large number of nontwin siblings or twins who were never separated. Twinning is unusual in humans, and separation of twin babies is even less likely. Counterintuitive though it may be, small rather than large samples are more likely to provide extreme results because extreme measures have more of a chance to average out when large samples are used. The effect of extreme results in small groups is exaggerated when the news media report on only a small group of cases in which there is a surprising resemblance between twins and not on others in which there are small and undramatic resemblances.

Studies of reunited twins may show genetic effects on intelligence or health but are not very good evidence that specific behaviors can be "in the

DNA." However, other sources of information support the idea that genetic factors are powerful. People with an unusual genetic makeup sometimes display uncommon behaviors, such as hand-wringing. Babies of different ethnic backgrounds may show different behaviors shortly after birth, when it seems there has been too short a time for differences to be learned.

More often, though, it appears that an individual's *phenotype*, or developed physical and behavioral characteristics, is determined by genetic factors and environment working together in complicated ways (Plomin, 2000). For example, children share their parents' genetic material, but the children's development is also shaped by experiences their parents choose for them, such as music lessons, low-fat meals, or severe physical punishment. The parents' choices for their children may be the result of the parents' own genetic makeup, their childhood experiences (either repeating them or rejecting them), or a combination of the two as well as many other factors. To some degree, parents' genetic makeup plays a role in their children's experiences as well as in their children's genetic characteristics.

Genetically determined characteristics of a child's appearance or behavior can also cause others to treat the child in predictable ways. A small, thin child may be treated with more care than a large, robust child who is rarely sick and does not seem to mind minor pains and injuries. The experiences of both the thin and the robust child are not random events but are indirectly related to each child's genetic makeup, so that the long-term effect of the genetic material is potentially much greater than the individual's physical characteristics alone.

As children become older, they are increasingly free to choose their own experiences and thus to shape their own development. Some of their choices may be determined by past experiences and some by genetic components. But certainly some choices in later childhood and adolescence come about because of genetic material as well as body type, activity preferences, or emotional tendencies that result from the biological inheritance.

Directly or indirectly, genetic factors can have a powerful effect on behavior, and in recent years developmental psychologists have placed much stress on this fact. However, it seems that, as is so often the case in psychology, the way the question is asked helps determine the answer. For instance, what would happen if you were to ask one group of parents to rate the similarities between their monozygotic (identical) twins and another group of parents to rate the similarities between their dizygotic (fraternal) twins? The ratings would be very different: The parents would report the similarities between the monozygotic twin pairs as very strong and the similarities between the dizygotic twin pairs as quite small. Ask trained observers to rate the twin pairs, however, and you'll get a different outcome. The monozygotic pairs would still be rated as more similar, and the dizygotic pairs as less similar, but the differences between the two would be a good deal less than the differences the parents reported. Parents seem to exaggerate the similarities between monozygotic twins and the differences between dizygotic twins (Roisman & Fraley, 2006). When questions about causes of behavior take these factors into account, genetic characteristics seem to play a smaller role in development, and shared environmental factors, such as parenting, seem to play a larger role. Perhaps some of the existing beliefs about genetic effects have given those factors more weight than they should have.

A curious issue about genetic effects involves the question of when in life a genetic factor is likely to come into play. We would expect genetic factors to play their strongest role early in life, before much learning has occurred, and environmental factors to have a greater effect as more learning takes place. But one study found higher correlations between intelligence test scores of elderly twins than between those of younger twins (McClearn et al., 1997). It seems that there may be genetic influences whose effects cannot be observed in children and adolescents.

Conclusion

It is possible for specific human behaviors to result from specific genetic makeups, but in most cases behaviors are the result of various combinations of heredity and experience. It's hard to see how a complex behavior like Susan's coffee drinking could be determined by genetic factors, and the possibility that the behavior was learned is suggested by the actions of her sister, who is not biologically related but behaves in the same way.

Critical Thinking

1. Use a child development textbook to define the term *passive gene-environment correlation*. Describe a scenario that shows this kind of connection between genes, experience, and developmental outcome.

2. Use a child development textbook to define the term *evocative gene-environment correlation*. Describe a relevant scenario that is an example of this type of correlation.

3. Use a child development textbook to define the term *active gene-environment correlation*. Describe a relevant scenario that is an example of this type of correlation.

4. In studies of formerly separated twins, how would similarities in a twin pair make the twin siblings more likely to reunite? How may the post hoc error be part of people's thinking about separated twins?

5. An article by Poduri, Evrony, Cai, and Walsh (2013) describes the roles of mutations and mosaicism in causing autism spectrum disorders and intellectual disabilities. Use the article or other sources to define mosaicism and state briefly how this condition relates to the discussion of genetic factors in development.

References

Kaplan, P., Wang, P. P., & Francke, U. (2001). Williams (Williams Beuren) syndrome: A distinct neurobehavioral disorder. *Journal of Child Neurology, 16*, 177–190.

McClearn, G. E., Johansson, B., Berg, S., Pedersen, N. L., Ahern, F., Petrill, S. A., & Plomin, R. (1997). Substantial genetic influence on cognitive abilities in twins 80 or more years old. *Science, 276*, 1560–1563.

Plomin, R. (2000). Behavioural genetics in the 21st century. *International Journal of Behavioral Development, 24*, 30–34.

Poduri, A., Evrony, G. D., Cai, X., & Walsh, C. A. (2013). Somatic mutation, genomic variation, and neurological disease. *Science, 341*, 43.

Roisman, G. I., & Fraley, R. C. (2006). The limits of genetic influence: A behavior-genetic analysis of infant-caregiver relationship quality and temperament. *Child Development, 77*, 1656–1667.

Claim 2

Although prematurely born babies are smaller than most and may need special medical care, the babies and their parents instinctively know how to interact with each other.

Ella had expected her baby to be born in November, but to her surprise and concern, Sammy arrived in late September, about seven weeks early. He was thus a *preterm* baby, born after about 32 weeks' gestation rather than between 38 and 42 weeks. Fortunately, he did not have any growth problems, and although he was smaller at birth than he would have been if he had waited a while longer, he was of average weight for his gestational age. Nevertheless, he needed to be cared for in the hospital's neonatal intensive care unit, which could help with any breathing or heart problems he might have and could feed him carefully. Ella was upset when she first saw tiny Sammy in a small transparent crib, with monitors of various kinds attached to his body. She was crying as she told her husband, Jeff, "He doesn't even seem like a real person, and I would be afraid to touch him. He can't even get to know us yet the way he should be doing, so how can we have a relationship with him when he's bigger?" Jeff naturally tried to reassure Ella. He said, "Come on, honey. He knows who we are instinctively. He'll be the same as any other kid when he gains a little weight."

Was Jeff correct, or do families of premature babies need more help than others do in psychological as well as medical areas?

The medical problems of babies born prematurely are always the first concern. Although most who are as far along as Sammy do well if they receive careful care, babies who are born early and with low birth weight risk damage to the brain, heart and respiratory problems, and intestinal infections. Whether young parents are aware of these dangers or not, they are usually quite disturbed by the appearance of the preterm baby and by the machinery and activities of the neonatal intensive care unit.

Relationships between infants and their parents are *transactional* in nature whether a baby is or is not born at full term; this means that each influences the way the other behaves, and over time each person changes and their interactions change, too. It's a reasonable guess that a baby's premature birth, and the worries it causes, could interfere with the usual transactional process and create undesirable developmental outcomes. Whether or not disturbed interactions with parents cause the problems is not clear, but preterm babies are at unusually high risk of having later difficulties like hyperactivity, depression, anxiety, and peer problems (Potilk, de Winter, Bos, Kerstjens, & Reijneveld, 2012). Because about 11% of babies worldwide are born prematurely (Blencowe et al., 2012), a sizeable problem may exist and need to be dealt with.

Although it is not certain that disturbed interactions cause the children's later problems, there has been enough concern about this possibility to generate work on treatments that may help keep parent-baby interactions active and positive. It's generally considered more effective to intervene in ways that prevent problems from developing than to try to solve the problems when they are already in place. One method of working with mothers and their preterm babies is to help the mothers provide "kangaroo care," in which "the infant, naked except for a diaper, is placed between the mother's [also naked] breasts" and held for an hour (Neu, Hazel, Robinson, Schmiege, & Laudenslager, 2014).

An important problem for the study of such early interventions is how to decide what to measure in either mother or baby. Very young babies do not show the behaviors like hyperactivity that will later be of concern, so how do we know at that early stage whether a treatment is doing any good? One way is to measure factors that indicate stress in either mother or baby, such as cortisol levels. Neu et al. (2014) measured the amount of cortisol in saliva to determine the effectiveness of kangaroo care. They used a randomized controlled design to compare a group of preterm babies receiving kangaroo care to another group who were also held but were wrapped in blankets. Both groups showed decreases in cortisol levels for both mothers and babies over time, with no advantage for kangaroo care.

A second intervention was studied by White-Traut et al. (2013). This randomized design compared mothers who were taught to hold their preterm babies, talk to them, and rock them several times a day with mothers who were given educational materials and received the same amount of attention from the researchers as the first group. The researchers reported that the mothers and babies in the "holding and talking" group interacted better (more like mothers and full-term babies) both during feeding and during play than those in the control group did.

Researchers who study preterm babies usually have difficulty finding as large a group of babies as they need for meaningful statistical analysis. There are also often problems with creating a randomized design; parents may not want to have their babies in the treatment group they have been assigned to, and they may not cooperate or follow treatments if they are not pleased with their assignment. This means that instead of having one or more large studies involving many babies and parents and allowing statistical analysis to discover patterns of outcomes, there are usually numerous small studies, not necessarily randomized, that are looking at a variety of interventions. As a result, a systematic research synthesis may be the best way to examine the existing information and to try to draw conclusions. In one such synthesis, Herd, Whittingham, Sanders, Colditz, and Boyd (2014) found only 12 articles using randomized designs on interventions that started soon after birth for preterm babies and their parents. They started with 972 possible articles whose titles suggested that they might be appropriate, but they rejected articles that did not use standardized measures of child behavior, as well as those that were not randomized in design or that looked at full-term babies. The authors were especially concerned with child behavioral outcomes, and some of the programs that were examined had small but significant effects on the children's behavior when they reached preschool age.

Conclusion

Although many preterm babies do very well both physically and psychologically, when compared to full-term infants they have a higher risk of developing later behavior problems. It's understandable that Jeff just wanted to soothe Ella, but in fact her fears may be somewhat justified. Fortunately, there has been some research on the kinds of preventive treatments that may help preterm babies develop appropriate behavior, and beginning a good program for Sammy soon may help guide his development and his parents' relationships with him.

Critical Thinking

1. What does it mean to say that preterm babies have a "higher risk of behavior problems"? Does this indicate that all preterm babies have behavior difficulties? Use a child development textbook to find several factors other than preterm birth that may contribute to the development of behavior problems.

2. Use a child development textbook or Internet sources to define the terms *systematic review* or *systematic research synthesis* and *meta-analysis*.

3. All of the studies cited here noted that not all infants tested at the beginning of an intervention were tested at the end. Name several factors that could be responsible for this attrition.

4. Herd et al. (2014) suggested that interventions for preterm babies might influence parents and babies best if they are relatively brief. Why did they argue this in their discussion section? Is this suggestion contrary to the usual assumptions about a dose-response relationship?

5. Search the Internet for statements about kangaroo care. Do the statements you find seem to agree with the conclusions of the Neu et al. article? Explain your answer.

References

Blencowe, H., Cousens, S., Oestergaard, M. Z., Chou, D., Moller, A.-B., Narwal, R., . . . Lawn, J. E. (2012). National, regional, and worldwide estimates of preterm birth rates in the year 2010 with time trends since 1990 for certain countries: A systematic analysis and implications. *Lancet, 379,* 2162–2172.

Herd, M., Whittingham, K., Sanders, M., Colditz, P., & Boyd, R. N. (2014). Efficacy of preventive parenting interventions for parents of preterm infants on later child behavior: A systematic review and meta-analysis. *Infant Mental Health Journal, 35*(6), 630–641.

Neu, M., Hazel, N. A., Robinson, J., Schmiege, S. J., & Laudenslager, M. (2014). Effect of holding on co-regulation in preterm infants: A randomized controlled trial. *Early Human Development, 90,* 141–147.

Potilk, M. R., de Winter, A. F., Bos, A. F., Kerstjens, A. M., & Reijneveld, S. A. (2012). Higher rates of behavioural and emotional problems at preschool age in children born moderately preterm. *Archives of Disease in Childhood, 97,* 112–117.

White-Traut, R., Norr, K. F., Fabiyi, C., Rankin, K. M., Li, Z., & Liu, L. (2013). Mother-infant interaction improves with a developmental intervention for mother–preterm infant dyads. *Infant Behavior & Development, 36,* 694–706.

Claim 3

If a child's problem is genetically caused, the problem will be present at birth and will stay the same throughout life.

Tom and Cara McDonald have been worried that their children may be at risk for genetic problems. Cara McDonald's grandmother had several miscarriages, and several of her other babies died in infancy. Cara's own mother had no problems, but an aunt had a child who died young. When little Jack McDonald is born in blooming health, the McDonalds relax and forget about their earlier worries.

Are genetic problems present at birth and in the same form throughout a person's lifetime? Or can a genetic problem show up later?

People frequently assume that any genetically caused problem is present at birth and will persist in much the same form throughout a person's life. Conversely, people think that a problem that becomes apparent later in life is caused by an experience with the environment. For instance, the idea that autism has a genetic cause is often rejected by families, who are often heard to make remarks such as this: "The child was perfectly normal at birth and for months afterward. Then he had an immunization or was sick with the flu or had some other experience, and he changed completely. There was no genetic problem because nobody else in our family is autistic—it was the experience that caused the trouble."

Of course, you can't rule out the possibility that an experience caused a child's autism or any other problem, such as cerebral palsy or mental illness, that may not have been diagnosed at birth. But neither can you rule out the possibility that a sudden change is at least partly determined by a genetic component. Even well-understood genetically caused problems do not necessarily have the same symptoms at different stages in development. Rett syndrome is an example of a cognitive and behavioral disturbance that is clearly caused by a genetic problem—in this case, a mutation in a specific gene on the X chromosome. Boys who have this mutation usually die very young, but girls survive. Initially, the girls develop normally, but in late infancy they begin to lose developmental ground. Girls with Rett syndrome display the basic steps in a number of developmental processes, with the beginnings of hand control, mastery of a few words, and walking. But these achievements do not last long. The girls lose the abilities they had developed, begin to wring their hands in a stereotyped way rather than make voluntary movements, and tend to become anxious and irritable as they regress behaviorally (Miller, 2006; Neul & Zoghbi, 2004).

Another good example of the different effects of genes at different ages is Williams syndrome, a condition that develops when certain areas of a chromosome are lost during a stage in the early development of a sperm or ovum. Williams syndrome is not fatal or terribly debilitating, so the ongoing development of affected individuals provides a display of changing genetic effects. Adults with Williams syndrome have some cognitive problems, especially in dealing with quantities. However, they have wonderful language abilities and are at the same time highly sociable and obviously lacking in some kinds of social skills. People with Williams syndrome do not have much social anxiety; thus, they do not feel awkward in social situations and do not pay attention to social signals. This ability to detect social signals provides people with much better social abilities, even though they may feel uncomfortable as a result of social anxiety.

What would you guess about the characteristics of people with Williams syndrome, who are talkative and fluent as adults? Do they learn to talk early? No; in fact, they have quite different characteristics as children than as adults. As infants and toddlers, people with Williams syndrome commonly go through several behavioral stages, each different from what you would expect of genetically typical children of the same ages. In the early months, babies with Williams syndrome are intensely colicky, crying frantically and unable to be soothed. Although many other babies experience the apparent stomach pain, distress, and crying referred to as colic, most babies have less severe cases that are resolved earlier than in cases of Williams syndrome. When children with Williams syndrome emerge from their colicky period, they make contact with other people through their intent stares and a voracious search for eye contact. Genetically typical infants are interested in eye contact, too, and use it for communication with others by the end of the first year, but they quickly move on to use speech as communication—an achievement that is delayed for another year or so in infants with Williams syndrome. When they do start talking, children with Williams syndrome quickly become charming and chatty conversationalists (Dobbs, 2007).

It is easy to tell the difference between the early nontalking stage shown by children with Williams syndrome and their later talkative stage. Although these children have the same genetic makeup from birth, they switch from being unusually silent to being unusually garrulous. Are there any other such reversals in Williams syndrome behavior as children age? One group of researchers looked at the poor number skills of school-age children with Williams syndrome and wondered how they had compared to typical children earlier in their lives. Of course, infants and toddlers cannot do arithmetic, but they can show by preferential looking whether they are paying attention to the number of objects in a group shown to them or simply to the kind of objects they see. When the researchers set up their experiment and compared babies with Williams syndrome to babies with Down syndrome and to genetically typical infants, the babies with Williams syndrome performed better than the others on detecting number differences—again, the opposite of the characteristics seen in their later lives (Paterson, Brown, Gsödl, Johnson, & Karmiloff-Smith, 1999).

If Rett and Williams characteristics are genetically caused, how can they come and go like this? Don't people have the same genetic makeup all of their lives? One possibility has to do with genes turning on or off, functioning or not functioning, a phenomenon that depends on many factors. A gene's activity can be affected by maturational changes, events such as dietary changes or sickness, or other experiences. When a gene is turned on, it helps the cell make a protein, which in turn assists with chemical processes, such as the cell's use of oxygen, and it may do this differently in some cells than in others. When a gene is turned off and the protein is not made, the cell's chemical processes are different than they are when the gene is turned on. Considering that behavioral characteristics result from the functioning of a group of cells, it appears that a change in genetic functioning has the potential to cause a reversal of behavioral characteristics.

However, most human characteristics, behavioral and physical, are caused by the complex effects of multiple genes interacting with complicated environmental events. Although the behaviors of people with Rett and Williams syndromes seem to be based on aspects of single genes, one must keep in mind that the determination of the Rett or Williams phenotype may depend on the influence on other genes when the most significant genes do not operate as they should. It is possible that changes with age in people with Rett and Williams syndromes—and, yes, people with autism—may occur because of a combination of events, both genetic and environmental. For example, high levels of stress hormones found in the bodies of girls with Rett syndrome (and measured in their urine) can possibly have a negative effect on brain development. Slowing or alteration of brain development can, in turn, influence the girls' ability to deal with numbers. More information about these factors may someday enable experts to develop helpful treatments for genetically caused behavior problems. In fact, there have already been efforts to use psychotherapy to help the obsessive-compulsive behavior associated with Williams syndrome (Klein-Tasman & Albano, 2007).

Conclusion

Genetic material does not necessarily function in the same way throughout a lifetime, so even a condition that appears to have come on very suddenly may be due to changes in genetic factors and not to the effects of either pleasant or unpleasant experiences. It is to be hoped that the McDonald baby has no genetic problems, but what can be seen at birth is not necessarily the only effect of genetic material.

Critical Thinking

1. Using a child development textbook, find two disorders that have genetic components but are not detectable until adulthood. Explain your choices. How can the fundamental attribution error make this more difficult to understand?

2. Why would boys with Rett syndrome die early, whereas girls with the disorder survive with disabilities? Use a child development textbook to find another disorder in which boys are more seriously harmed than girls. What do the two disorders have in common?

(Continued)

(Continued)

3. What role would you expect the intense stare of children with Williams syndrome to play in evoking adult reactions? How might the adults' reactions affect the child's later language development and use?

4. Using a child development textbook, find information about attachment behavior and the friendliness of toddlers with Williams syndrome, as described in the Dobbs (2007) article referenced in this section. What differences do you find between the social behaviors of Williams toddlers and genetically typical toddlers?

5. How would longitudinal studies be helpful in determining how genetically caused characteristics change in the course of life?

References

Dobbs, D. (2007, July 8). The gregarious brain. *New York Times Magazine*, pp. 43–47.

Klein-Tasman, B. P., & Albano, A. M. (2007). Intensive, short-term cognitive-behavioral treatment of OCD-like behavior with a young adult with Williams Syndrome. *Clinical Case Studies, 6*, 483–492.

Miller, G. (2006). Getting a read on Rett syndrome. *Science, 314*, 1536–1537.

Neul, J. L., & Zoghbi, H. Y. (2004). Rett syndrome: A prototypical neurodevelopmental disorder. *Neuroscientist, 10*, 118–128.

Paterson, S. J., Brown, J. H., Gsödl, M. K., Johnson, M. H., & Karmiloff-Smith, A. (1999). Cognitive modularity and genetic disorders. *Science, 286*, 2355–2358.

Claim 4

Unborn babies are not influenced much by the environment outside the mother's body.

Malinda is pregnant with twins and is getting very big and clumsy. She needs to rest a lot and has time to think about the babies. "Do they listen when I play music?" she wonders. "Sometimes I think they kick in rhythm to it. And what if people talk loudly? I had a fight with my husband the other day, and we called each other some nasty names. We made up later, but I wonder if the babies heard the argument and remember it. My grandmother used to say a baby could get a strawberry mark if a mother ate too many strawberries. I'm sure that's not true, but I wonder about these other things."

How much do Malinda's soon-to-be-born babies actually experience?

Can unborn babies figure out anything that is happening around them? Do they learn from and remember events that occurred during gestation? Or do they start absolutely from scratch with their first experiences on the day they are born?

The unborn human being is in a peculiar position, both literally (upside down, at least toward the end of gestation) and figuratively. Surrounded by protective membranes and cushioning amniotic fluid, the fetus is defended from all but the most direct blows. Even during the early embryonic period, before the membranes and fluid are present, the developing organism is thoroughly protected from impact by the tissues of the mother's body. If a normal pregnancy could be easily damaged by external physical forces, many babies would be lost to injury and abortion clinics would not exist.

On the other hand, an unborn child can be seriously damaged by infectious agents and toxic substances that cross the placenta, an organ that filters out most, but not all, potentially harmful materials. Harm can thus come to the fetus from some aspects of the environment that penetrate the mother's body, and if this harm includes damage to the brain, later cognitive development may be compromised. The developing individual can even be predisposed to diseases that will not appear until adulthood (Phillips, 2006).

But what about the harmless aspects of the environment? Not every effect of the outside world is a dangerous one. Can the fetus be influenced by external events, either directly or indirectly? Harmful effects are defined by the damage to the physical development of a fetus or by the creation of long-term behavioral or intellectual problems. Are other harmless effects shown in behavioral changes, either temporary or lasting? The abilities of prematurely born babies to see, hear, taste, and smell certainly suggest that a fetus past a certain age of gestation has the sensory capacity to respond to stimulation. Of course, for stimulation to occur, the stimulus must reach the unborn through the tissues of the mother's body, the membranes, and the fluid that surrounds the fetus and fills his or her mouth, nose, and ear canals. Sounds, tastes, and the physical pressures of touch can all do this. Animal studies and some work on human beings have shown that flavorful foods eaten by the mother transfer in taste and smell to the amniotic fluid, as they do later to mother's milk. If a pregnant mother eats garlic, lemon, coffee, or chocolate-flavored foods, the unborn baby experiences those flavors as they pass over the tongue in the amniotic fluid. Rat pups prefer to drink milk flavored with particular tastes that were given to their mother during her pregnancy, and some researchers have speculated that humans like the flavors they experienced prenatally when certain foods were part of their mothers' diets. The taste of the amniotic fluid acts as a "flavor bridge" that encourages a preference for foods frequently served at a family's table (Mennella, 1995; Mennella & Beauchamp, 1993).

Taste experiences are delivered through the amniotic fluid. The flavors' sources are actually inside the mother's body because the mother consumed them. But what about the influence of events that remain external to the mother? Can the fetus hear what is going on in the outside world?

Sound waves can travel through a mother's body and through the amniotic fluid—in fact, they travel faster through solids and liquids than they do through the air. The sounds of a mother's heartbeat are known to penetrate the uterus, and, rather less romantically, the sounds of her stomach and intestines must do so also. Sounds that come from outside the body are also carried into the uterus, but they are muffled by the mother's tissues and partially masked by other simultaneous sounds, such as the maternal heartbeat. The fetus is not in the ideal situation for listening to details of sounds, especially if the mother has high blood pressure, which changes the transmission of sound to the fetus (Lee, Brown, Hains, & Kisilevsky, 2007).

Because sound, however muffled, can penetrate to the unborn baby and because many hearing functions develop months before birth, it is possible for a baby to "listen" to external sound events, such as people speaking or music. But whether the fetus is actually affected by what he or she hears is still unclear. To prove such an effect, the unborn baby's behavior needs to change in a measurable way, either immediately or in a way that can be detected after birth.

Some years ago, a remarkable study concluded that babies can learn from speech sounds heard before birth—not what words mean but rather some information about the sounds and rhythms of language. In their complicated and careful study, DeCasper and Spence (1986) prepared two stories: the familiar *Cat in the Hat* and an alternative version called *Dog in the Fog*. (A third story they used is left out of this discussion for purposes of brevity.) Women who were about 7.5 months pregnant were asked to record the two stories. After they had done so, the women were assigned one of the stories to read aloud twice each day until childbirth. The reading was to be done in a quiet place and at a time when the fetus was "awake" and moving around. These precautions were to ensure that the fetus could hear as clearly as possible and that he or she was as likely as possible to be "listening" to the stories.

About two days after the babies were born, the babies were tested for reactions to their mother's recordings of *Cat in the Hat* and *Dog in the Fog*. Each baby was given a nipple with a switch inside it, and by sucking faster or slower the baby could activate the switch and turn on one or the other of the recordings. The researchers wanted to find out whether the babies would change their sucking rates more readily if the change let them hear the familiar story that had been read before they were born or if they would respond more to a chance to hear the unfamiliar story. Their responses were also compared to those of babies who had not heard the stories before they were born. The babies whose mothers had read aloud before they were born changed their behavior more rapidly when the action let them hear the familiar story than when the change turned on the unfamiliar story. Whether the story was *Cat in the Hat* or *Dog in the Fog* did not matter. The babies worked to hear the story that had been read aloud before they were born, suggesting that they had learned from what they heard.

The idea that mothers can "bond" with their unborn babies by talking to them or tapping or rubbing their pregnant bellies is discussed in popular books (Stoppard, 2008), but no research evidence exists to support the idea of intentional maternal-infant communication before birth.

Conclusion

Before birth, babies can experience tastes and sounds and may learn from experiences in ways that can affect their later behavior. It's possible that Malinda's twins will learn a preference for the music she plays before they are born or for some speech sounds, but they do not understand the words themselves when they hear people speaking.

Critical Thinking

1. If unborn babies learn from sounds, as DeCasper and Spence (1986) concluded, the same should be true of prematurely born babies of the same gestational ages as the read-to fetuses in the DeCasper and Spence study. Describe how you would carry out a similar study to test the effects of hearing a story on prematurely born babies. Use a child development textbook to identify problems of premature babies that your study might need to consider.

2. Use a child development textbook to find information about habituation. Do the facts about habituation suggest that newborn babies would prefer the familiar story or an unfamiliar one? A familiar taste or an unfamiliar one? Explain your answer.

3. In the DeCasper and Spence study, the researchers gave about half of the babies a chance to listen to the familiar story first and the novel story second. For the other half of the group, they reversed the order. What was the point of doing this?

4. Why did DeCasper and Spence assign each mother a story to read aloud only after she had recorded both stories? Explain your answer.

5. Some of the studies on prenatal taste experiences were performed on unborn animals. Using the bibliography of a child development textbook, look up the titles of studies cited as relevant to prenatal and newborn development. What proportion appear to have involved human subjects and what proportion involved animals? Are there problems or advantages to this situation? Keep in mind that the goal of studying child development is the understanding of events in human life.

References

DeCasper, A. J., & Spence, M. J. (1986). Prenatal maternal speech influences newborns' perception of speech. *Infant Behavior and Development, 9*, 133–150.

Lee, C. T., Brown, C. A., Hains, S. M. J., & Kisilevsky, B. S. (2007). Fetal development: Voice processing in normotensive and hypertensive pregnancies. *Biological Research for Nursing, 8*, 272–282.

Mennella, J. A. (1995). Mother's milk: A medium for early flavor experiences. *Journal of Human Lactation, 11*, 39–45.

Mennella, J., & Beauchamp, G. (1993). Early flavor experiences: When do they start? *Zero to Three, 14*(2), 1–7.

Phillips, D. I. W. (2006). External influences on the fetus and their long-term consequences. *Lupus, 15*, 794–800.

Stoppard, M. (2008). *Bonding before birth*. New York: DK.

Claim 5

As the date when her child will be born gets closer, a mother-to-be needs to be more careful about alcohol and drugs because the risk of birth defects increases throughout pregnancy.

Twenty-year-old Jennifer did not plan to become pregnant, but she decided to go forward with the pregnancy that surprised her and her boyfriend. While considering what to do about the pregnancy, Jennifer continued her usual life and did not tell too many people what was happening. Now, at about five months into her pregnancy, her clothes are getting tight, and even the people she has not told are beginning to get the picture. When she goes out to a bar one night, a friend tells her, "Hey, you better taper off. Your baby is getting big, so you shouldn't be drinking."

Is Jennifer's friend right about this?

The idea that an unborn baby becomes more vulnerable as it progresses toward birth and life as a "real person" is one that strikes people as intuitively correct. Most people know that in sufficient quantities, drugs and alcohol can do real harm to adults; thus, people assume that as an unborn child begins to resemble an adult more closely, its needs and vulnerabilities become more like those of adults, too.

The idea that a baby is more vulnerable to harm as it nears birth also matches the subjective experience of pregnant women. In the early weeks and even early months of pregnancy, women usually do not "feel pregnant." They have no real sense of a developing organism inside their bodies. Instead, they feel like their ordinary nonpregnant selves, but selves who are a little sick, queasy, or extra tired, as if coming down with the flu. Some pregnant women find it hard to believe that anything they do can affect a growing child, whose existence is not even obvious. In the second trimester (fourth through sixth month of pregnancy), most women experience *fetal embodiment*—a sense of the unborn child as within and a part of the mother's body—and an accompanying sense of worry about possible harm to the baby. In the last trimester of pregnancy, the baby's growth and movement capture a lot of the mother's attention, and she usually begins to think about the baby as a separate person from herself, potentially threatened by dangers, such as the events of birth. Many mothers are aware of what an unborn baby does, whether it is awake, kicking and moving, or quiet. If the baby is quiet for too long, the mother may become anxious and seek help and assurance that her unborn child is still alive.

Unfortunately, the actual vulnerability of an unborn baby follows quite a different pattern from the mother's feelings about it (Meyer, Yee, & Feldon, 2007). The possibility that birth defects will be caused by drugs, alcohol, or disease is by far the greatest in the *early* part of the pregnancy, from about day 18 to day 56 after conception. Day 18 is only a few days after the mother misses her first menstrual period. By the time the mother feels worried about injury to the fetus, much less danger to development is possible.

To understand this situation, examine the events in early development. As the fertilized ovum moves into the uterus, it divides into a clump of cells that are much like each other; though there is some differentiation, the cells are *equipotential*—they have the possibility of developing into any of the various cells that will make up the body. After implantation in the wall of the uterus, during about day 14 to day 18 after conception, the cells begin to divide and differentiate so that new cells that are produced are not necessarily identical to the cells that gave rise to them. During the *embryonic* period of development, all of the types of cells that will be needed are produced, and the foundations for all of the body's organs are established—if an organ system is missing at this time, it will not develop later. After day 56, when the *fetal* period begins, much less differentiation occurs.

Major birth defects, such as the absence of a limb, the development of the heart or intestines outside of the chest, or a cleft palate, can occur because of an environmental effect that interrupts differentiation and prevents the formation of a needed cell type. Such environmental events may be avoidable (e.g., alcohol or drug use) or not so avoidable (e.g., exposure to a contagious disease or a food toxin). In all cases, the event stops a part of cell differentiation, and as a result, a body part never develops as it should (Shonkoff & Phillips, 2000).

Although many women are not certain that they are pregnant during this especially vulnerable time, they may experience a form of protection that is outside their control and often unpleasant: *morning sickness* or *pregnancy sickness*—an unaccustomed queasiness or even vomiting that can occur at any time of day, not just in the morning. Pregnancy sickness often includes sensitivity to unusual flavors and strong smells, especially smells of food. Perhaps this increased sensitivity prevents women in early pregnancy from consuming foods that may be partly spoiled or contaminated. A slightly deteriorated food may be eaten by a nonpregnant person, who notes that it's a bit "off" but not too bad; a woman in early pregnancy may find the taste so disgusting that she refuses to eat it. Unfortunately, people cannot depend on smells and flavors to provide complete protection because some dangerous food contaminants do not change the food's taste.

Why doesn't differentiation start again after the contaminated food, or drug or toxin, has passed through the mother's body? This would be an excellent way to prevent birth defects if it could be managed, but it is not the way early development works. Genetic information encoded in the cells defines *what* differentiation will happen and *when* it will occur. The schedule of differentiation is built into the species and cannot be changed. If a process is interrupted, there is no time in the schedule to repeat or correct it; instead, that process—the differentiation of a type of cell—is bypassed, and as a consequence the foundation of a body part fails to be built, resulting in a birth defect.

One part of an unborn baby's development continues to be vulnerable into the period when the mother becomes most concerned, the last trimester—brain development. The complex human brain results from other complicated processes in addition to differentiation of new cell types. Brain cells move from place to place to form elaborate patterns, such as the six cell layers of the cortex. The brain cells also form multiple connections with one another, enabling them to send messages from one part of the brain to another. These developmental processes can also be disrupted by environmental events (e.g., contagious disease), but the result of the disruption is a functional problem—as in the case of mental retardation, for example—not an obvious physical defect, such as a shortened limb.

Of course, normal development depends on the presence of needed factors, not just the absence of harmful ones. A mother's diet plays an important role in supporting developmental change as well as physical growth (Ricciotti, 2008). But again, as is the case for alcohol and drugs, the timing of dietary and other effects on development helps to determine the outcome (Brodsky & Christou, 2004).

In addition to the effects of drugs and alcohol on the still-developing brain during the fetal period, drinking and drug use during late pregnancy are likely to continue after childbirth. Although a baby's physical development is no longer directly affected by the mother's intake of toxins (unless the mother is breastfeeding), it is clear that drug and alcohol use indirectly interfere with the sensitivity and responsiveness of caregivers and therefore have a real impact on later child development.

Do pregnant women take these facts into consideration? One study of women in Denmark concluded that almost 90% reduced their alcohol intake when they became pregnant—but 40% of them still had one alcohol binge during the pregnancy (Kesmodel, Kesmodel, Larsen, & Secher, 2003). Although this is not the best outcome, it does show that education about drinking in pregnancy is having an effect.

Conclusion

The most vulnerable period of prenatal development actually occurs very early, before many women are even aware that they are pregnant. At this time, environmental events are most likely to cause major birth defects. If any harm was to come to Jennifer's baby as a result of prenatal alcohol exposure, much of it has probably already happened, although problems of brain development are still possible. However, even if her present drinking does no harm, Jennifer would do well to develop drinking habits that allow for the baby's need for sensitive, consistent care.

Critical Thinking

1. Using a child development textbook for information, define the term *teratogen*. Are all birth defects caused by teratogens? Explain your answer.

2. Would you expect a specific type of birth defect, such as cleft palate, to occur because of the kind of teratogen encountered or because of the

(Continued)

(Continued)

timing of the encounter? Use the book *From Neurons to Neighborhoods* (Shonkoff & Phillips, 2000) to find information about this issue. Explain.

3. It was once commonly believed that a pregnant mother's experiences (e.g., being frightened or really wanting a certain kind of food) could "mark" her baby in some way. What problems of critical thinking were at work in this belief?

4. Could you use the information in this section to determine the cause of a particular child's birth defect? Explain your answer.

5. What confounded variables might make it difficult to investigate whether birth defects are caused by alcohol or drugs? (Remember, confounding variables are factors that commonly accompany the events under study—in this case, alcohol and drug use. Confounding variables make it difficult to know which of many possible events actually caused an outcome.) You should use a child development textbook to find information about the role of genetics in habitual alcohol use.

References

Brodsky, D., & Christou, H. (2004). Current concepts in intrauterine growth restriction. *Journal of Intensive Care Medicine, 19*, 307–319.

Kesmodel, U., Kesmodel, P. S., Larsen, A., & Secher, N. J. (2003). Use of alcohol and illicit drugs among pregnant Danish women, 1998. *Scandinavian Journal of Public Health, 31*, 5–11.

Meyer, U., Yee, B. K., & Feldon, J. (2007). The neurodevelopmental impact of prenatal infections at different times of pregnancy: The earlier the worse? *The Neuroscientist, 13*, 241–256.

Ricciotti, H. A. (2008). Nutrition and lifestyle for a healthy pregnancy. *American Journal of Lifestyle Medicine, 2*, 151–158.

Shonkoff, J., & Phillips, D. A. (Eds.). (2000). *From neurons to neighborhoods: The science of early childhood development.* Washington, DC: National Academy Press.

Claim 6

Assisted reproductive technologies (ART) offer reliable ways for couples to have healthy children in spite of fertility problems.

Tyrha and Ray had been hoping to start a family for two years. They were getting pretty discouraged and depressed, and Tyrha, who was 36, could hear her biological clock ticking. When she told Ray of her distress, he tried to be comforting even though he was worried, too. "If it comes down to it, we can have one of those procedures like IVF [in vitro fertilization]. I know they're expensive, but we have money saved," Ray said. "And I know you think those babies might not be healthy, but why not? They get off to a good start before they're implanted in the mother."

Is Ray right in thinking that ART is a sure way to have a healthy baby?

It's a long time since 1978, when the first baby was born after an ovum was fertilized outside the mother's body and then implanted in the uterus. In that time, more than 4.5 million children have been born after reproductive assistance (International Committee for Monitoring Assisted Reproductive Technology, 2009). This long period of observation and large number of events have made it possible to answer some important questions about ART—although we need to keep in mind that over the years there have been many changes in ART methods and in their success. For example, the chances of having a live baby as a result of ART were less than 20% in the 1980s and are now about 40% for women under 35, though less for older women (Servick, 2014).

For many medical issues, it's possible to develop an "animal model" in which methods are tested on an animal species that closely resembles human beings in some way. Although ART methods can be used with animals, some of the questions we'd like to ask about the risk of ART for long-term child health factors are difficult to answer by studying animals. For example, if there are cognitive effects of ART, especially subtle ones, we can probably not understand them by looking at mice. But it is possible to know from animal studies that IVF animals, when adult, can have higher levels of heart disease, high blood pressure, and diabetes than "natural" animals (Servick, 2014).

It's also possible to know, on the basis of both animal and human studies, that ART is associated with somewhat more problems apparent at the time of birth than are usually seen. Helmerhorst, Perquin, Donker, and Keirse (2004) looked at 25 studies that compared babies born after ART to those born after nonassisted conception. More problems were apparent for ART pregnancies than for nonassisted pregnancies—although it is clear that only 4% or 5% of ART babies have these problems.

The Helmerhorst et al. (2004) study found that death of the newborn occurred significantly more often among ART singletons (not multiple births) than among single-born babies from nonassisted conceptions. However, twins were more likely to die after nonassisted conception than after ART. Cesarean sections were more likely after ART, but the effect was stronger for singletons than for twins. The rate of spontaneous abortion (miscarriage) is about 20% higher after ART conception (Frankfurter, 2013).

The Helmerhorst et al. (2004) study also found that twice as many ART babies were born prematurely than was the case for nonassisted conceptions. This effect was especially strong for those who were born at less than 32 weeks gestational age, a level of prematurity that requires careful medical treatment in a neonatal intensive care unit and that may be accompanied by complicating events like brain bleeds, sometimes causing death or long-term problems like deafness. About 40% more of the ART infants than of the nonassisted conceptions were also small for gestational age (SGA), as compared to established standards for prenatal growth as it should be at particular points after conception. (SGA babies are more likely than others to have malformations ranging from very mild to serious and to require additional care.) Cerebral palsy, damage to the nervous system that affects voluntary movement, is another outcome that is more likely for ART babies.

A feature of ART that may be responsible for the problems of some babies is *multiple gestations*. When ova are fertilized outside the mother's body, there are multiple developing cells that are implanted into the uterus. Although all of these sometimes "take," a number—even all—may die, but it is common for several to survive and develop. Even without ART, multiple gestations (twins, triplets, or more) are more likely to be born prematurely and to have associated problems than singletons are. Transferring a single fertilized ovum rather than a group can help prevent some of the problems associated with ART (Skora & Frankfurter, 2012).

Can all of the problems seen in increased numbers in ART pregnancies be blamed on ART itself? It's possible that some developmental difficulties do come from the techniques used in ART; for example, the developing cells are kept in a "broth" that contains more nutrients than are available in the uterus, which may not duplicate the best conditions for development. The method of injecting a sperm into the egg may also be a problem (Servick, 2014).

However, as we try to understand the effects of ART, it's important to realize that some factors affecting development may not be as obvious as others. For instance, why were couples infertile to begin with? Were any of the characteristics that made them need to seek ART also likely to interfere with development after a pregnancy had begun? One study (Kapteijn et al., 2006) asked whether conditions that caused subfertility (two years without conception in spite of unprotected intercourse) might, in themselves, have ill effects on pregnancies that did occur. They compared spontaneous pregnancies among subfertile women to ART pregnancies in a similar group and found that although there seemed to be some effect of subfertility, developmental problems could not be explained without an effect of ART itself.

ART methods have become much more sophisticated since the 1980s, with positive effects on outcomes. Will newly proposed techniques follow the same pathway of development? A recently proposed method to allow a woman carrying harmful mitochondrial DNA to have a healthy baby would involve "three parents," using DNA from a father, a mother, and an egg donor. The nucleus, with its genes, of an ovum from a mother with faulty mitochondrial DNA would be removed and inserted into an ovum with healthy mitochondrial DNA. Theoretically, a resulting baby would not only be healthy but could have children who carried the healthy DNA. But questions about the possible outcome arise because of a related technique used as part of a fertility treatment in the 1990s, which resulted in some normally developing children but one with autism and one with a missing X chromosome (Vogel, 2014). The "three parent" solution is still under discussion, but some researchers are requesting permission to try it in human beings.

Conclusion

Couples with fertility problems are sometimes so determined to become parents that they will grasp at every possible source of help. ART is much more likely to lead to a pregnancy and a live-born child than it used to be, but it is not realistic for Ray to assume that having enough money will enable him and Tyrha to conceive and deliver a healthy child. Fertility does decline with age, and there is not yet a magic solution to this difficulty.

Critical Thinking

1. How does the post hoc fallacy come into thinking about the outcomes of ART procedures?

2. Use a child development textbook or the Internet to find information about multiple gestations (twins, triplets, etc.). What characteristics do multiple gestations share with ART pregnancies?

3. Do sperm have mitochondrial DNA? How does this fact enter into the "three parent" solution?

4. What are confounded variables? What variables are easily confounded in the study of ART outcomes?

5. Why would ethical guidelines for psychologists prohibit the use of randomized controlled trials in the study of ART?

References

Frankfurter, D. (2013, March 4). Adverse perinatal events need to be discussed with patients. *Fertility Weekly,* 9–10.

Helmerhorst, F. M., Perquin, D. A. M., Donker, D., & Keirse, M. J. N. C. (2004). Perinatal outcome of singletons and twins after assisted conception: A systematic review of controlled studies. *British Medical Journal, 328,* 261–265.

International Committee for Monitoring Assisted Reproductive Technology. (2009). World collaborative report on assisted reproductive technology, 2002. *Human Reproduction, 24,* 1909–1919.

Kapteijn, K., de Bruijn, C. S., de Boer, E., de Craen, A. J. M., Burger, C. W., van Leeuwen, F. E., & Helmerhorst, F. M. (2006). Does subfertility explain the risk of poor perinatal outcome after IVF and ovarian hyperstimulation? *Human Reproduction, 21,* 3228–3234.

Servick, K. (2014). Unsettled questions trail IVF's success. *Science, 345,* 744–746.

Skora, D., & Frankfurter, D. (2012). Adverse perinatal events associated with ART. *Seminars in Reproductive Medicine, 30*(2), 84–91.

Vogel, G. (2014). FDA considers trials of "three-parent embryos." *Science, 343,* 827–828.

Claim 7

Genetic relationships are a powerful factor in social and emotional interactions, so people recognize and are attracted to blood relatives even if they have never met them before.

While she was a senior in high school, Amy had become pregnant and given birth to a baby whose adoption had already been arranged. She later married and had two other children, but she still thought often about her first child. She knew he was a boy and thought of him as "Moses" because of the Old Testament story about Moses's adoption. Amy confided her thoughts to a close friend and told her that she was always looking around in crowds to see teenagers of the age "Moses" would now be. She wondered if she would recognize him or whether he would know her. Her friend commented, "I'll bet you would know each other. I was reading that people who are genetically related look and smell familiar to each other and can seek each other out even if they've been separated for a long time. And I'm sure his adoptive parents have never really felt familiar to him."

Was Amy's friend right in thinking that Amy and "Moses" would know each other if they met? Would they feel familiar, and would their connection be different than the relationship between "Moses" and the adoptive parents who had cared for him all his life?

The idea that genetic connections make relationships easy is a popular one and has been applied in discussions about adoption. For example, one author (Verrier, 2011) argues that adopted children, even infants, feel what she calls "genetic confusion" as they encounter a mother who is biologically different from the birth mother. According to Verrier, "At birth a baby knows his mother through the senses: smell, touch, sight of mother's face, tone of voice, heartbeat, resonance. No matter how wonderful the adoptive mother, she doesn't pass the sensory test. The baby is confused, terrified, angry, then sad, helpless, hopeless, alone." From this unfortunate beginning in genetic confusion, says Verrier, arise difficulties between adoptive parents and children, especially because the adoptive mother, too, is genetically confused by the "alien" child.

In addition to concerns about "genetic confusion" in adopted children, some have suggested that Assisted Reproductive Technologies (ART) might cause difficulties for offspring who were genetically different from their parents because sperm or ova had been donated or a surrogate mother had carried the baby through gestation (Golombok, 2013). If *(if!)* genetic confusion exists in adopted children, we would expect the problem to be equal or even worse for those whose genetic relationships to parents are not only convoluted but are quite difficult to understand.

However, there are several reasons to think that "genetic confusion" is not an issue either in adoption or in ART births. First, Verrier's statements about a newborn baby's fear and anger when he sees "the wrong mother" are based on imagination, not fact. Newborn babies do not behave differently when held by their birth mothers, by their fathers, by nurses, by grandmothers, or by interested neighbors. They quickly learn their mothers' smells and prefer them, but they do not already know them at birth. Their limited vision at birth means that they are not likely to see faces well enough to recognize them for some weeks—and of course, before birth they could have had no experience of faces at all. In addition, although newborn babies can respond loudly to pain or frustration, they do not show fear in any usual sense of the term for many more months, so it does not make sense to claim that they are afraid when in contact with a mother who does not resemble them genetically.

Family therapists and other authors have pointed to the problem of secrecy in adoption as well as in ART methods and surrogacy and have argued that families who maintain secrecy about the facts of adoption or donor conception have adverse effects on the children (Imber-Black, 1998; Wincott & Crawshaw, 2006). The concerns expressed in these discussions have not been about genetic information in and of itself

but about the roles of secrets in family life and the problems of relationships in which one party knows a secret and the other does not. In
both adoption and donor conception, the possibility that a child will
accidentally discover the secret can produce anxiety that affects parents'
attitudes toward children. This factor is far more likely than "genetic
confusion" to cause relationship difficulties between adoptive parents
and children.

Although openness in adoption has increased and continues to increase,
lessening the problem of secrecy for adoptive families, the increasing use
of ART methods creates the potential for more complex problems because
even parents who do not want to keep a child's background secret may
have trouble explaining the family history. Rather than a simple adoption
scenario, there are a range of family possibilities such that a child may
know of no other person with a similar history. As Golombok (2013)
has pointed out, "Children born to gay men through surrogacy may have
two 'mothers' and two 'fathers'—a gestational mother, a genetic mother,
a genetic father, and a social father—but no mother in the family home"
(p. 62). Nevertheless, some parents in these situations do create simple
stories or explanations for their young children, and the outcome of their
efforts is positive. Blake, Casey, Readings, Jadva, and Golombok (2010)
interviewed parents and children about their discussions of the children's
donor conception starting at age 4 and found that the children were emotionally neutral about the information but did not understand it well even
at age 7. (The title of this article, "Daddy Ran Out of Tadpoles," shows
how these parents tried to bring the complex explanation down to the children's level.) Those who were told about their background in their teens
or later were more likely to be angry about being lied to by the mother,
but they felt sympathetic toward the father (Jadva, Freeman, Kramer, &
Golombok, 2009). In these families, the major issue seems to have been
a sense of betrayal when there had been secrecy, rather than a sense of
"genetic confusion."

Conclusion

Amy's friend is probably not correct in saying that Amy and "Moses"
would recognize their genetic connection, nor in saying that "genetic confusion" would have meant that "Moses" would not have the kind of relationship with adoptive parents that he would have had with Amy. However, it's
easy to see why Amy would feel comforted by these ideas.

Critical Thinking

1. Golombok (2013, p. 61) argues that the idea of the importance of genetic connections comes from studies of parents who had no genetic connections with their children, and the children had been maltreated before adoption or were exposed to some of the tensions of stepfamilies. What fallacy would be at work if authors assumed that genetic connections were the issue even when other factors clearly existed?

2. The studies by Blake et al. (2010) and Jadva et al. (2009) involved interviews with small numbers of parents and children. Would you expect people agreeing to interviews to be different in some ways from those who would not participate? How might such differences affect the conclusions of these studies?

3. Use the Internet or other sources to find three other websites that reference Verrier's (2011) claims. What else do those sites have in common?

4. Use a child development textbook to find out about children's early understanding of human reproduction. Would you expect 4-year-olds to understand conception and birth? Why or why not?

5. What are the problems with assuming that waiting until a late age to tell a child about donor conception is the cause of the child's feelings about the parents? What fallacy may be a problem here?

References

Blake, L., Casey, P., Readings, J., Jadva, V., & Golombok, S. (2010). "Daddy ran out of tadpoles": How parents tell their children they are donor conceived, and what their 7-year-olds understand. *Human Reproduction, 25,* 2527–2534.

Golombok, S. (2013). Families created by reproductive donation: Issues and research. *Child Development Perspectives, 7*(1), 61–65.

Imber-Black, E. (1998). *The secret life of families.* New York: Bantam Dell.

Jadva, V., Freeman, T., Kramer, W., & Golombok, S. (2009). The experiences of adolescents and adults conceived by sperm donation: Comparison by age of disclosure and family type. *Human Reproduction, 24,* 1909–1919.

Verrier, N. (2011). *Identity and relationships.* Available at http://nancyverrier.com/identity-and-relationships/.

Wincott, E., & Crawshaw, M. (2006). From a social issue to policy: Social work's advocacy for the rights of donor-conceived people to genetic origins information in the United Kingdom. *Social Work in Health Care, 43*(2–3), 53–72.

Claim 8

Babies work hard to be born.

Marcus heard two people in his office talking about a New Age treatment called "rebirthing," and he asked them to explain the concept. "You wrap a person up in a blanket, and then they wiggle and kick to get out of it, just like they did when they were born. It's like starting all over again as a new person." Marcus wasn't sure whether wiggling out of a blanket would make anyone start anew, but he thought a baby might have to fight to be born, so he could see that this method was like being born all over again. But as he thought it over, he wondered how a baby could wiggle to be born but couldn't crawl until 5 or 6 months of age.

Was Marcus right to question the notion of a struggle to be born?

Do babies wiggle and kick their way out of the birth canal? People often assign intentions to unborn infants (e.g., "I guess he'll be born when he decides to"), and the idea that a baby achieves birth through his or her own efforts may be a way people have of thinking of babies as competent and independent even before birth. The belief that a baby is in charge of birth also shows up in some fringe psychotherapies, such as rebirthing, in which a child or an adult pushes through a narrow passage in an imitation of the birth process, sometimes while helpers push rhythmically against the "baby" as if mimicking the contractions of the uterus. The goal of this ceremony seems to be a symbolic new beginning, thus leaving behind the problems of earlier life.

In reality, the baby during birth is passively subjected to the physical forces of the uterus and eventually to the pressures of the mother's voluntary pushing. The first step in the process is one that no infant could accomplish voluntarily: the gradual enlargement of the cervical opening. As the baby lies head down (typically) in the uterus, contractions of the powerful uterine muscles repeatedly force the baby's head downward against the ring of muscle that has held the bag-shaped uterus closed. Slowly, the repeated pressure of the head stretches the cervix to a width that the head can pass through. Because the head is the largest and least flexible part of the fetus, the rest of the body can follow the head through the same opening.

As the head moves down into the vagina, the process becomes more complicated, but the baby remains passive—acted upon rather than acting. The head and body need to pass through a channel that is solidly backed by the mother's pelvic bones. Whereas the cervix was able to stretch to let the baby be moved out of the uterus, the bony structure of the pelvis prevents the tissues of the vagina from yielding as much under pressure. Instead, the baby's head has to yield and the body to shift position for the birth to be successful.

The baby's skull is not a solid bony structure of the kind seen in adult skeletons but instead is a series of bony plates, each incompletely developed and quite soft compared to adult bones. These plates are placed under considerable pressure as the uterus continues to contract, push the baby's body down, and thus press the baby's head against the bony structures behind the tissues of the birth canal. The skull yields under these pressures and is gradually molded into a longer, narrower shape that is able to pass through the narrow outlet between the mother's pelvic bones. (In most cases, the "deformed" skull returns to its rounder shape in a few days without any help.)

At this point in the birth process, the baby's physical makeup and position become especially important, but the baby does not contribute any intentional movements. There is turning and twisting to be done, but these movements occur mechanically because of physical pressures, not because of the baby's efforts.

The oval shape of the human female pelvic outlet makes it easier for the head to pass through when the baby "looks" toward the mother's back. But if the baby's head were straight on the shoulders, this position would mean that the shoulders would be cross-wise in the narrow part of the pelvic outlet. For the shoulders to line up with the long axis of the pelvic outlet—and pass through—the baby needs to be in essence looking over its shoulder, with its face toward the mother's back. This position is typically produced gradually as the baby's body is slowly moved into the right position by the repeated pressure of contractions. The baby must have a normally flexible neck, or the repositioning will not be possible.

What is the baby doing all this time if not trying to be born? The baby is actually being the greatest help to the birth process by inhibiting movements and going along with the mechanical pressures exerted on his or her body. Unlike newly born or older babies, who respond to stress by fighting and yelling, babies during birth display the paralysis reflex. Babies in the birth canal move very little and use no more oxygen than usual—almost as if they have gone to sleep in the midst of the pushing and pressure (Lagerkrantz & Slotkin, 1986).

Before and during birth, babies are very unlikely to fight or make an effort to be born. They have a limited amount of oxygen, which they receive from the mother's lungs via her bloodstream and the umbilical cord. Babies outside the womb breathe and can take in oxygen faster when it is needed for a vigorous effort. Conversely, if an unborn baby tries to increase activity beyond a certain point, the baby will start to asphyxiate as the need for oxygen surpasses the supply. The fetus cannot make his or her mother breathe faster or use any source of oxygen other than the mother's lungs to increase the oxygen supply. Therefore, the unborn baby's environment in the uterus limits it to a quiet, passive response to strong stimulation like that of birth.

Although young humans tend to be resilient and able to recover from harmful influences, it is a mistake to think of babies as "in charge" of their development and birth. On the contrary, fetuses and newborn infants are passive recipients of a wide variety of factors that affect birth and health outcomes, including ethnicity and other genetic factors and the mothers' use of drugs and alcohol, her diet, and her level of prenatal care (Shiao, Andrews, & Helmreich, 2005). Preterm births due to infection or other pregnancy complications are among the most serious problems for infants, and it would be quite unreasonable to imagine that a weak, thin, premature baby would be able to struggle to be born.

Conclusion

Babies do not work to be born but instead become quiet and passive during the process, a strategy that aids birth much more effectively than any effort or movement could. Marcus's officemates misunderstood how babies behave during birth, and their misunderstanding made them accept a practice that is probably not helpful and is potentially harmful.

Critical Thinking

1. How might an apparently minor problem in a baby, such as a stiff neck, affect a birth? How would a baby's position in the uterus head up or head down affect what happens during birth? Explain.

2. Because adults dislike stress and physical pressure, they may think that birth is painful and unpleasant for a baby. Using a child development textbook, find information about birth by Cesarean section. Do the differences between Cesarean and vaginally born babies suggest that the latter have suffered during the birth process? (Don't forget about the baby's production of stress hormones, which is discussed in Lagerkrantz & Slotkin, 1986.) Explain your answer, and state how overgeneralization may confuse thinking about this issue.

3. How is a baby's brain protected when the skull is pressed and molded during the birth process? Does birth entail dangers to a baby's brain other than physical pressure?

4. Find out how long different parts of labor and delivery last. What is the period of time when pressure on a baby's head is most intense? Consult a child development textbook to provide evidence for your answer.

5. Consider the source of oxygen for a fetus before and during birth. What does this situation imply for becoming passive under the stress of birth, rather than crying and struggling? How do matters change when the baby cries for the first time?

References

Lagerkrantz, H., & Slotkin, T. H. (1986). The "stress" of being born. *Scientific American*, *254*, 100–107.

Shiao, S.-Y. P. K., Andrews, C. M., & Helmreich, R. J. (2005). Maternal race/ethnicity and predictors of pregnancy and infant outcomes. *Biological Research for Nursing*, *7*, 55–66.

Claim 9

When a baby has genetic problems, there are no pre- or postnatal methods for treatment.

Melody was a college sophomore whose younger sister, Cayla, had Down syndrome. As a result of her family's experiences with Cayla, Melody was very concerned about genetically caused developmental disabilities and handicapping conditions. She felt as if most people had no idea that children with genetic problems were more like other people than they were different—or at least that was true of Cayla. When her psychology professor pointed out that it would be impossible to "fix" all the cells with a genetic defect in someone's body, Melody did not speak up, but she felt a good deal of turmoil as she tried to think through her own opinion. She thought the professor meant that someone like Cayla could not be helped in any way. But she had seen Cayla develop over the years and knew that her sister could manage much better than most people had expected her to.

Is it correct to say that there are neither medical nor psychological treatments that can improve the functioning of an individual whose genetic makeup is causing developmental problems?

Throughout history, human beings have feared the birth of children with atypical development and their very probable loss early in life. In the 1970s, along with legalization of abortion, prenatal diagnosis by means of amniocentesis (and, later, other methods) began to allow parents to be aware of serious genetic problems like Down syndrome and, in many cases, to decide to terminate pregnancies. These decisions were often based on the many physical problems and early deaths associated with Down syndrome, as well as with the difficulties Down syndrome individuals were likely to experience with education and with self-sufficiency in adulthood because of their intellectual disabilities.

Medical treatment for physical difficulties has enabled a large number of Down syndrome individuals to live into middle age and later in recent years. For example, the tendency to respiratory infections that used to cause early deaths can now be counteracted by antibiotic and other treatments. As more parents expect their Down syndrome children to survive (and perhaps fewer choose to terminate these pregnancies), there is increasing interest in treatment methods that may improve the children's capacity for learning and memory, thus helping them to engage better socially and even to become more self-sufficient.

Because Down syndrome is genetically caused and is accompanied by physical symptoms, medical treatments are still under investigation. One of these involves the drug ELND500, originally developed as a possible treatment for dementia in later life but currently being studied as a way to help mental impairment by getting rid of "plaques" that form in the brain. Another treatment, still far from usable, actually involves "turning off" the extra chromosome that causes Down syndrome by taking neural stem cells, treating them, and reinserting them into the patient (Underwood, 2014). Although it is not possible today to "fix" every cell's mistaken genetic information, it may be possible at some point either to use drugs that counteract some of the genetic effects or to correct some kinds of genetic errors.

There is some room for optimism about medical treatment of Down syndrome and other genetic problems in the future. But what about psychological and educational treatments? Children with Down syndrome or other genetically caused difficulties do not stop developing and learning, although their development is slowed compared to genetically typical children. Is it possible to use their ability to learn to help them overcome some of their delays and also to improve their interactions with other people?

An early problem for Down syndrome children is that they are slow to develop independent walking. Walking without having to hold someone's hand or to hold onto furniture is an important step in toddlers' experience of the world. It's not just about physical activity (though that's important) but about being able to see things and move comfortably at the same time, which is much harder to do when on all fours. The walking toddler is able to explore the world freely, to go where he or she wants to go, and to hold objects and even look at them while walking. One method of helping handicapped children develop independent walking involves the use of a treadmill. Of course they can't just be placed on a treadmill as an adult is, but when they are supported and have their feet in contact with the moving surface, they reflexively perform alternating stepping movements. These movements help to strengthen leg muscles and have been shown to help bring nonwalking children along to the capacity to walk independently. In one report (Smith & Bompiani, 2013), treadmill practice helped a Down syndrome child who had not walked independently become able to walk 10 steps by herself by the time she was 16 months old, an achievement that gave her access to intellectual and social activities that were impossible for her earlier.

Although independent walking is an important developmental event for Down syndrome children, most parents and teachers are more concerned about steps that are more obviously cognitive. Cognitive delays are a major factor in preventing Down syndrome individuals from living independently as adults and reaching normal developmental milestones like school graduation and employment. However, Down syndrome children are not all the same in their cognitive development, with some showing serious delays and others testing much closer to the rest of the population. In one study (Couzens, Haynes, & Cuskelly, 2012), the researchers looked at characteristics of the children and the environment to find factors that were associated with better or worse cognitive development. They found that one important factor that helped boost cognitive growth was maternal education; Down syndrome children with more educated mothers did better cognitively. A second factor was "behavior style" or temperament of the child, a characteristic that is probably biologically determined. Children who tended to be emotionally negative had trouble persisting in the face of frustration and were less likely to perform well on cognitive tests.

The results just mentioned suggest that Down syndrome children's experiences contribute to their cognitive development. De Graaf, van Hove, and Haveman (2013) showed that Down syndrome children placed in regular schools rather than special education did better academically, especially with respect to reading.

So far in this essay, Down syndrome has been used as an important example of a genetic problem influencing development. But it's important to realize that treatment needed for one genetic syndrome is not necessarily the same as what is needed for others. One study (Steele, Scerif, Cornish, & Karmiloff-Smith, 2013) compared Down syndrome children with those with Williams syndrome, which is caused by deletion of genes from a specific chromosome. Children from both groups have trouble with reading, but Down syndrome children have poor language skills and good spatial skills, while Williams children have the reverse situation. These differences are present even before reading instruction begins, so Steele and her colleagues suggest that different instructional emphases are needed for the two groups, rather than treating their reading difficulties as if they had the same causes.

Conclusion

Although it is true that there is presently no method for "fixing" defective genes, Melody was right in thinking that Down syndrome children and others with genetic problems can be treated in ways that will help them develop to their fullest potential. Without treatment and instruction, inside and outside the family, they may do very poorly. It's possible that in the future there may be methods for changing genetic functioning. There is also ongoing work toward understanding genetic problems better and designing effective treatments for specific concerns.

Critical Thinking

1. According to the Underwood (2014) article, one of the problems of systematic studies on drug treatment for Down syndrome is obtaining informed consent from Down syndrome individuals. What rules govern informed consent to research? Are these different for adults and for children or for people with intellectual disabilities?

2. What are some of the concerns reported in the Underwood article that might make it more difficult to get informed consent for research from Down syndrome individuals?

3. The article by Smith and Bompiani (2013) mentions Cochran reviews. What are these, and what are they used for?

4. In the De Graaf et al. (2013) article, what do the authors say about how children were placed in regular or special schools? Could the reasons for their placement affect the outcome of this study?

5. The Couzens et al. (2012) article reports that higher maternal education is associated with better development for Down syndrome children. Give three possible explanations for this association.

References

Couzens, D., Haynes, M., & Cuskelly, M. (2012). Individual and environmental characteristics associated with cognitive development in Down syndrome: A longitudinal study. *Journal of Applied Research in Intellectual Disabilities, 25*, 396–414.

De Graaf, G., van Hove, G., & Haveman, M. (2013). More academics in regular schools? The effect of regular versus special school placement on academic skills in Dutch primary school students with Down syndrome. *Journal of Intellectual Disability Research, 57*, 21–38.

Smith, B. A., & Bompiani, E. (2013). Using a treadmill intervention to promote the onset of independent walking in infants with or at risk of neuromotor delay. *Physical Therapy, 93*, 1441–1446.

Steele, A., Scerif, G., Cornish, K., & Karmiloff-Smith, A. (2013). Learning to read in Williams syndrome and Down syndrome: Syndrome-specific precursors and developmental trajectories. *Journal of Child Psychology and Psychiatry, 54*, 754–862.

Underwood, E. (2014). Can Down syndrome be treated? *Science, 343*, 964–967.

Claim 10

Except for their reproductive organs, there are no differences between boy and girl babies before or soon after birth. Gender differences occur as a result of different experiences for boys and girls.

Tom and Marni were expecting their first baby soon and they knew it would be a boy. They had already chosen the name "Alex," after Tom's father. As they discussed the coming birth, Tom acknowledged that he was anxious about being a father. "I'll have to teach him all about being a boy and then about being a man," he said. "I'm not sure I know how to do this." Marni dismissed Tom's concerns completely. "Of course you have to do a lot of things to be a good father," she answered. "But teach him how to be a boy? He *is* a boy! And girls are girls! They just automatically know how to be who they are. You don't have to worry about teaching them." But Tom continued to be concerned. He didn't see how boy and girl babies could be different except for the obvious physical features. They were both weak and helpless—and a boy would need to overcome that and get strong and adventurous, as Tom and his father both were.

Are boy and girl babies already different before they are born?

It's obvious that boy and girl babies began their development from conception with one important difference: their sex chromosomes. Girls are girls because they have two X chromosomes, whereas boys have one X and one Y, the Y carrying the testis-determining factor that makes the individual male. But do different pairs of sex chromosomes create other differences as well, or are there other factors at work that can cause differences in development?

Whenever we are trying to understand the effects genetic material may have on development, it's important to think in terms of *gene-environment interactions*. Genes are always at work within a surrounding environment, and environments can have different effects when there is different genetic material present. *Evocative* gene-environment interactions occur when genetically caused characteristics create environmental differences, which in turn shape development. Such evocative effects are most obvious when we think about older babies and young children. For example, a cheerful, friendly baby may attract positive adult attention and may thus have more of the experiences that help with language development, while a baby with more negative mood quality may be talked to and played with less. The friendly baby *evokes* more of the adult attention that can foster language.

It's less easy to see how genetic material can evoke environmental differences before birth, but in fact it does do this in a very important way, if we include the internal environment that surrounds the brain and affects other body parts. Because they have the Y chromosome with its testis-determining factor, unborn boys are already producing significant levels of male hormones (androgens). Androgens help to shape the developing brain as well as the reproductive organs in ways that lead to typical gender differences at birth (Alexander & Wilcox, 2012). These hormones increase the growth rate in boys but may slow lung development (Mage & Donner, 2006). In addition, even after birth, boys' androgen levels stay high and even approach the levels seen in early puberty before they drop to low levels at 5 or 6 months of age, while girls' levels drop further from their original low level (Forest, Cathiard, & Bertrand, 1973).The Y chromosome thus continues to "evoke" a difference in internal environments that helps to shape development for some months after birth.

What are the results of the differences in androgen levels? They create differences between unborn and newborn boys or girls in a number of ways. The girls are thinner for their length than the boys and have less prominent chins. The girls also have greater control over their fingers and express more reaction to pain with their crying, as well as showing more pain response to injections on a standardized scale (Bellieni et al., 2013). Newborn girls cry longer than boys do when they hear a female infant crying (Alexander & Wilcox, 2012).

An additional important measure of differences between male and female fetuses is *habituation.* This term refers to the way fetuses and infants respond to a sensory stimulus like a tone. When they first hear it, they are attentive; if the stimulus is something they can see, they scan it visually for a while. However, after several repetitions of the stimulus, they pay less attention, and even if the stimulus is taken away and then returned, they look at it only briefly, but will again pay close attention to a new stimulus. When this process has taken place, they are said to have habituated to the original stimulus. It turns out that male and female fetuses are different in their habituation to a sound, with females habituating more quickly than males (Hepper, Dornan, & Lynch, 2012). Because habituation seems to be related to cognitive abilities, this difference seems to be an important one.

Can these early differences between boys and girls explain later gender differences? Some of the obvious later differences have to do with a higher mortality rate for boys than for girls in the first year of life, a higher rate of autism in boys than in girls, and a higher rate of mood disorders in women than in men. Other differences in social, sensory, and motor behavior have been reported (Alexander & Wilcox, 2012). Some of these are apparent in children so young that it is hard to imagine how cultural factors could have influenced them. On top of these, though, there are culturally sanctioned beliefs about how boys and girls ought to be, as mentioned by Tom in the earlier vignette, with his concerns about strength and adventurousness. These are more obvious when children are older, but in fact can be at work in early infancy; for example, it may be the culturally approved belief that boys can be handled more roughly that causes boys to have more head injuries than girls as a result of being dropped in the first three months after birth (Greenes, Wigotsky, & Schutzmann, 2001).

Conclusion

It is clear that there are a range of differences between boys and girls not only when they are newborn, but even before birth. Tom will find that he does not have to—and actually cannot—teach these. However, little Alex's development into an adult will also be guided by cultural rules about how boys and girls should be treated and about how men and women should behave. Tom and Marni will be giving both direct and indirect instruction that will help Alex develop from the male characteristics he had at birth to some version of the characteristics of manhood his culture approves of. Tom's job will be an important one, but perhaps not exactly what he now thinks it will be.

Critical Thinking

1. In the 1970s, it was not unusual for psychology professors to have their students read "The Story of X" (Gould, n.d.). Have a look at this story and comment on the view of early sex differences that is conveyed. How does this compare with the material cited in the present essay?

2. Use a child development textbook to find a definition of habituation. How did Hepper et al. (2012) measure habituation in unborn babies?

3. Girls with congenital adrenal hyperplasia are exposed to unusually high levels of male hormones during prenatal development. Use the Internet or other sources to find two studies on behavioral differences between these and other girls. What conclusions about the role of prenatal hormones can you draw from the studies you find?

4. The Introduction to this book mentioned the critical thinking problem of the "seductive idea" *infant determinism*. When researchers try to trace the foundations of later sex differences by looking at unborn and newborn babies, are they being influenced by infant determinism? Why or why not?

5. Use a child development textbook to find types of gene-environment interactions other than the evocative type. Do the other types appear to apply to the issue of development of sex differences? Why or why not?

References

Alexander, G. M., & Wilcox, T. (2012). Sex differences in early infancy. *Child Development Perspectives, 6*(4), 400–406.

Bellieni, C. V., Aloisi, A. M., Ceccarelli, D., Valenti, M., Arrighi, D., Muraca, M. C. . . . Buonocore, G. (2013). Intramuscular injections in newborns: Analgesic treatment and sex-linked response. *Journal of Maternal-Fetal and Neonatal Medicine, 26,* 419–422.

Forest, M., Cathiard, A., & Bertrand, J. (1973). Evidence of testicular activity in early infancy. *Journal of Clinical Endocrinology and Metabolism, 37,* 148–150.

Gould, L. (n.d.). *The story of X.* Available at www3.delta.edu/cmurbano/bio199/aids_sexuality/babyx.pdf.

Greenes, D. S., Wigotsky, M., & Schutzmann, S. A. (2001). Gender differences in rates of unintentional head injury in the first 3 months of life. *Ambulatory Pediatrics, 1,* 178–180.

Hepper, P. G., Dornan, J. C., & Lynch, C. (2012). Sex differences in fetal habituation. *Developmental Science, 15,* 373–383.

Mage, D. T., & Donner, M. (2006). Female resistance to hypoxia: Does it explain the sex differences in mortality rates? *Journal of Women's Health, 15,* 786–794.

Part II

Infants and Toddlers

Claim 11

Parents need to have contact with their babies right after birth so that they can bond with them.

When Eric and Tina's little girl, Emma, was born, there were some minor problems for both mother and baby. Emma was taken away to be watched and cared for in a special nursery, and her parents did not get to hold her until the next day. Now Emma is a happy, healthy, lively 2-year-old. When Eric was asked how she was doing, he replied, "Oh, very well, especially considering that we never got a chance to bond with her."

Does a parent's relationship with a child really depend on immediate contact after the child is born?

Many of the beliefs discussed in this book date back centuries, but the claim that parents require early contact to bond with their babies began in the 1970s. It had its origin in a much-publicized research project carried out by M. H. Klaus and J. H. Kennell (1982; Klaus, Kennell, & Klaus, 2001). Although these researchers later noted some errors of analysis and interpretation and tried to soften the impact of their report, the public continues to favor a simplified version of the story.

To understand the issues involved requires a good definition of bonding. Bonding is one of those things that few can define, but everybody thinks they "know it when they see it." The researchers (Klaus & Kennell, 1982) who originally used the term later tried to clarify that they were not comparing human relationships to chemical glues. Bonding, they later said, was not necessarily instantaneous nor was it a process that made each member of a pair equally concerned and involved with the other. Instead, *bonding* is an emotional development in which an adult begins to have powerful, positive feelings toward an infant, to be preoccupied with, concerned with, and prepared to make any sacrifice for that baby. Although most parents develop these strong positive feelings, some do not (Sluckin, 1998).

Bonding may begin in anticipation of a birth or an adoption, but it progresses through contact with the baby who is the object of the bonding. Bonding may involve very quick development of strong feelings, like falling in love at first sight, or it may take weeks or months to develop. In either case, however, the issue is an emotional change in the adult, not in the infant, although the baby's later emotional development is influenced by the care of a devoted—or an indifferent—caregiver.

Unfortunately for researchers' understanding of bonding, the adult's emotional change is not signaled by some simple observable event. There is no litmus test for bonding, although many attempts have been made to assess the nature of maternal-infant interaction and the way this interaction reflects the mother's emotions (Horowitz, Logsdon, & Anderson, 2005). Emotional changes often lead to behavior changes, so one can look for behaviors that might indicate bonding. Generally, bonding is associated with increased attention to the baby, such as looking, talking, and touching. But these actions are very much affected by individual personality and cultural factors. For example, a naturally quiet or depressed mother may not talk much compared with a more outgoing person or one in better mental health. Without a measure of the mother's behavior before birth, there is no way to know which behavior is the effect of bonding and which is the effect of other factors in the mother's life.

Cultural factors and social expectations also play a part in bonding. A middle-class American woman (who has heard all about bonding) may look at and talk to her baby as frequently as she thinks makes her a good mother, but women from some traditional societies may avoid too much looking and talking, wishing as they do to avoid attracting the attention of harmful spirits to their babies. For these traditional women, avoiding looking too much at their babies may indicate their deep emotional involvement, whereas looking freely might indicate that they are indifferent.

Because it is so hard to measure some bonding-related behaviors, and much harder to measure bonding itself, early research on this topic looked at other factors that could be measured easily, such as the timing of a mother's first contact with her infant after birth and aspects of the baby's development. Researchers speculated that bonding might only be possible when infants are extremely young. However, in the United States at that time, customary practice gave most mothers only a glimpse of their babies shortly after birth. According to hospital routine, babies were taken to a nursery, where the staff pediatrician, who usually came in only once a day for this purpose, examined the infant before the child had more contact with the mother. (During this time in history, fathers were not significantly involved at this point of newborn care.) Such practices would be less than ideal if it were true that early contact was needed for bonding purposes.

As the issue of timing of mother-infant contact received more attention, researchers became interested in comparing how mothers and babies would react in two different situations—an arrangement by which mother and baby spent time together in the first few hours after birth versus the then-customary delayed contact. A change in hospital policy in one city made it possible to carry out a study that was close to the ideal of a randomized comparison. As the hospital switched from a delayed-contact to an early-contact policy, researchers were able to compare mothers and babies with births in the last days of the old policy to those with births in the first days of the new policy. It seemed reasonable to think that chance alone determined whether a baby was born during one week or during the next week, so any differences between the groups of mothers and babies ought to be related to their experiences with early or delayed contact. In fact, the early-contact babies were later reported to perform better on several measures, including language development at age 5 years, and the mothers were judged to be more attentive and affectionate.

Discussion of this research focused on the idea that the mothers had responded to early contact with their babies by better bonding, that bonding had led to improved relationships and more attentive and sensitive baby care, and that improved care had resulted in improved child development. But should you conclude that all of this is correct—that early contact causes bonding, bonding causes good child care and development, and therefore all families need to have early contact with their babies? No, there are several problems with those conclusions. Very few mothers and babies were in the study, causing statistical problems. (Most statistical tests are intended for use with large numbers of participants and have problems with the biases that may be associated with small groups.) It was difficult to know how to interpret certain measures, such as the length of breastfeeding time. And all of the mothers were very young and poor and experiencing practical problems, such as where to live and how to care for their babies. Problems like these are not characteristic of older, more educated, more affluent mothers, who may not respond in the same way to early contact as the younger mothers did. Mothers' care of infants and infant development are probably affected by many factors working together, rather than simply by early contact and the events referred to as "bonding." For example, the mothers' own childhood experiences may affect the ways they think about and respond to their children (Jefferis & Oliver, 2006).

Do adoptive or foster mothers also bond with children they did not carry or give birth to? Some researchers have examined this by looking at the mothers' levels of oxytocin as they handled their babies, as well as their behavioral expressions of delight in the babies (Bick, Dozier, Bernard, Grasso, & Simons, 2013). They found that foster mothers who produced high levels of oxytocin when cuddling their babies also showed more delight in the babies, and this occurred even though the mothers were not with the babies until at least two weeks after their births. Again, this suggests that there is no "magic" in early contact.

However, parents usually receive a lot of pleasure from holding their babies very soon after birth, and this is a good enough reason to allow and encourage early contact with healthy babies.

Conclusion

It is hard to measure how parents "fall in love" with their babies, and existing research does not make it very clear that early contact is necessary for good relationships and development. Emma was developing very well, and obviously her parents were doing the right things for her. Eric and Tina might have been saved some worry if they had not believed that early contact could make such a big difference in their daughter's progress.

Critical Thinking

1. Using a child development textbook for information, comment on the importance of a mother's age, education, and socioeconomic status for her baby's development. How might these factors be related to bonding?

2. Describe the differences between attachment and bonding. Use evidence from a child development textbook in your description.

3. Use the Internet to access four or five commercial websites offering information about infant and child care and parenting. How do the sites define bonding and attachment?

4. With respect to the research discussed in this essay, should you be concerned about confounding variables and generalizability? Explain your answer.

5. When people assume without evidence that pregnancy and childbirth are essential to a mother's emotional response to her baby, what critical thinking problems may be involved?

References

Bick, J., Dozier, M., Bernard, K., Grasso, D., & Simons, R. (2013). Foster mother–infant bonding: Associations between foster mothers' oxytocin production, electrophysiological brain activity, feelings of commitment, and caregiving quality. *Child Development, 84,* 826–840.

Horowitz, J. A., Logsdon, M. C., & Anderson, J. K. (2005). Measurement of maternal-infant interaction. *Journal of the American Psychiatric Nurses Association, 11,* 164–172.

Jefferis, P. G., & Oliver, C. (2006). Associations between maternal childrearing cognitions and conduct problems in young children. *Clinical Child Psychology and Psychiatry, 11,* 83–102.

Klaus, M. H., & Kennell, J. H. (1982). *Parent-infant bonding.* St. Louis, MO: C.V. Mosby.

Klaus, M. H., Kennell, J. H., & Klaus, P. (2001). *Bonding: Building the foundations of secure attachment and independence.* New York: Perseus.

Sluckin, A. (1998). Bonding failure: "I don't know this baby, she's nothing to do with me." *Clinical Child Psychology and Psychiatry, 3,* 11–24.

Claim 12

Babies are born with emotional attachments to their mothers and can recognize their mothers at once.

Linda was very excited about her first baby, soon to be born. "I've carried her all this time, and I just can't wait to get a look at her! It will be so wonderful when she sees me and knows I'm her mommy! We'll just look and look at each other."

Linda's excitement is a very positive sign, but will she be disappointed with her baby's response to her? Will the baby know her? How might you tell?

Attachment and recognition are not the same thing, although of course a baby would have to recognize a person in some way before he or she could show attachment. Because recognition has to come first, examination of this claim must begin with the baby's relevant experiences and abilities for recognition. Can a newborn baby recognize his or her mother—by sight or in any other way?

Recognizing a person involves remembering a previous experience with him or her, either a visual experience of the face or some other detail, such as posture or movement. Memory for another person can also be based on recognition of the voice or a characteristic smell or taste (e.g., the taste of the mother's milk). Or memory and recognition can be based on touch sensations, such as skin texture, warmth, or pressure exerted in holding. After a few weeks of life, a baby has had many opportunities to learn about sensory experiences with parents and other caregivers, but at the time of birth a baby has had no opportunities for the experiences of touch, sight, or smell and only limited experiences for taste (through the amniotic fluid) and hearing (sound waves passing through the mother's body). Newborns can perform some complex perceptual tasks (e.g., noticing that an object they see has changed in both shape and movement; Laplante, Orr, Vorkapich, & Neville, 2000), but this does not necessarily mean that they can deal with all the characteristics that make up a human face or voice, even if they had seen or heard the person before.

It is possible that newborns can recognize their mothers' voices. Babies' hearing is much better developed than their vision, and they have already experienced hearing the sound waves that travel through their mother's body into the uterus—even though their mother's voice must sound a lot different after it passes through skin, muscle, and fluid than when it is heard through air. There does seem to be evidence that newborns can recognize their own mother's voice. Infants will work (by sucking on a nipple) to hear their mother's voice rather than that of other women (DeCasper & Fifer, 1980). However, it is impossible to know whether the baby's response shows simply the recognition of a voice the baby has heard before or whether the baby recognizes his or her mother as a person who has a special role in the baby's life. Because babies tested weeks after birth do not seem to respond with very different emotions to their mothers than to other people, it seems most unlikely that newborns have such a complex set of feelings and thoughts as those associated with emotional attachment.

Within days after birth, infants recognize the smell of their mother's milk and turn toward it, if they have been breastfed. (Bottle-fed babies do not do this.) Breastfed infants possibly learned the smell after birth, although some evidence suggests that unborn babies learn the smells and tastes of their mother's food through their experiences with the amniotic fluid inside the uterus (Mennella & Beauchamp, 1993).

As for recognizing the mother by sight, newborn infants have such limited vision that they would probably have difficulty recognizing an individual face, no matter how well known it is, for several reasons. For one, babies are only able to get a well-focused visual picture when objects are between 8 and 12 inches from their eyes. Anything too close or too distant is just a blur. The ideal looking distance is achieved when a caregiver holds a baby and bends his or her face toward the child's—and because well-cared-for infants frequently experience this type of contact, they have plenty of opportunities to become familiar with their mother's face or that of another frequent caregiver. Within a few weeks, babies can show that they remember their mother's face in one specific way; given several faces at which to look at different times, babies spend the most time looking at their own mother's face.

Infants also experience hearing their caregivers' voices, either talking or singing. Within a few months, babies may become interested or calmed in response to their mother's singing (Shenfield, Trehub, & Nakata, 2003), but it is not clear whether this response happens at birth.

What about attachment, though? Newborns seem to have some ways of recognizing familiar experiences with another person. Do these experiences have any emotional meaning for babies? Is a familiar person an important person, from a baby's viewpoint? Keep in mind how the baby feels, not how the mother feels. A mother would be distraught if she thought her baby had been kidnapped or was very sick. Does the baby feel any type of similar concern about separation from the mother, the father, or any other family member? *Attachment* is usually defined as a type of emotional connection where there is distress about separation and increased comfort when the attached person is reunited with the other.

Although there are standardized techniques for evaluating a 12-month-old's emotional attachment to an adult (Ainsworth, Blehar, Waters, & Wall, 1978), no such methods exist for newborns. Generally, emotional attachment is thought to be indicated when one person tries to stay near another or shows distress and grief when separated from another. Newborn babies have little ability to try to stay near someone because they cannot walk or even crawl. They can only maintain contact by crying and getting an older person to come to them. However, newborns seem to cry because of physical discomfort, not because someone leaves them. They will accept feeding and care from any adult, not just from their mother. If separated from their mother (e.g., by adoption), the youngest infants do not appear to grieve or to be distressed. Only after about 8 months of age are babies likely to show intense disturbance over abrupt, long-term separations. They cry, look sad, and have trouble sleeping and eating, unlike the youngest babies. These facts suggest that newborns have no emotional attachment to their mother but develop this important emotional response over a number of months of contact.

The evidence seems to show that newborns have no emotional attachment to the mother and only limited recognition of her. Yet many readers have observed that a baby's mother can calm a crying newborn when other adults are unsuccessful. Doesn't this mean that the baby knows and cares for his or her mother? In light of the previous evidence, this does not seem likely, and an alternative explanation must be considered: that the mother behaves in ways that other adults do not. The mother is genuinely concerned and highly motivated to comfort her baby and therefore persists in rocking, humming, and patting when others give up. In addition, the mother, who is often the primary caregiver, quickly develops experience with her baby and within a few days may be more aware than others of "what works" to soothe her baby.

The belief that newborns are emotionally attached to their mother has important implications for practical decisions about adoption, foster care, and infant day care. Babies in the first months of life are not likely to show distress when separated from their mother. This means that infant distress in a new situation means something about the situation itself—for example, a day care center may have too few or inexperienced caregivers, and a baby may protest against clumsy or even rough handling. A baby who complains in the first months of life generally has something specific to complain about. He or she is not anxious about separation, and certainly the infant of this age is not trying to control or manipulate adults.

New mothers who expect their babies to show strong attachment behaviors right away may be disappointed, withdraw from their baby, and start the new relationship on a rocky pathway. It is important for parents and other adults to understand that attachment is a gradual process. Mothers who experience depression during pregnancy or after their baby is born may be especially vulnerable to sad feelings about a baby who "doesn't love" them in the way the mothers believed would happen. Fortunately, newborns typically do enough to make parents feel that their baby cares about them. They look at adults' faces and eyes when nearby and often become calm and relax in response to a parent's attempts to soothe them. These responses are good enough to start the parent-child relationship, and soon babies are so active and responsive that their parents are locked into their emotional connection. As the months go on, babies become attached and show the attachment in their behavior.

Conclusion

Newborn babies do not really recognize their mothers and do not show any emotional attachment to them. However, Linda's baby should behave sociably enough toward her, so she will probably not feel disappointed. Before long, the two will develop an affectionate relationship.

Critical Thinking

1. Using a child development textbook as a source, create a definition of emotional attachment that works for the material discussed in this essay. To work, your definition needs to apply to the relationship between adult caregivers and infants or young children, and it needs to focus on the feelings of the babies, not the adults.

2. Is your definition an operational definition? *Operational definitions* involve the ways an observer can measure whether an event or a phenomenon is present—for example, you might operationally define *anxiety* in a child in terms of the amount of time that a child spends crying and looking away from a person or an object. If your definition of attachment was not an operational definition, change your definition so it involves measurement of some kind.

3. Find and read the DeCasper and Fifer (1980) article. How did the authors choose the mothers and babies who participated in their study? If they had chosen differently, how might the outcome of the study have been affected?

4. Find and read any article that describes the Strange Situation, discussed by Ainsworth and her colleagues (1978) and most child development textbook authors. For which age group was this observational technique designed? Would you expect either younger or older children to behave in the same way as the group in the study? Citing information in your textbook or other sources, describe several reasons why you might expect children of other ages to behave differently.

5. Use information from a child development textbook to describe some ways in which you could test the vision of newborn babies. Remember that they cannot name letters of the alphabet as adults can, nor can they point to right or left as preschool children do during a vision test.

References

Ainsworth, M., Blehar, M., Waters, E., & Wall, S. (1978). *Patterns of attachment.* Hillside, NJ: Lawrence Erlbaum.

DeCasper, A., & Fifer, W. (1980). Of human bonding: Infants prefer their mothers' voices. *Science, 208,* 1174–1176.

Laplante, D. P., Orr, R. R., Vorkapich, L., & Neville, K. E. (2000). Multiple dimension processing by newborns. *International Journal of Behavioral Development, 24*, 231–240.

Mennella, J., & Beauchamp, G. (1993). Early flavor experiences: When do they start? *Zero to Three, 14*(2), 1–7.

Shenfield, T., Trehub, S. E., & Nakata, T. (2003). Maternal singing modulates infant arousal. *Psychology of Music, 31*, 365–375.

Claim 13

When mothers of young babies are depressed, the problem is caused by the changes in hormones they experience after the birth.

Tom was worried about his wife, Evie. She had been sad and depressed for weeks, since not long after the birth of their now 2-month-old daughter. Evie cried easily and seemed overwhelmed by caring for the baby and even by getting herself dressed or talking to friends. She was tired, but she didn't sleep much, even when the baby was sleeping. Was this what they called postpartum depression? Was it dangerous? And when would it ever end? Tom asked Evie's mother what she thought, but she did not seem concerned. "It's just her hormones," she said. "When they get straightened out, she'll get right back to her old self." But it seemed to Tom that this was all taking a much longer time than he had seen in friends' wives and in his sister when she had her children.

Is depression in young mothers a matter of hormonal changes?

There are a variety of emotional difficulties following childbirth, and the more serious ones are given the name "perinatal mood disorders" (PMD). Most new mothers experience a few days at least of the "baby blues," when they feel vulnerable and emotionally fragile as well as not completely well physically. Perhaps 10% continue to have these feelings after a few weeks, at a level that amounts to postpartum ("after birth") depression. Depressed young mothers have a sense of worthlessness and inadequacy but are also irritable and unsociable, and they are often dismayed by unwanted thoughts of harming their babies. A small percentage experience a severe emotional disturbance called "postpartum psychosis," in which they may hallucinate voices telling them to hurt or kill the baby—and in a few cases they obey the voices. For example, in the unfortunate case of Andrea Yates that brought so much attention to PMD, a mother who had experienced emotional disturbance after the births of each of her children drowned all five of them in the belief that they should go to God while innocent (see Cohen, 2012).

In addition to the small but real danger of harm to the baby by a mother with PMD, these emotional disorders make it difficult for mothers to socialize and play with their babies in ways that are known to encourage good infant development. Probably as a result, babies of depressed mothers show delays in language development (Kaplan et al., 2014) and are thus at risk for both social and cognitive development problems. It's clear that maternal depression early in a child's life has the potential to do moderate to serious developmental harm, and understanding how it occurs could open the door to important interventions that would improve families' lives in many ways.

It is not surprising that hormonal changes have been emphasized in explanations of PMD. Each case of PMD is preceded by a birth, and each birth is the beginning of a cascade of hormonal changes in the mother. High levels of progesterone and estrogen, present and necessary during pregnancy, are rapidly reduced following birth and are excreted in urine and in breast milk (sometimes causing the swelling of the breast area in very young nursing babies, as they ingest reproductive hormones with their mothers' milk). The hormones oxytocin and prolactin increase as mothers breastfeed. Most of the hormonal changes are over in a week or so, but breastfeeding mothers continue to experience some hormonal differences from their prepregnant state, as shown by the fact that most do not menstruate as long as the baby is exclusively breastfed (although they may ovulate after a few months).

Still, it is clear that although all new mothers experience hormonal changes, most do not have even moderate PMD and recover quickly from the "baby blues." Is there something special about the women who do go on to PMD or about their situations? It's possible that depressed mothers have some unusual brain characteristics that make them vulnerable to the effects of hormone changes, but it's also possible that personal and situational factors, like the temperament or early behavior of the baby and other family members, may either protect against depression or make it more likely to occur (Sword, Clark, Hegadoren, Brooks, & Kingston, 2012).

What about parents who do not go through hormonal changes or other problems during and after pregnancy? Do they experience anything like PMD? We can answer this question to some extent by looking at adoptive mothers and at fathers. Both experience some of the challenges of caring for a young infant, but neither has had the physical strain of pregnancy and childbirth, and neither has known changes in reproductive hormones like those that follow pregnancy and birth.

It might be thought that women who have long wanted a child and who have adopted, perhaps because of infertility, would be very happy with this outcome. However, it appears that mood disorders are approximately as frequent in adoptive mothers as in birth mothers (Mott, Schiller, Richards, O'Hara, & Stuart, 2011). Sleep deprivation was a factor in both groups of mothers, but adoptive mothers were more likely to be depressed if they had a history of infertility, past psychological disorders, and less than the highest marital satisfaction—in spite of the absence of the reproductive hormone changes characteristic after childbirth.

Are fathers depressed following the birth of a child? A review by Tuszynska-Bogucka and Nawra (2014) reports that some are and notes the existence of the www.SadDaddy.com website devoted to their concerns. Swain, Daytin, Kim, Tolman, and Volling (2014) referenced work estimating that about 10% of fathers in the United States experience depression in the first year after a child is born. Again, as in the case of adoptive mothers, these negative moods occur in the absence of the dramatic hormonal changes that follow childbirth but in the presence of the real challenges of child care, such as sleep deprivation.

Conclusion

Evie's mother was probably wrong in thinking that hormonal changes were responsible for her daughter's postpartum depression and that the solution was just to wait for the hormonal changes to be complete. Although hormonal changes may be one factor in PMD, evidence from adoptive mothers and from fathers tells us that other causes are also at work in creating mood disorders in young parents. The potential for harm to development—and even direct harm to the child—as a result of parental depression is high enough that help should be sought for depressed young mothers—and fathers, too.

Critical Thinking

1. It's been common for people to assume that hormonal changes in mothers happened just as a result of pregnancy and childbirth. Look at the papers by Swain et al. (2014) and by Tuszynska-Bogucka and Nawra (2014) to see information about hormonal changes in both men and women that appear to result simply from being with a baby. (There is no need to read the whole paper in either case, but you can find sections that address this question.)

2. When mothers are depressed, they may feel that there is something wrong with their babies. Explain how the fundamental attribution error may be at work here.

3. The paper by Mott et al. (2011) suggests that the experience of a history of infertility may make an adoptive mother more prone to depression. How could you test this idea with a nonrandomized study? (Hint: what are some reasons for adoption other than infertility?)

4. According to www.SadDaddy.com, "as many as 1 in 4" new fathers experience depression. How does this estimate compare to the statement in the Swain et al. (2014) paper?

5. Find information on the Internet about the Andrea Yates case. Use the Internet and other sources to find information about whether the killing of the children could have been predicted and prevented.

References

Cohen, A. (2012). How Andrea Yates lives, and lives with herself, a decade later. *The Atlantic*. Available at www.theatlantic.com/national/archive/2012/03/how-andrea-yates-lives-and-lives-with-herself-a-decade-later/254302/

Kaplan, P. S., Danko, C. M., Everhart, K. D., Diaz, A., Asherin, R. M., Vogeli, J. M., & Fekri, S. M. (2014). Maternal depression and expressive communication in one-year-old infants. *Infant Behavior & Development, 37*(3), 398–405.

Mott, S. L., Schiller, C. E., Richards, J. G., O'Hara, M. W., & Stuart, S. (2011). Depression and anxiety among postpartum and adoptive mothers. *Archives of Women's Mental Health,14*, 335–343.

Swain, J. E., Daytin, C. J., Kim, P., Tolman, R. M., & Volling, B. L. (2014). Progress on the paternal brain: Theory, animal models, research, and mental health implications. *Infant Mental Health Journal, 35*(5), 394–408.

Sword, W., Clark, A. M., Hegadoren, K., Brooks, S., & Kingston, D. (2012). The complexity of postpartum mental health and illness: A critical realist study. *Nursing Inquiry, 19*(1), 51–62.

Tuszynska-Bogucka, W., & Nawra, K. (2014). Paternal postnatal depression: A review. *Archives of Psychiatry & Psychotherapy, 2*, 61–69.

Claim 14

It's been proved that it's always better for parentless children to be placed in foster care rather than in orphanages or similar institutions.

Valerie was concerned about a friend who was planning to adopt a child from an orphanage in Ethiopia. She remarked to another friend, Olivia, that this could be a big mistake. "I read that kids who have been in orphanages are always really damaged," she said. "It stands to reason that the staff in orphanages are mean to the kids and don't really care what happens to them. Besides, there are all those awful pictures of how the children were abused in those old Romanian orphanages. But I also read that kids who have been in foster care are much better off and easier to deal with. I'm not planning to adopt, but if I did I'd be sure the baby had been in a foster home." Olivia couldn't really remember how long ago those pictures of children in Romania had come out, but she wondered whether the orphanages were still the same today. She also wondered how these children could be studied and what anyone had actually found out about them.

Is it clear that parentless children will develop much better if they are cared for in foster homes rather than in institutions?

In the 1990s, shocking pictures emerged from Romania, showing the conditions in which children had lived in orphanages during the Ceauşescu regime that had collapsed not long before. Observers were horrified by images of young children tied to their cribs and older ones naked and in groups, gazing in puzzlement at the camera ("A lost boy," 2014). A study of Romanian children adopted by British families (Rutter et al., 2010) later showed that of the children who were adopted, the majority caught up in their development over the years and did well, but some did not. It was difficult to know whether cases of poor development had to do with the orphanage experience or with preexisting problems—perhaps even the problems that had caused them to be placed in the orphanage to begin with. (Most of the children were not orphans in the literal sense; they usually had at least one parent alive who, for some reason, was not caring for the child.)

As time went on, Romanian orphanage conditions improved somewhat, but studies of adoptees from those institutions were still showing less than ideal developmental progress (Rutter et al., 2010). At the beginning of the 21st century, a team of researchers from the United States proposed an unusual study, the Bucharest Early Intervention Project (BEIP; Zeanah et al., 2003). Unlike most studies of treatments for at-risk children, this was designed as an experimental study with randomized assignment of orphanage children to two groups. One group of children was to stay in the usual care of the orphanage, which involved poor conditions with frequent changes of staff, making it difficult for a child to develop any stable relationships with caregivers. The other group was to be assigned to highly trained and carefully selected foster families who would be paid for the children's care and who could consult frequently with experts knowledgeable about the expected early problems. The foster children would have only a few caregivers and plenty of opportunity to develop warm, stable relationships with them.

The conclusion drawn from the BEIP (Fox, Almas, Degnan, Nelson, & Zeanah, 2011) was that the quality of children's development was significantly helped by experience with foster care, and that the foster children progressed much better than those who remained in orphanage care. The BEIP researchers and others have recommended against institutional care for parentless children and have advocated greatly expanded foster care systems in many countries.

Meanwhile, however, another study (Whetten et al., 2014) presented conclusions that contradicted the recommendations based on the BEIP study. The Whetten study used random sampling (but not random assignment to groups) to investigate the development of parentless children in five low- to middle-income countries. The researchers looked at 1,357 children who were living in institutions and at 1,480 orphaned or separated children living in foster families. The institutional children were significantly taller for their ages and were rated by their caregivers as having better physical health than the family children, and the family children were rated by their caregivers as having fewer emotional problems. The authors concluded that institutional care does not universally reduce well-being and development of parentless children.

Because the Whetten et al. (2014) study did not have a randomized design, it is subject to all the problems of nonrandomized designs, including confounding of variables. It is not safe to conclude that a correlation between good development and institutional care means that the type of care caused the difference between the two groups. The BEIP study, with its randomized design, should be free of these problems—but it is not. The difficulty with the BEIP design is that although it appeared to be comparing children's development with respect to a single variable, the care location, it inadvertently introduced a second variable—the funding, training, and number of the caregivers each child encountered. The institutional group children were in a situation where financial resources were scarce, there was no special training for the staff, and each child met many different caregivers over time. The foster family group members were with a well-trained, well-funded, consistent, and unchanging small number of caregivers. These facts mean that there should have been four, rather than two, groups whose development was compared: a standard, low-quality orphanage group; a low-quality, poorly trained and funded, foster family group; a high-quality institutional group with adequate funding, training, and consistent staff; and a high-quality foster family group. Only a design of that type could let us avoid the confounding of care location and care quality.

An important issue about these studies is that the ages of children may make a great deal of difference to their care needs. Older children have important relationships with their peers and may thrive in group care (e.g., elite boarding schools). Infants and toddlers do better if they are with a small number of regular caregivers, and the National Association for the Education of Young Children (1996) has recommended that day care for the very young should involve small groups of children with a single caregiver, rather than larger groups with more caregivers who "circulate" to all children who need them rather than stay with the familiar small group. When children are cared for in an institution over many months or years, it can be difficult to provide familiar caregivers both night and day for long periods of time. Caregivers in institutions most often work in shifts and go home to their own families when off duty. Pay is usually poor, encouraging high staff turnover (followed by the entrance of unfamiliar caregivers) when staff members see a chance to be paid more. Many institutional caregivers are young women in their childbearing years who may leave the job when they have babies, creating additional turnover and new unfamiliar caregivers for the infants and toddlers. Foster families can often provide more consistent, stable care, with one of a small number of adults always present, night and day, and for long periods of time. However, foster families have their own lives and may have reasons for abruptly deciding to give up care of a foster child, including the birth of a baby or the need to care for an older family member. (Some foster families specialize in certain age ranges and will decide to decline further care for a child who gets "too old.") In some parts of the United States, foster mothers may also be employed outside the home, and foster children may spend hours of each day in out-of-home care. For all these reasons, there is no certainty that infants and toddlers will have an appropriate number of caregivers, whether they are in an institution or a foster family, although it would probably be a good deal easier to achieve this in foster care.

Conclusion

The research does not clearly support Valerie's belief that institutional care for orphaned and separated children is always a cause of serious developmental problems. Unfortunately, the research needed to draw this conclusion is quite difficult to do, and no study done yet has provided the highest possible level of evidence in one direction or another.

Critical Thinking

1. What does it mean to isolate a variable? Did the BEIP study (Fox et al., 2011) do this effectively? Explain your answer.

2. Look at the BEIP (Fox et al., 2011) and the Whetten study (Whetten et al., 2014). What were the ages of the children in the two studies? How might the ages of the children make a difference to the results of these studies?

3. In what countries were data collected for the Whetten study (Whetten et al., 2014)? Comment on two or three cultural differences that might have made the outcomes different for this study and the BEIP (Fox et al., 2011). (Although Wikipedia is not always a good source, it might help you on this question.)

(Continued)

(Continued)

4. In the Whetten et al. (2014) study, caregivers were asked to assess children's emotional problems. How might these assessments (not the problems themselves, but the caregivers' evaluations) have been affected by the nature of life in a large group as opposed to life in a foster family?

5. Is the BEIP study (Fox et al., 2011) or the Whetten et al. (2014) study more likely to be affected by the "post hoc, ergo propter hoc" fallacy? Explain.

References

"A lost boy finds his calling." (2014). *The Washington Post*. Available at www .washingtonpost.com/sf/style/2014/01/30/a-lost-boy-finds-his-calling/.

Fox, N. A., Almas, A. N., Degnan, K. A., Nelson, C. A., & Zeanah, C. H. (2011). The effects of severe psychosocial deprivation and foster care on cognitive development at 8 years of age: Findings from the Bucharest Early Intervention Project. *Journal of Child Psychology & Psychiatry, 52*, 919–928.

National Association for the Education of Young Children. (1996). *Developmentally appropriate practice in early childhood programs serving children from birth to age 8*. Available at http://www.naeyc.org/resources/position_ statements/daptoc.htm.

Rutter, M., Sonuga-Barke, E. J., Beckett, C., Castle, J., Kreppner, J., Kumsta, R., . . . Bell, C. A. (2010). Deprivation-specific psychological patterns: Effects of institutional deprivation. *Monographs of the Society for Research in Child Development, Serial No. 295, 75*(1), 1–229.

Whetten, K., Osterman, J., Pence, B. W., Whetten, R. A., Messer, L. C., Ariely, S., . . . The Positive Outcomes for Orphans (POFO) Research Team. (2014). Three-year change in the well-being of orphaned and separated children in institutional and family-based care settings in five low- and middle-income countries. *PLoS ONE, 9*(8). Available at http://www.plosone.org/article/ info%3Adoi%2F10.1371%2Fjournal.pone.0104872.

Zeanah, C. H., Nelson, C. A., Fox, N. A., Smyke, A. T., Marshall, P., . . . Koga, S. (2003). Designing research to study the effects of institutionalization on brain and behavioral development: The Bucharest Early Intervention Project. *Development & Psychopathology, 15*, 885–907.

Claim 15

A baby's sleeping position can cause or prevent sudden infant death syndrome.

Angie's mother always told her that it was a good idea to keep her baby in bed with her at night. That way, she said, Angie could nurse the baby frequently and everybody could get some sleep. But when Angie took the baby to the pediatrician for her first checkup, she saw a lot of posters and pamphlets that said parents should not take a baby into their bed. To Angie's surprise, the resources also said not to put a baby to sleep face down in a crib. The pamphlets warned that sleeping with parents or in a prone (face down) sleeping position might result in SIDS—sudden infant death syndrome. Naturally, Angie was terrified at the idea that she might find her baby dead in her crib one morning. But when she tried to put her little daughter to sleep on her back, the baby cried and could not seem to relax.

What could she do? Is the face down position really so risky? After all, Angie and all of her brothers and sisters had slept that way as infants and had developed well.

T his claim is one that involves many variables, confused or confounded with one another in ways that make it quite difficult to conclude that a particular factor has caused an outcome. This is often the case when people try to understand the effects of practices that parents have chosen. Parents do not make their choices—of sleeping position or other caregiving techniques—at random but instead make decisions that are connected with their own personalities, cultures, education, and lifestyles. Each of those broader factors brings with it more variables that can influence an infant's life and health, so deciding on cause and effect can be almost impossible.

Sudden infant death syndrome (SIDS) is a term used to describe the unexpected death of an infant during sleep, without any serious signs or symptoms of illness even a few hours before death. Also called "crib death," this phenomenon most often occurs in babies between 2 and 4 months of age. The victims may have had slight colds, but otherwise they appeared healthy. Death by SIDS is rare, with a rate of 0.7 occurrences per 1,000 babies in the United States in 2000. (Figures on problems of this kind are surprisingly hard to get because they involve the time-consuming collection of information in counties and then in states and finally calculations that show the rate for the entire country.)

Though SIDS is rare, the possibility of SIDS is a source of anxiety for parents, who are deeply concerned about protecting their babies and fearful of finding them unresponsive in their cribs. Parents' natural concerns are worsened by the knowledge that SIDS deaths have sometimes been followed by accusations that the death was due to neglect or even to murder. Because some such accusations have turned out to be true, the most innocent parents may be regarded with suspicion by friends and neighbors and may even suspect each other, adding serious anxieties to their grief for their lost infant.

In the early 1990s, reports from other countries, such as New Zealand, suggested that the prone (face down) sleeping position might be a factor in SIDS and that the rate of SIDS deaths might be reduced by putting babies to sleep in the supine (face up) position and making sure that no soft bedding could interfere with a baby's breathing. SIDS rates were reported to decrease when parents used a supine sleeping position for their babies in the first few months of life. (Babies eventually learn to turn over by themselves, so there is a limit to how long their sleeping position can be managed—but SIDS becomes much less likely after 4 months of age, in any case.) Subsequently, pediatricians and government officials in the United States began to promulgate the Back to Sleep program, a parent education program advocating the supine sleeping position. They argued that infants whose sleeping posture was supine were much less likely to die of SIDS. However, not all parents use the supine position, and not all physicians recommend it (Moon, Kington, Oden, Iglesias, & Hauck, 2007).

SIDS rates dropped after the Back to Sleep program began. Can this fact be interpreted to mean that supine sleeping caused the change in SIDS mortality? It is unusual for a single factor to be the cause of a developmental outcome—for example, a child's growth in height and the age when a child first walks have multiple causes—and it would be surprising if SIDS deaths had a single cause. But another issue is of importance here: that SIDS rates in the United States were already decreasing during the periods 1989–1991 and 1995–1998, before the Back to Sleep movement was well under way. Whatever factors were causing that decrease may have been responsible for the continuing reduction in SIDS rates in later years. Sleeping position may have been one among many factors—or it may not have been a causal factor at all.

Statistical analysis of data can explain many things, but it alone cannot tell whether one factor caused another. The only way to determine causality is through experimental work that can control for confounded variables. However, continuing analysis of data on SIDS shows that multiple factors seem to be connected with this type of infant mortality. For example, the presence of environmental tobacco smoke is associated with an increased SIDS rate. Surprisingly, babies are *less* likely to die of SIDS when they are sucking pacifiers.

Factors such as secondhand smoke, pacifiers, and sleeping position may directly affect the likelihood that a given baby will die of SIDS, or these factors may simply be associated and confused with other confounding variables. For example, more educated parents are less likely to smoke near their babies, so it is not possible to know whether the effect of environmental tobacco smoke on SIDS is a direct one or whether the parents' educational level makes them reluctant to smoke *and* causes them to behave differently in some other, unidentified way that is relevant to SIDS. For example, although researchers have concluded that bed sharing with adults is not actually an important risk factor for SIDS (Kattwinkel, Havek, Moon, Malloy, & Willinger, 2006), they do conclude that both breastfeeding (McVea, Turner, & Peppler, 2000) and the use of pacifiers (Schwartz & Guthrie, 2008) make SIDS less likely. These factors are also connected with educational level.

Other issues to consider are classification and reporting of infant deaths. Could the dropping SIDS rate indicate that infant deaths are being categorized in different ways than before, so the reported figures are changed even though there is no "real" change in the rate? Statistical analysis of possible causes of SIDS would certainly be affected by including or excluding particular deaths from the SIDS category. Deaths of infants that fit the rather general earlier description may or may not be classified as SIDS. In fact, at least two other classifications are possible when a sleeping infant is found dead and no obvious reason for the death is evident (there are actually three, if murder is included). One such category is "accidental suffocation and strangulation in bed" (ASSB); deaths in the second category are classed as "cause unknown/unspecified." U.S. infant death statistics show that during the 1990s, SIDS rates decreased and the rates of the other two categories did not change; from 1999 to 2001, however, the continued decline in SIDS rates was accompanied by an *increase* in rates of death from the other two categories. The changed rates may thus have resulted from decreased classification and reporting of infant deaths as due to SIDS and increased classification and reporting in the other categories, rather than a real change in the hard-to-determine actual causes of death (Shapiro-Mendoza, Tomashek, Anderson, & Wingo, 2006).

Conclusion

Although most parents want to follow all possible advice about protecting their babies from SIDS, including using a supine sleeping position, it is by no means certain that changes in sleeping position have been the cause of changes in SIDS rates in the United States. In fact, at this point, decreased reported SIDS rates may result primarily from changes in classification and reporting of infant deaths. Angie may decide that her baby's health and comfort—and her own—are best achieved by using a pacifier and avoiding exposure to tobacco smoke and that the risk of SIDS is very small, indeed. Alternatively, she may decide that she wants to follow her pediatrician's recommendations and may work to help her baby feel more comfortable in the supine position. It's difficult to make the leap from some research to everyday practice, and parents' decisions are usually based on opinions of their own.

Critical Thinking

1. Describe three possible confounded variables that would confuse conclusions from your study if you compared families who offer their babies pacifiers with those who do not. Explain why these factors make it difficult to know whether pacifier use has any effect on SIDS.

2. Use the Internet or other sources to find how cigarette smoking has declined in the United States since 1990. How does this change appear to be related to the decrease in SIDS? Describe how a graph of the two changes would look.

3. Using a child development textbook for information, discuss one or two other early childhood problems that might have their known rates affected by classification (diagnosis) and reporting. Explain your answers.

4. Babies sleeping with parents are most likely to die unexpectedly when the two are sleeping on a couch or in an armchair. What characteristics of parent or baby could cause this sleeping arrangement? What characteristics could cause infant death? Would some of those characteristics also be associated with infant death? Use a child development textbook to find information about factors such as temperament. The article by Kattwinkel et al. (2006) is also helpful.

5. Use the Internet or other sources to define the term *proxy measure*. Babies are reported to be less likely to have SIDS if they are fully immunized, even though SIDS does not involve death from any of the contagious diseases prevented by immunization. Is immunization possibly a proxy measure for some other important factor? What might the factor be? Is post hoc reasoning a possible problem of critical thinking about this issue?

References

Kattwinkel, J., Havek, F. R., Moon, R. Y., Malloy, M., & Willinger, M. (2006). Bedsharing with unimpaired parents is not an important risk for sudden infant death syndrome: In reply. *Pediatrics, 117*(3), 994–996.

McVea, K. L. S. P., Turner, P. D., & Peppler, D. K. (2000). The role of breast-feeding in sudden infant death syndrome. *Journal of Human Lactation, 16*, 13–20.

Moon, R. Y., Kington, M., Oden, R., Iglesias, J., & Hauck, F. R. (2007). Physician recommendations regarding SIDS risk reduction: A national survey of pediatricians and family physicians. *Clinical Pediatrics, 46*, 791–800.

Schwartz, R. H., & Guthrie, K. L. (2008). Infant pacifiers: An overview. *Clinical Pediatrics, 47*, 327–331.

Shapiro-Mendoza, C. K., Tomashek, K. M., Anderson, R. N., & Wingo, J. (2006). Recent national trends in sudden, unexpected infant deaths: More evidence supporting a change in classification or reporting. *American Journal of Epidemiology, 163*(8), 762–769.

Claim 16

Parents should not talk baby talk to their children because it slows their language development.

Al became very annoyed with his mother-in-law when he heard her cooing to 3-month-old Carlie. "How is she ever going to learn to talk when she hears that baby-talk stuff all the time? Besides, it sounds so stupid. I'm embarrassed to hear you. Just talk normally when you're around the baby, okay?" Carlie's grandmother was offended, but to keep the peace she did not argue with Al. She thought to herself, "What in the world is wrong with him? Everybody talks to babies that way! Besides, I can tell that Carlie likes it because she gets quiet and looks and listens. But he's the father, so when he's around I won't talk like that—if I can help it."

Who was right? Does Al have good reason to think that his daughter's speech will be affected by what she hears now? Is baby talk a problem?

As is the case with many myths and misunderstandings, the accuracy of this claim depends on exactly what someone means by it. One interpretation of *baby talk* is the use of common childish mispronunciations of ordinary words, such as *basketty* for spaghetti or *muvver* for mother. It's obvious that if parents always say *basketty*, their child will not have many chances to hear the correct pronunciation of *spaghetti*, but most children will learn how to say this word before they ever take a date to an Italian restaurant. Baby talk can also mean family words for private functions, such as toileting. Children whose families use their own terms eventually learn the adult versions, but it is probably kindest to teach them what other people say before they go to preschool or visit a friend's house, where they may need to communicate their needs to adults.

Baby talk can also mean a specialized form of speech, probably found in all human groups, a form that follows different rules from the rules adults use to talk to other adults. This kind of baby talk is sometimes called *motherese* or infant-directed talk (IDT), and it is different in a number of ways from adult-directed talk (ADT). When speaking IDT, adults raise the overall pitch of their voice, produce changes in intonation by going from high to low pitches and back again, and speak sometimes loudly and sometimes softly. IDT conveys the maximum of emotional involvement but does not necessarily carry much other information.

People speaking in IDT also emphasize and repeat important words— "Where is the *doggie*? Do you see the *doggie*? What a nice *doggie*!" Sentences in IDT are shorter and simpler than they are in ADT, and, surprisingly, they are very grammatical, unlike the sloppily constructed and error-filled speech adults use when speaking to other adults. Adults who are speaking to babies also use dramatic and exaggerated hand gestures and facial expressions that parallel their speech patterns.

IDT can be annoying and even embarrassing to adults who overhear it. Listeners may feel that IDT has a silly quality that cannot be good for language development—certainly they would not want a baby to grow up to talk that way. If one adult spoke to another in the IDT pattern, offense would probably be taken and the speech interpreted as condescending or patronizing. These negative emotional reactions cause many adults to state their disapproval of baby talk.

To evaluate whether IDT is a good method for speaking to babies, however, one needs to observe how babies react to it, not just how adults feel about it. Babies typically respond to IDT with extreme interest and attention. Their eyes brighten and they smile and look at the speaker with interest and animation, whereas they react to ADT with a blank or serious expression and look elsewhere for entertainment (Bryant & Barrett, 2006).

A baby's interested expression has an important effect on adult caregivers—and on other children, too, although not as much (Rabain-Jamin, 2001). Caregivers like to talk to responsive babies and quickly give up the effort if a baby pays no attention. So, when using IDT and gaining a baby's interest, caregivers are likely to talk to the baby longer than they would otherwise do. Hearing lots of speech helps a baby's language abilities to develop, so there is a benign circle at work. Adults who use IDT capture a baby's attention, and the baby's attention stimulates the adult to keep talking. The more the adult talks during a baby's first year of life, the more the baby's understanding and use of spoken language will progress. In fact, the IDT type of baby talk encourages language development rather than slowing it (Barinaga, 1992).

For good language development, infants need to be able to hear the sounds of language and listen to the words—and listening will not last long if the baby does not find the speech *sounds* engaging and interesting. Among the first aspects of speech the baby must learn are the *phonemes*, or smallest meaningful sound units, of their parents' language. The very young baby listens (or fails to listen) equally to all kinds of voice sounds, but each language uses only some of those possible sounds. By listening to speech, the baby learns that an /s/ sound at the end of a word has a meaning, but a hiccup is not speech, even though the sound comes out of a person's mouth. Speech that attracts the baby's attention, such as IDT, helps infants figure out which mouth noises are part of language and which are not.

For young babies, the specific words an adult says and the topic of discussion are of very little importance. The youngest babies have no understanding of the words adults speak, and even older babies understand only a few words, such as their own names. If babies listen—and as a result eventually learn words and grammar—they do it because IDT sounds and behaviors attract their attention.

Of course, there are many individual differences in the experiences babies have with spoken language. Studies have shown that later-born children are exposed to somewhat different kinds of speech than those heard by firstborn children (Oshima-Takane & Robbins, 2003). There is no single "speech diet" that is absolutely essential for language learning, but language that responds to infant interest does seem best, just as sensitivity and responsiveness in all areas seem to foster infant development.

As language development progresses and young children begin to understand words, they become more interested in what adults say and less interested in the way they say it. As children respond less to IDT, their adult caregivers modulate their speech to a less exaggerated, less emotion-conveying form and begin to concentrate on new types of speech that attract the attention of toddlers and preschoolers. Children of these ages would rather hear an exciting story than have an adult speak in a high-pitched voice, and adults usually respond by giving the children what they want.

Conclusion

Babies' language development in the first year is actually helped by baby talk in the form of infant-directed talk, which attracts babies' attention and encourages them to listen and learn about their parents' language. Al would do better not to object to the way his mother-in-law talks to Carlie, and if he would look at Carlie's face while she listens, he would see that she is fascinated by infant-directed talk, however strange it may sound to an adult.

Critical Thinking

1. Infants and toddlers often turn with interest toward television commercials, even when they have been ignoring the ordinary program just before the commercial. Using a child development textbook for information, describe what commercials and IDT have in common. Are there also some differences between IDT and commercial presentations? Explain your answer.

2. Bryant and Barrett (2006) studied responses to IDT in a number of different cultural and language communities. Why did the authors want to examine various language backgrounds? Why was it not sufficient to consider IDT among English-speaking families? Explain your answer.

3. Use a child development textbook to read about maternal depression. Would depression make a mother more or less likely to use IDT with a baby younger than 1 year old? What effect on a baby's language development would maternal depression likely have? Explain your answer.

4. What training should day care providers receive about IDT? Explain your answer.

5. Use a child development textbook to read about steps or stages in language development. At what age would you expect children to be more interested in a story and information rather than voice pitch and repetition? Explain your answer.

References

Barinaga, M. (1992). The brain remaps its own contours. *Science, 258,* 216–220.

Bryant, G., & Barrett, C. (2006). Infant preference for both male and female infant-directed talk. *Psychological Science, 18*(8), 740–745.

Oshima-Takane, Y., & Robbins, M. (2003). Linguistic environment of second born children. *First Language, 23,* 21–40.

Rabain-Jamin, J. (2001). Language use in mother-child and young sibling interactions in Senegal. *First Language, 21,* 357–385.

Claim 17

Being exposed to two different languages is confusing for babies and interferes with normal language development.

Jun and Elena were both young mothers who had come to the United States from other countries. Both were fluent in English, but neither had English as her first language. They were discussing their wishes to give their babies the best possible start in life and wondering whether their concern with having the babies learn Korean (in one case) and Greek (in the other) was in conflict with what the babies needed for good language development. "I always heard that babies would get confused if they heard people speaking more than one language, and that would slow their development," said Jun. "I know," said Elena. "I heard that too. But my parents don't even speak English. How can it be good for a person not to be able to talk to their grandmother or understand their roots? My little guy will be just a stranger in Greece if he can't speak the language. But I try to speak English around him most of the time, in case two languages do really cause problems."

Are Jun and Elena right to be concerned about this issue? Are there disadvantages to hearing more than one language at an early age? Could there be some advantages for children who have this experience?

Jun and Elena may have heard of research about children of bilingual families, like a study by Hammer, Davison, Lawrence, and Miccio (2009), which found that when mothers whose first language was Spanish spoke English to their young children, they did not increase the children's English vocabulary but did decrease their Spanish vocabulary. But like so many child development research questions, this one is much more complicated than it appears at first glance, and work on it needs to include a wide range of variables. Who are the speakers of each language? Are they talking to the child or just overheard as they talk to someone else? How much of the time is each language heard? Is the speaker of each language a native speaker who knows the language very well, or does the baby hear one language spoken by someone who is not perfectly familiar with it? And what are the effects of all these different factors?

These questions have been difficult to answer because most research did not collect data on these points, although recently researchers have begun to explore the effects of amounts of exposure in each language (De Houwer, 2009). Most research has depended on the retrospective reports of parents and other caregivers. However, Place and Hoff (2011) used a Language Diary method to record details of 25-month-old children's bilingual experiences. They asked caregivers to keep a log of what the children heard, for example the number of 30-minute periods in which the child heard only Spanish or only English; who was speaking; and whether there was a particular context, like bedtime or mealtime. The researchers reminded the caregivers when it was time to record language events and collected data over seven weeks or more.

In Place and Hoff's (2011) study, there were big differences between families in the proportions of English and Spanish the children heard. These varied from 10% Spanish and 90% English to the reverse proportions. The families were also different in the speakers of languages, some having an English-speaking mother and a Spanish-speaking father, some having the opposite, and some having both parents native speakers of Spanish. These variations enabled the researchers to examine correlations between factors like proportion of a language heard and vocabulary and grammar development for that language. Not surprisingly, skill in a language was correlated with the proportion of time the child heard that language. But less predictable outcomes were also seen. Children's English skills were better when they had more conversational partners with whom they spoke only English, when they heard English from larger numbers of speakers, and when more of their English experience was with people whose first language was English.

A common critical thinking problem is the tendency to look for negative effects only when we think a factor may be harmful or for positive effects only when we think it may be beneficial. It would be easy to make this kind of mistake with respect to bilingual language development because we are so concerned about good language skills, their impact on reading and school performance, and lifelong problems that may ensue if language develops poorly. But some researchers have been interested in possible positive effects of bilingual experience and have shown that there are some desirable outcomes.

Kovacs (2009) investigated factors in the development of false-belief reasoning. This is the capacity to understand that a person may act in a certain way not because he or she wants the outcome that occurs but because of a mistaken assumption. For example, the child may be shown a person who puts a treat into a hiding place and leaves the room. Another person comes and moves the treat to another hidden place. When the first person comes back, a child (usually 4 years old or more) who can do false-belief reasoning will know that he or she will look in the wrong place and fail to find the treat; a younger child is likely to expect the person to look in the new hiding place. Kovacs compared children who were bilingual in Hungarian and Romanian to monolingual children and found that bilingual children did significantly better on a false-belief task than monolingual children did, but they were about equally capable at a control task that did not require them to understand false beliefs.

One study (Adi-Japha, Berberich-Artzi, & Libnawi, 2010) looked at children's ability to draw an object that doesn't really exist—a real flower, then a flower that isn't a real one, or a real house, and a house that isn't a real one. For example, some nonexistent flowers were described by children as a heart flower, a lion flower, a camel flower, and so on. Monolingual children do not do this task well until about age 7, but children who were bilingual in English and in Hebrew or in Arabic and in Hebrew did the task at age 4 or 5 years. The researchers considered this outcome to be the result of cognitive flexibility encouraged by bilingual experiences.

Bilingual children need to pay more attention than monolingual children to cues other than speech that will tell them which language is being spoken, for example, who is speaking, what the circumstances are, and the speaker's facial expression or other gestures. A study by Yow and Markman (2011) looked at children's ability to figure out where a toy was hidden when the researcher stood near the wrong box but gazed at the right box. Monolingual children managed this by age 5, but bilingual children as young as 2 years were able to do the task.

Conclusion

Jun and Elena certainly had reasons to be concerned about children's development in a bilingual environment, but the research on this topic suggests that the effects of hearing two languages depend very much on the details of the experience. Whether an adult is or is a not a native speaker of a language seems to have a considerable effect on his or her success as a "teacher" of the language to young children. But it might have made the two young mothers feel better about bilingual exposure for their children if they had realized that some research indicates real cognitive advantages for young bilingual children, including improved understanding of communications other than language.

Critical Thinking

1. In the study by Place and Hoff (2011), would you expect that the parents' language abilities would affect the children's, rather than the other way around? What do these authors say on this point in their discussion section?

2. Use your textbook or other sources to define *infant-directed speech* or *child-directed speech*. How might it be more difficult for a nonnative speaker of a language to produce infant-directed speech in that language? What would this mean for children's bilingual experience and its effects on language learning?

3. Describe several confounding variables that could influence the outcomes of these correlational studies. Be sure that of the variables you name, all are confounded with one or more of the factors discussed earlier, such as amount of experience with people whose first language was English.

4. Kovacs (2009) looked at whether the bilingual children had bigger vocabularies than the monolingual children (they did not). Why would she have been concerned about this possible confounding variable?

5. How might bilingual parents model for their children or instruct them on attentiveness to what other people know or think? Could you argue that people who are likely to enter a bilingual marriage are already good at or interested in such attentiveness? How is such an argument relevant to the issue of how best to work with bilingual children? The article by Castro and Espinoza (2014) may be helpful in answering these questions.

References

Adi-Japha, E., Berberich-Artzi, J., & Libnawi, A. (2010). Cognitive flexibility in drawings of bilingual children. *Child Development, 81*, 1356–1366.

Castro, D. C., & Espinoza, L. M. (2014). Developmental characteristics of young dual language learners: Implications for policy and practice in infant and toddler care. *Zero to Three, 34*(3), 34–40.

De Houwer, A. (2009). *Bilingual first language acquisition*. Bristol, UK: Multilingual Matters.

Hammer, C. S., Davison, M. D., Lawrence, F. R., & Miccio, A. W. (2009). The effect of maternal language on bilingual children's vocabulary and emergent literacy development during Head Start and kindergarten. *Scientific Studies of Reading, 13,* 99–121.

Kovacs, A. M. (2009). Early bilingualism enhances mechanisms of false-belief reasoning. *Developmental Science, 12,* 48–54.

Place, S., & Hoff, E. (2011). Properties of dual language exposure that influence 2-year-olds' bilingual proficiency. *Child Development, 82,* 1834–1849.

Yow, W. Q., & Markman, E. M. (2011). Young bilingual children's heightened sensitivity to referential cues. *Journal of Cognition and Development, 12,* 12–31.

Claim 18

It's a problem, and possibly means autism, if babies don't make eye contact in the first few weeks of life.

A mother wrote the following to a child development blog author: "I have read that there are some 'red flags' to watch out for in case your child has autism. My daughter is 5 weeks old, and she does not make eye contact when she is nursing or when I hold her face-to-face with me. Sometimes she smiles when she looks at the wall, but she doesn't smile at me. I'm really worried that she may be autistic, and I also read on a website that not making eye contact could mean she has Reactive Attachment Disorder. I know it's early to tell, but is this anything to worry about?"

Is this mother's concern about eye contact realistic? Can anyone assure her at this point that her little girl will develop typically, not autistically, in the future?

As parents have become more and more concerned about autism, the idea of the "red flag," or warning by which they can diagnose their own children, has become more common. For example, one Internet list of "red flags" ("Autism: 9 warning signs every parent should know," 2015) refers to a lack of social connection or interaction, lack of eye contact, lack of babbling or speech, failure to respond to his or her name quickly, lack of smiling in response to smiles, playing with toys by lining them up or flicking or spinning them, arm flapping and other odd movements, repetition or echoing of words, and lack of imitation.

One problem with these "red flags" is that it is often unclear to parents at what age and how regularly the behavior should appear in typical development. For example, arm flapping and toe walking, which may be symptoms of autism, are also very common among typically developing year-old children, who may flap when excited or trying to communicate, and who may toe-walk just for the fun of it, just as they try out walking backward or sideways. Typical and atypical behavior can overlap a great deal, and to some extent the behavior of older autistic children resembles the behavior of younger typically developing children. In addition, even the best-developing children (or even adults) do not do everything in exactly the same way every time.

For many parents, the focus of their fears is on eye contact, the event in which each of a pair of human beings looks at the other's eyes at the same time. This is more technically referred to as *mutual gaze,* or sometimes as *eye gaze* (when you look for information about this behavior, you may find more material by looking for these terms than by looking for "eye contact"). Mutual gaze is a very important signaling mechanism for communication between humans, although we can get along without it, as people of all ages with serious visual impairments show us. However, autistic individuals, who have many communication problems of various kinds, do often display less mutual gaze than people developing more typically, so it's not surprising that parents who worry about autism look to mutual gaze events to confirm or alleviate their fears.

But a problem with this "red flag" is that autistic individuals do sometimes make eye contact, and typically developing people of any age do not do it all the time or for prolonged periods. Whether any baby looks at an adult's eyes depends on a variety of factors. One is the infant's age and developmental level, with increasing use of mutual gaze from birth onward. Another has to do with the conditions for looking at another person. Young infants require brighter light to get a clear image than older people do, and in the early weeks they have a very limited focal distance, so a face nearer than 8″ or farther than 12″ is much more difficult to see than one between those distances. After the first few months, babies like to look at smiling, responsive faces, and when they see a "still face" they soon avert their eyes and even begin to cry. Temperamental shyness makes a difference to the amount babies gaze at faces (Matsuda, Okanoya, & Myowa-Yamakoshi, 2013). At later ages, there are cultural differences in the mutual gaze patterns of parents and their children (Schofield, Parke, Castañeda, & Coltrane, 2008), and some cultural groups pay little attention to infant gaze but encourage communication in other ways (Akhtar & Gernsbacher, 2008).

In order to know whether a baby's eye contact was similar to that seen in typically developing (rather than autistic) children, we need to have some idea about the developmental changes seen in most infants, and there is some information about this. Newborns prefer to look at photographs of faces with open rather than closed eyes and at faces with eyes looking directly at them rather than faces with averted eyes. Babies of 4 weeks may gaze at someone's eyes, but they do not do this reliably or more than briefly. By 9 weeks, they tend to look at someone's eyes more when he or she is speaking than otherwise. By about 3 months, babies are more likely to smile when someone makes eye contact with them and to stop smiling when the person averts the gaze (Beier & Spelke, 2012).

To understand how changes in mutual gaze take place over time, it is useful to study a group of babies longitudinally. Leeb and Rejskind (2004) did this by testing the amount of eye contact with a stranger observed in 70 babies, first when they were an average of 52 hours old and second when they were about 15 weeks old (when only 23 were available). The investigators measured the total seconds of eye contact in a three-minute test period and tested each baby with a male and with a female observer. Infant girls made eye contact for only a little more than a total of 20 seconds out of the 3 minutes during the first (52 hours) observation, while boys spent almost 30 seconds. However, at 15 weeks, the boys increased their mutual gaze time by only a small amount, whereas the girls increased theirs to about 85 seconds out of the 180-second observation period. When the researchers examined changes in the duration of each episode of eye contact, they again found girls increasing the periods for which they looked at the observer's eyes a great deal, in comparison to the boys, who continued to look in short "bursts" rather than in a sustained way. Both boys and girls looked longer at a female observer than at a male, but this difference was much more marked for girls.

Leeb and Rejskind's (2004) findings suggest that something basic like sex determines a great deal of infant mutual gaze behavior. However, when preterm and full-term babies are compared, they also show different eye contact patterns. Preterm 3-month-olds looking at their mothers break eye contact by averting their eyes more than full-term babies do, and the mothers do the same thing (Harel, Gordon, Geva, & Feldman, 2011). This suggests that something about the babies' experiences may also have affected their behavior.

Why is mutual gaze important, in itself or as a clue to the development of autism? It may be that mutual gaze serves as an introduction to the ability to use gaze as communication. A moment of mutual gaze seems to help babies follow another person's gaze as it moves to look at an object or another person (in other words, to learn the important skill of *joint attention*). When a baby looks where another person is looking and observes the happy, angry, or frightened expression on that person's face, he or she can use that communication to learn facts and attitudes about the world. In one study (Bedford et al., 2012), observers noted whether a baby looked where another person was looking and how long her attention was held by the object being looked at. Babies who were later diagnosed as having autism or other social-communication problems were no different from typically developing babies in their ability to follow another's gaze at either 7 or 13 months, but at 13 months had their attention held by the object less well.

Conclusion

To be able to use eye contact to tell the difference between typically developing babies and those who will later be diagnosed as autistic, we would need a lot of information about how both groups develop. So far, there is not enough information about development of eye contact over time in either group. The mother who wrote to the blog cannot compare her baby's use of mutual gaze to that of any large group of babies, and even if she could, very little is known about typical development of this skill at such an early age, so even professionals with a high level of training cannot make the autism diagnosis so early. (And, if they did, chances are high that in later months the child would be seen to be developing in typical fashion.)

Critical Thinking

1. Use a child development textbook to find a description of the "still face" effect. How would an adult's "still face" encourage or discourage a baby's eye contact? Explain how this is an example of a transactional process.

2. In the paper by Leeb and Rejskind (2004), parents were asked to bring the babies dressed in "gender-neutral" clothing, not pink or blue gender-related colors. Why was this precaution taken?

3. The title of the Leeb and Rejskind paper refers to "perceived gender differences." Read the procedure section of the paper and explain why the authors referred to "perceived" differences, rather than simply to differences.

4. Several of the papers mentioned in this section used longitudinal designs. What is the advantage of using longitudinal rather than cross-sectional designs for studies of the development of mutual gaze or of any behaviors that are symptoms of autism?

5. Look at the paper by Pellicano and Macrae (2009) and describe what they concluded that typically developing children can do when they use mutual gaze to understand the world but that autistic children cannot do as well. Does this difference between typically developing and autistic children suggest that lack of eye contact for communication is the major problem in autism? Explain your answer.

References

Akhtar, N., & Gernsbacher, M. A. (2008). On privileging the role of gaze in infant social cognition. *Child Development Perspectives, 2*(2), 59–65.

Bedford, R., Elsabbagh, M., Gliga, T., Pickles, A., Senju, A., Charman, T. . . . & the BASIS team. (2012). Precursors to social and communication difficulties in infants at risk for autism: Gaze following and attentional engagement. *Journal of Autism and Developmental Disorders, 42,* 2208–2218.

Beier, J. S., & Spelke, E. S. (2012). Infants' developing understanding of social gaze. *Child Development, 83*(2), 486–496.

CBS News (2015). Autism: 9 warning signs every parent should know. Retrieved from www.cbsnews.com/pictures/autism-9-warning-signs/every-parent-should-know/8/.

Harel, H., Gordon, I., Geva, R., & Feldman, R. (2011). Gaze behaviors of preterm and full-term infants in nonsocial and social contexts of increasing dynamics: Visual recognition, attention regulation, and gaze synchrony. *Infancy, 16*(1), 69–90.

Leeb, R. T., & Rejskind, F. G. (2004). Here's looking at you, kid! A longitudinal study of perceived gender differences in mutual gaze behavior in young infants. *Sex Roles, 50*(1/2), 1–14.

Matsuda, Y.-T., Okanoya, K., & Myowa-Yamakoshi, M. (2013). Shyness in early infancy: Approach-avoidance conflicts in temperament and hypersensitivity to eyes during initial gazes to faces. *PLoS ONE, 8*(6), 1–7.

Pellicano, E., & Macrae, C. N. (2009). Mutual eye gaze facilitates person categorization for typically developing children, but not for children with autism. *Psychonomic Bulletin & Review, 16*(6), 1094–1099.

Schofield, T. J., Parke, R. D., Castaneda, E. K., & Coltrane, S. (2008). Patterns of gaze between parents and children in European American and Mexican American families. *Journal of Nonverbal Behavior, 32,* 171–186.

Claim 19

It's harmful to preschoolers' psychological development if they make overnight visits to estranged parents.

Isabel was talking to her former sister-in-law, her ex-husband Rob's sister. The two women were still friendly, and Isabel wanted to explain why she did not want 3-year-old Alex to stay with Rob overnight. She told Caroline, "I was reading that psychologists think these overnight visits really mess little kids up. And I could see how cranky Alex was after the one time he went to Rob's overnight. I don't have anything against Rob and I'm not saying he did anything wrong, but these little guys don't like separation from the people they're attached to, especially at night. Alex has a fit about going to bed anyway, and I don't think Rob knows how to handle that. But even if he didn't hate going to bed, I figure that if people who do psychological research say not to do it, they probably know what they're talking about." Of course Caroline tended to be on her brother's side in this, but she did also have to wonder why it would be so bad for Alex to sleep at the apartment of the person who had often put him to bed until 6 months ago. However, she didn't think she could convince Isabel, so she kept quiet.

Is there evidence that overnight visits to noncustodial parents are bad for preschool children?

It used to be assumed that young children of divorced couples in the United States would stay in their mother's custody, have occasional visits with the father during the early years, and only later begin to spend days at a time with him. This assumption began to diminish in the 1970s, as the restrictions of traditional sex roles loosened and the role of the father received more attention and value. An article by Horner and Guyer (1993) examined the issue of infant overnight stays with the father and advised that children can get used to sleeping in different places (as they do if they go to day care) but suggested that breastfed babies should not stay overnight until they are weaned. However, not long afterward, Solomon and George (1999) reported research from which they concluded that babies who "overnighted" with divorced or separated parents had no significant differences in attachment from babies from similar families who did not have overnight visits, and that although there were more attachment problems in babies from divorced families than from families where the parents were married, these probably had more to do with the parents' difficult interactions than they did with visiting, not visiting, or even divorce or separation.

In 2011, a special issue of a professional journal, *Family Court Review*, contained some articles that advised strongly against overnight visits with noncustodial parents, not only for the infants who were discussed earlier, but for preschool children as well (McIntosh, 2011). This topic received increased discussion because of its relevance for court decisions about custody and shared parenting by divorcing couples, but the research remained unclear. For example, in a longitudinal study by Tornello et al. (2013), infants who had frequent overnights were found to be more often insecurely attached, but later behavior problems were associated only with early insecurity, not with overnight visiting in itself.

Warshak (2014) reviewed a large number of studies intended to provide information about the possible effects on young children of overnight visits with divorced or separated parents, and he concluded that there was no acceptable evidence that problems were caused by overnight visiting. On the contrary, he cited evidence that relationships with parents were protected by young children's frequent overnight visits. Nielsen (2014) gave a similar analysis and concluded that statements about evidence that such visits are harmful amount to a "woozle"—a belief that something is true simply because we have seen the statement many times (just as in the Winnie-the-Pooh stories, Pooh and Piglet become convinced that they are following a group of "woozles" when they see their own tracks in the snow as they go around and around some trees).

The "overnight" question is typical of quite a few issues about young children's psychological development. Research on such issues is, to some extent, dependent on people's values and wishes; if no one cared much about the possible outcomes, chances are that the questions would never be asked, and the fact that they are asked means that there may be some strong feelings involved. Those feelings can make some researchers careless, and even with the best possible research work, people trying to apply the research results may distort them to fit the outcome they desire. An additional problem is that researchers and interpreters of research may feel under pressure (by the courts, for example) to produce nice, clear "science" that will make it possible to avoid the messy legal process of deciding the best interests of children. That kind of pressure and the rewards that can come with offering a scientific solution can influence thinking about complex problems.

The "overnight" question and similar questions share a particular research problem. For many practical and ethical reasons, research on issues like child custody and parenting is virtually never done in the form of randomized studies. (You can imagine what any judge would say if requested to randomly assign couples in her court to overnight visits or no overnight visits, no matter what the judge thinks is best for particular children!) Instead, research must deal with case studies or with information drawn from large studies that collect a variety of data. In the Tornello et al. (2013) study, the data the authors used came from the Fragile Families and Child Wellbeing Study, which looked at young children born primarily to low-income, racial/ethnic-minority parents. Statistical methods are used to extract information of interest from the data available in studies of this kind, but this approach can tell us only about correlation between factors, not whether overnight visits cause problems.

It would be ideal for courts to have evidence about the effects of overnight visits that was not only clear-cut, but that could also be generalized to children whose parents are likely to appear in court. As it happens, there are relatively few high-conflict couples who ask for courts to mediate their disagreements about custody. Most divorcing or separating couples are able to agree on parenting plans and do not ask for legal help on this. Would it be reasonable for a judge to generalize from information about a wide range of families to these unusual high-conflict people, in order to determine the best decision for their children? This might not be a good idea, and the same applies to generalization from the low-income, minority families studied by Tornello et al. to affluent families who are more likely to appear in court when in conflict.

There is one more very basic question about generalization. Is it appropriate to generalize from information about infants, and to try to use that information to draw conclusions about children up to the age of 4, as some of the work on this topic has done? The answer is "probably not," as developing speech and memory make it much easier for preschool children to handle changes and transitions than it is for infants of 6 to 12 months.

A final point: It should be noted that the existing evidence about advantages and disadvantages of overnight visits for preschoolers does not generalize to families in which there has been domestic violence. Where there has been violence, stability and safety for the child should be the first considerations, and visiting should be supervised or should be delayed until safety can be guaranteed.

Conclusion

Isabel is mistaken in thinking that there is clear research evidence to support her decision not to let her son visit his father overnight. Although there has been much discussion on this point, there is an absence of well-designed research that concludes that Isabel should try to delay such visits. It would be wise for both parents to discuss how visits can best be conducted and whether Alex's crankiness actually had any connection with any part of the visit, or whether (as Warshak, 2014 pointed out) this may simply be the irritability often seen in children of his age and would have occurred whether there was a visit or not.

Critical Thinking

1. Warshak (2014) refers to "cherry picking" as a way in which biased reporters use research evidence to draw the conclusions they want. What does this term mean, and what is an example of the way Warshak suggests it may have been done in discussions of overnight visiting for young children?

2. Nielsen (2014) also refers to the practice of "cherry picking" but does not use the term. Give one example she cites in her paper to show that evidence has been used selectively in making decisions about children.

3. Nielsen (2014) states that case studies are useless for understanding effects of events on children's development or making decisions about parenting. Explain her reasoning about this.

4. What is the null hypothesis in the studies described in this section? Consult a research methods textbook if you are not sure what this means, and discuss why a null hypothesis cannot be "proved."

(Continued)

(Continued)

5. Young children can have a number of experiences that resemble some aspects of overnight visits with a divorced parent. Starting to attend day care or preschool is one of them. Look at information provided by the National Association for the Education of Young Children (www.naeyc .org) and discuss how it might be applied to make any transition easier for children and parents.

References

Horner, T., & Guyer, M. (1993). Infant placement and custody. In C. Zeanah (Ed.), *Handbook of infant mental health* (pp. 462–479). New York: Guilford.

McIntosh, J. (2011). Guest editor's introduction to the special issue: Attachment theory, separation, and divorce. *Family Court Review, 49,* 418–425.

Nielsen, L. (2014). Woozles: Their role in custody law reform, parenting plans, and family court. *Psychology, Public Policy, and Law.* http://dx.doi.org/10.1037/law0000004.

Solomon, J., & George, C. (1999). The effects on attachment of overnight visitation in divorced and separated families: A longitudinal follow up. In J. Solomon & C. George (Eds.), *Attachment disorganization in atypical populations* (pp. 243–264). New York: Guilford.

Tornello, S. L., Emery, R., Rown, J., Potter, D., Ocker, B., & Xu, Y. (2013). Overnight custody arrangements, attachment, and adjustment among very young children. *Journal of Marriage & Family, 75,* 871–885.

Warshak, R. (2014). Social science and parenting plans for young children: A consensus report. *Psychology, Public Policy, and Law, 20,* 46–67.

Claim 20

Toddlers drop food on the floor because they want to make their parents angry.

Twelve-month-old Andrew had a way of infuriating his mother, Annie, at mealtimes. He would eat happily for a while, with Annie spoon-feeding soup or cereal that he couldn't handle by himself. Then he would eat pieces of cheese, cooked vegetables, dry cereal, or toast, polishing them off happily but messily. However, meals ended with a grand climax of throwing things. Whatever was left on the high-chair tray—including leftover spoons covered with applesauce—would go overboard. Andrew obviously did this on purpose, leaning over the side of the chair as he released each object and watching carefully as it bounced, crumbled, or splashed on the floor. Annie was angered by all the work this made for her, and she yelled at Andrew and occasionally even smacked him, but he kept doing it. What angered Annie even more was the thought that he knew she was angry but kept dropping things anyway.

Was Andrew dropping food with the intention of aggravating his mother?

Having to clean up a puddle of applesauce or pick green beans out of a shaggy rug would probably annoy most parents—especially if the mess occurred, as it usually does, at the end of a long day of work and family chores. However, parents' annoyance, predictable as it may seem to any adult, may have nothing to do with a young child's wishes or intentions. In fact, even preschoolers may have trouble recognizing emotional expressions (Russell & Widen, 2002).

Even adults do things that result in undesirable and unanticipated consequences. Because human beings of all ages experience unintended results of their actions, it would seem like a good idea to entertain some alternative hypotheses about why people do the things they do and whether certain results are unintentional. A toddler's eating habits may be maddening, but that may not be the toddler's plan. Adults should consider the possibility that young children have intentions when they drop or throw food, but those intentions may not include frustrating and irritating their caregivers. Why, then, would they do something that, to adult eyes at least, appears so silly and pointless?

One possible explanation was offered many years ago by the eminent Swiss developmentalist Jean Piaget. Piaget suggested that children in the first part of their second year of life are powerfully motivated to cause interesting events to occur. (These are, of course, events that are interesting to toddlers, not events that are particularly interesting to older people.) According to Piaget's theory of cognitive development, children do not understand that they can cause things to happen until they are about 1 year old. When they do catch on to this fact, they are intensely motivated to test it out repeatedly, just as, in Piaget's view, they have a strong need to practice and repeat any new achievement.

Having discovered their ability to initiate interesting events, young children find that they cannot do everything with equal ease. They are limited in what they can do by their own physical and motor development. A 1-year-old cannot build a machine with interlocking blocks, draw a recognizable picture, or turn on a computer. If restrained in a high chair at mealtime, the toddler cannot run around in circles, pull off shoes and socks, or try to brush the dog's teeth. Most of the things a high-chair-bound child can do involve dropping or throwing of available objects—food and eating utensils. Dropping or throwing objects is interesting and yields some important new information about the physical world: For example, liquids like soup or milk, if dropped, make little noise and redistribute in novel patterns across the floor; a spoon, on the other hand, makes a noise but does not change in size and may show only a slight alteration in shape.

The desire to learn new and intriguing information about the world provides a strong alternative motivation, one that explains why toddlers drop food without intending to anger adults. But other aspects of this claim should be considered by comparing the child's feelings with those of an adult. Why might it be that an adult would want to make someone else angry, and is it possible for a toddler to share the beliefs and social skills that this vengeful adult has? Working to make someone else angry actually involves a quite complicated understanding of others' thoughts and emotions. An adult who can successfully and intentionally act to make others angry must be able to conceptualize how the other people would feel in a given situation, even though the feeling might not be the same one that the person would experience. In addition, if the would-be annoying person has any sense, his or her intention will be to produce feelings of anger and frustration but not of sufficient intensity to provoke retaliation. People do not usually want to make other people so angry that they respond with a punch; instead, people who inflict vengeance want their victims to simmer in helpless, uncomfortable rage, unable to do anything about it. To manage this requires careful and skillful anticipation of the degree of anger created and the likelihood that victims will fight back.

Such complex assessment of others' responses is only possible for people with a well-developed theory of mind—those who can predict with some accuracy how another person will think and feel (Fonagy, Gergely, Jurist, & Target, 2002). Toddlers have taken the first steps in developing theory of mind. However, they have little understanding of the meaning of applesauce on the floor and a tired and frustrated parent. Toddlers would not plan to throw food or anticipate the anger as a result of food throwing and the punishment as a result of anger, even if the action has sometimes had that effect in the past. In fact, toddlers still rely heavily on their parents' sensitivity to communications to help establish the understanding of others' thoughts that will help in later conflicts (McElwain & Volling, 2004).

Curiously, early steps in theory of mind include a stage in which children assume that what any person does is what they want to do (rather than something that happens by accident or through lack of knowledge). This *desire psychology* stage is exactly parallel to adults' assumption that a baby who makes them angry has wanted to make them angry. Although adults have probably developed much further and can show advanced theory of mind in ideal circumstances, fatigue, frustration, and anger sometimes combine to limit adults to a much more childish view of other people.

As a final point in this section, consider toddlers' responses to angry parents. When children think that angry behavior is a joke, they may laugh, but on the whole they do not seem either pleased or amused when their parents are angry. It seems unlikely that they would intentionally provoke anger if they do not enjoy it. Angry shouting or physical punishment causes crying and emotional upset, of course. But children show distressed reactions even to adults who are suppressing anger, clenching their teeth, not looking at the child, or not speaking. Most young children respond to this confusing and threatening behavior by trying to approach the parent and by crying or becoming withdrawn if rebuffed. Young children do not seem to enjoy any aspect of angry parents, so it seems unlikely that they would make intentional efforts to annoy. However, a child might be defiant without having the intention of causing anger, and a certain amount of this behavior may actually indicate good development. According to some research, toddlers who are actively resistant are also likely to behave positively toward their mothers, and children of depressed mothers are less likely to show resistant behavior (Dix, Stewart, Gershoff, & Day, 2007).

Conclusion

Although toddlers sometimes make their parents angry by throwing food, the children probably have a very different intention resulting from their level of cognitive development. Toddlers' development of theory of mind is not sufficiently advanced to allow the performance of deliberately annoying behavior, although well-developed toddlers may display resistance to what parents want. Annie would still be tired and frustrated with thrown food, but she might feel better if she understood that Andrew is not trying to make her life difficult.

Critical Thinking

1. Read more about Piaget's theory in a child development textbook. Would Piaget have said that babies younger than 12 months of age have no knowledge of cause and effect? Explain the steps of development as babies come to understand how they cause changes in other people's moods or behavior. (This is not a question about development of theory of mind. Concentrate on the general idea of causing change, not the idea of knowing what the moods or beliefs are.)

2. Do you think parents who believe in this claim (that toddlers behave in intentionally annoying ways) are more or less likely to punish their child than those who do not accept this belief? What about parents who take the point of view described in the article by Dix et al. (2007)?

3. Use a child development textbook or one of the references in this section to find a description of the development of theory of mind. At what stage of theory of mind are the adults operating when they believe that a child who makes them angry actually wants to make them angry? Considering that adults can think about minds at the same level as children do, what do you conclude about development?

4. What observable behavior would cause you to conclude that a child intends to annoy an adult? You may want to consider first which adult behaviors make you think that another adult wants to annoy you, but don't forget to consider the child's probable level of theory of mind. Explain your answer. Watch out for the fundamental attribution error.

5. Do the points discussed in this essay imply that parents should simply clean up children's messes and allow them to drop food as long as they want to? What are possible alternatives that would meet the needs of both parents and children? Keep in mind that children need to practice steps in cognitive and motor development. You may want to review these developmental steps with the help of a child development textbook.

References

Dix, T., Stewart, A., Gershoff, E. T., & Day, W. H. (2007). Autonomy and children's reactions to being controlled: Evidence that both compliance and defiance may be positive markers in early development. *Child Development, 78,* 1204–1221.

Fonagy, P., Gergely, G., Jurist, E. L., & Target, M. (2002). *Affect regulation, mentalization, and the theory of the self.* New York: Other Press.

McElwain, N. L., & Volling, B. L. (2004). Attachment security and parental sensitivity during infancy: Associations with friendship quality and false-belief understanding at age 4. *Journal of Social and Personal Relationships, 21,* 639–667.

Russell, J. A., & Widen, S. C. (2002). Words versus faces in evoking preschool children's knowledge of the causes of emotions. *International Journal of Behavioral Development, 26,* 97–103.

Claim 21

It is important for parents to work with babies and teach them how to walk.

Ron and Shawna were spending a lot of time with their little boy, Eli. Eli was just 11 months old and really wanted to use his legs. If held on an adult's lap, he stiffened his legs to stand up, and if put on the floor he would pull himself up by the furniture and "cruise" along sideways. He could walk a little way when holding an adult's hand but did a lot better when holding both hands of a person walking behind him. "This is breaking my back!" Shawna said. "I hope he walks by himself soon. But I know we have to teach him how to do it." Ron noticed other parents at the park encouraging their babies to toddle back and forth between them, and he looked forward to the time when Eli could do that.

Were Ron and Shawna right? Did Eli have to receive instruction and practice to be able to walk?

It's charming to see a baby who is just beginning to walk alone, staggering back and forth between Mom and Dad, sometimes with an older brother or sister getting into the act. Baby is proud and perhaps a bit surprised at this new skill; parents are pleased and a little anxious. They all smile at one another and get ready to deal with a fall—it's a nice picture of family life at its best. The baby's ability to move is also a good index of general development, and as such it was once much investigated and is regaining interest after a period of less research activity (Thelen, 2000).

Are parents teaching their baby to walk when they supervise, smile, and hold their baby's hands? How do these behaviors compare to other actions that we call teaching? If parents wanted to teach in the ways people often use with children, they might demonstrate how to walk and tell their baby "Do it like this." They might reward their baby with a bite of cookie for every step taken and punish their baby when he or she crawled. These actions are usually considered to be connected with teaching. But do parents do these things and do them in the same manner, regardless of their culture (Solomons, 1978)? And would the baby not begin to walk if adults gave no instruction, rewards, or punishments?

In fact, babies can walk without having experienced much in the way of "teaching." Walking is a development that depends on maturation much more than instruction. Babies walk when certain physical changes have occurred to make walking possible: Their body proportions need to have altered from what they were at birth so that their lengthening legs and trunk counterbalance their large head, which makes it all too easy to fall over; their nervous systems need to have developed from the top down so that control over the lower as well as the upper body becomes possible; and their leg muscles need to have increased in strength to support their heavy upper body.

Like other new tasks, walking depends on a baby's motivation. Babies don't depend on adults to interest them in new skills; rather, they become interested on their own. Unlike older people, babies are interested in doing new things, even if those activities bring no specific reward, and they may even persist despite some discomfort or punishment. The term *mastery motivation* describes a baby's deep desire to perform difficult tasks and become more competent. Healthy babies are interested in walking when they are physically ready and will work very hard at it even if no one pays attention to them. Even babies with some physical handicaps strive to become mobile.

It seems, then, that healthy babies learn to walk without being taught. One might even say that they "mature" to walk rather than "learn" to walk. But does that mean that the doting parents of a new walker are completely useless in their baby's skill development? No. On the contrary, they teach some very important things.

The parents' smiles, attention, and readiness to help tell the young child that new abilities are important to loving caregivers, who share their child's joy in mastery and developmental progress. Pleasure in success and patience and tolerance about failure become shared parts of essential parent–child interactions. The foundations are laid for positive future relationships with teachers and others outside the family. Trying new things becomes associated with pride and pleasure, rather than with fear of failure and shame.

Parents' fascination with developments such as walking also teaches the parents to provide scaffolding for their children's other new achievements. First-time parents, especially, may be unsure of how to assist their child's developmental progress while simultaneously allowing their child to feel independent. The development of walking provides an excellent example of this complex parental skill and lets parents practice smoothing the developmental process without intruding on the child's activity. One simple but important contribution a parent can make is to keep looking at the young walker, giving the child a face to look at and a constant focus that helps maintain balance. Just as figure skaters and dancers keep their gaze on an object while they twirl, young children who keep looking at one thing do a better job of keeping their balance—and, of course, a parent's smiling face is an easy thing to focus on. Parents also provide scaffolding by foreseeing and removing problems—for example, taking up rugs that a baby might trip on and checking to be sure that their baby's shoes and socks are big enough for fast-growing feet. As parents discover these ways to support walking skill, they also learn how to provide similar scaffolding for many later types of learning, whether in school, sports, or social environments.

A baby's body type makes a difference in walking ability: Slender babies place their feet in a more mature way than do chubbier babies. But most babies fall a lot. According to one study, 14-month-olds fell an average of 15 times in 1 hour of free play. Parents are generally sympathetic about these little falls, but they cannot do much about them except make sure their baby is walking on surfaces that will not do any harm. Some other more complicated aspects of walking take time to develop, too (Garciaguirre, Adolph, & Shrout, 2007). For example, many new walkers like to carry objects or toys, such as teddy bears, around with them, but they do not do a very good job of adjusting their balance, so they may need to be monitored carefully when walking outdoors or stepping onto a carpet.

What about children whose handicapping conditions make walking more difficult? Children with Down syndrome, for example, tend to have loose joints and weak muscles as well as a general slowness in development. Do they need to be "taught" to walk? Once again, encouragement and excitement from adults can help with the motivation to conquer difficult tasks and, especially, the ability to bounce back and try again after failure.

But much of what is needed from adults is scaffolding of special tasks that toddlers with disabilities can gradually master. Children with Down syndrome may have poor vision that interferes with their ability to move, and corrective lenses can help with this. Special seats can help put children with disabilities into positions that encourage them to work toward independent movement (Williamson, 1988). Exercise on treadmill-type devices can strengthen leg muscles and help children with disabilities progress more rapidly toward mobility (Thelen & Ulrich, 1991). These methods support a child's development and learning, but they are not what is usually meant by "teaching."

In recent years, the practice of putting babies to sleep in a supine position in order to try to prevent SIDS has apparently resulted in delays of motor development. Although these resolve by age 2 without help, there are methods that parents can use to encourage earlier motor development. One program has been experimentally demonstrated to speed up motor development. It involves spending 15 minutes a day between the end of second and beginning of the third months putting the baby into a prone position and encouraging her to lift her head, holding her or sitting her upright and swaying her back and forth, and helping the baby move her hands to the midline (Lobo & Galloway, 2012).

The basic pattern of walking is the same for four-legged animals, humans, and other two-legged creatures like birds. Primitive patterns of muscular activity involved in stepping are a part of brainstem and spinal cord functioning and are seen in the reflexive stepping movements of newborn humans when they are held in an upright position with their feet touching a surface. However, walking does not really begin until the brain reaches a certain level of maturity and can coordinate different sensory events (Grillner, 2011).

Conclusion

Healthy children develop walking through a process of physical maturation and are not taught how to walk through their parents' efforts, although parents can contribute by helping the child practice movements and by helping with experience in the prone position. Efforts to help a child practice walking and other motor skills can encourage a child to try new things, and these experiences can help parents develop better approaches to use in support of later learning. Ron and Shawna are not actually teaching Eli how to walk, but they are teaching him (and themselves) some important things about learning and teaching.

Critical Thinking

1. Using a child development textbook as a source, describe what the Russian psychologist Lev Vygotsky said about the role of adults in children's learning. How do Vygotsky's ideas contribute to practical understanding of toddlers' development of walking?

2. When toddlers first begin to walk, they may do well when an adult watches but fall soon after the adult looks away. How would you explain this fact, using ideas from this section?

3. In the study by Lobo and Galloway (2012), a method taught to parents helped babies achieve motor milestones earlier than a comparison group did. The experimental method included encouraging babies to lift their heads when in the prone position. What could parents do in order to be encouraging? Would this kind of encouragement also apply when babies are beginning to walk? What other encouragement could be used with the older babies?

4. Using material from Thelen (2000), describe the evidence that shows that increasing muscle strength is related to the ability to walk independently.

5. Using a child development textbook, define the term *scaffolding*. Choose a motor skill other than walking and provide an example of scaffolding an adult might use to help a child develop the skill. Williamson (1988) provides examples drawn from work with toddlers with disabilities.

References

Garciaguirre, J. S., Adolph, K. E., & Shrout, P. E. (2007). Baby carriage: Infants walking with loads. *Child Development, 78*, 664–680.

Grillner, S. (2011). Human locomotor circuits conform. *Science, 334*, 912–913.

Lobo, M. A., & Galloway, J. C. (2012). Enhanced handling and positioning in early infancy advances development through the first year. *Child Development, 83*, 1290–1302.

Solomons, H. C. (1978). The malleability of infant motor development. *Clinical Pediatrics, 17*, 836–840.

Thelen, E. (2000). Motor development as foundation and future of developmental psychology. *International Journal of Behavioral Development, 24*, 385–397.

Thelen, E., & Ulrich, B. (1991). Hidden skills: A dynamic systems analysis of treadmill stepping during the first year. *Monographs of the Society for Research in Child Development, 56*(1, Serial No. 223).

Williamson, G. (1988). Motor control as a resource for adaptive coping. *Zero to Three, 9*(1), 1–7.

Claim 22

It is a good thing for an infant or a toddler to have experience with many caregivers, not just one or two.

Twelve-month-old Emma's mother, Holly, was telling her friend about Emma's child care center, which Emma had recently started attending when her mother went back to work full-time. Holly said how much she approved of the center's policies. "They have lots of different people taking care of the kids, and different ones on different days. I think that's a great way to make Emma independent and friendly. Anyway, I wouldn't want her to get attached to a caregiver and not want to be with me so much. She cries a lot when I leave her there, and when I look in the window she's in a corner by herself, looking sad, but I'm sure she'll get used to it soon. Some of the other kids are really friendly and want me to pick them up as soon as I go in."

Is Holly right in her approval of the child care center's policies?

Many of today's parents of young children attended day care or preschool when they were children, but of course they cannot clearly remember the experience. When they think about group care for their infants and toddlers, they may simply take their memories of kindergarten or first grade and apply them to younger children as a way of imagining proper child care for the very young. American parents tend to be concerned about their children's education, so it is not surprising that they take school as a model for infant and toddler care. One of the rules about school is that children should obey and respond to all the adults there—their own teacher, other teachers, the principal—so the idea of accepting many caregivers may be an important one in parents' thinking. Many parents reason that there should be similarities between their very young children's experiences and those the parents remember of their own experience, but professional groups such as the National Association for the Education of Young Children (NAEYC; 2005), do not agree.

The number of caregivers working with infants and toddlers has a special significance because of the connection with the children's development of attachment and healthy understanding of social relationships. Infants and toddlers who have a small number of consistent caregivers usually form a secure attachment to those adults, and after the age of about 8 months are much slower to accept unfamiliar people than they used to be. When young children are surrounded by a large, unpredictable group of caregivers, they may be less likely to develop secure attachment and may not show the same emotional changes that are characteristic of children with a few, consistent caregivers.

Although child development professionals feel that the emotional change to preference for familiar people is healthy and desirable, parents may perceive it as a matter of concern. Some young parents think their children will remain as friendly and outgoing as they were at 4 or 5 months of age. They are surprised and worried when an older baby begins to avoid strangers and fear that this behavior will be a permanent personality trait. Other parents need to use child care services, but they want their young children to have emotional attachments only to the parents—not to their other caregivers. Such parents may want infants and toddlers to have many different caregivers so that they do not have a chance to become attached to anyone else. Some parents may simply consider attachment behavior to be a nuisance, associated as it is with intense emotional reactions to separation or to the approach of strangers. Parents with this concern may believe that having many caregivers makes a child friendly, outgoing, independent, and adventurous—all characteristics that are preferred by many American parents. Young parents may consider a child who has strong attachments to a small number of caregivers to be unfriendly, clingy, shy, and overly dependent—characteristics they do not favor. (Behavior may be different among children in cultures where it is customary to have many caregivers, however; Whaley, Sigman, Beckwith, Cohen, & Espinosa, 2002.)

It is not easy to carry out research to clarify which child care situation best encourages good early development. The big question is, do infants and toddlers benefit from having many caregivers, as some parents believe, or do they do best with a smaller number of adults caring for them? This question is not likely to be answered through difficult experimental procedures that randomly assign some children to experiences with many caregivers and others to a care situation with a few consistent care providers. Such studies are simply not very practical. It is much easier to compare children from day care centers where each child interacts with many adults to those from settings where each child has only one or two caregivers who provide predictable care. However, with this kind of comparison, many other confounding variables are likely to affect the children in the two child care settings, so it is difficult to draw clear conclusions from these simple comparisons. Most often, information about the effects of multiple caregivers is based on generalizations from clinical work and from past child care arrangements, such as those in England during World War II, neither of which may actually be typical of modern child care experiences (Freud & Burlingham, 1973). But the sources available suggest that toddlers are calmer and happier and learn more effectively when they have had a chance to develop secure relationships by frequent interactions with small numbers of adults. These sources of information do not indicate that children with many caregivers are independent or friendly as a result of their care.

To further complicate the research issue, information from the sources mentioned earlier has been applied by organizations such as the NAEYC to establish guidelines advocating a small number of consistent caregivers for young children. Child care programs accredited by NAEYC (2005) must follow those guidelines and as a result have characteristics that certainly affect the types of children enrolled and that may affect the children's development. Such high-quality, accredited programs are usually more expensive and more selective of both children and teachers than many other programs. If children in these accredited programs show excellent cognitive and social development, caution should be taken when making the assumption that the small number of caregivers caused good development. It is possible that the programs accept few children with developmental problems, increasing the number of good outcomes; it is also possible that parents who can afford high-quality programs are also able to foster their children's development in other ways. In fact, it may be that being a well-developed child from a well-functioning family is the cause of the good experience with the program, rather than the other way around. It would be a mistake to think that research has clearly answered questions on this topic.

So far, I have discussed the possible direct effect of multiple (or few) caregivers on children's social and cognitive development. But what about less direct effects? An example of a less direct effect involves the result of a caregiver's familiarity with a child's characteristics, familiarity that would increase with amount of time spent in interactions with the child and decrease if many caregivers shared that time. Although adults and infants make many mistakes as they try to communicate, they are more persistent in their efforts if they know each other well. Adults are not as likely to give up on understanding a particular baby when they have the confidence that comes from many successful communications in the past. If a caregiver has too many infants to care for, or if the caregiver has no time to get to know them, or if staff turnover means that all the caregivers are new to all the babies, chances are that the adult will not have the energy or interest to work toward communication about physical or emotional needs. Other factors, such as physical crowding, can also affect children's responses and make them more difficult to care for (Legendre, 2003).

Conclusion

Young children probably benefit from better individual care and chances to form secure attachments when they have a small number of caregivers. However, the difficulties of research in this area make it hard to present clear evidence for this claim. There is no good evidence that having multiple caregivers is advantageous, so it is probably wisest for parents to seek child care that exposes children to small numbers of adults whom children can get to know. Holly's assumption that toddlers are "friendly" when they approach a stranger is a misunderstanding of early development and not a good reason to choose this child care center for Emma.

Critical Thinking

1. Using a child development textbook for information, describe the kinds of experiences that seem to foster attachment. Why would these experiences be less likely to occur with multiple caregivers?

2. A parent education pamphlet says that children who are securely attached will not cry when left at the child care center. Comment on the accuracy of this statement, using a child development textbook to support your position. What role does temperament play in this behavior? How about age?

3. Read an account of group child care during World War II (e.g., Freud & Burlingham, 1973) What are three ways in which the experiences of those

infants and toddlers were different from those of children in modern child care centers?

4. Find information about early language development in a child development textbook. Explain the benefits of infant caregivers' persistence in efforts to communicate. Use the concepts of communicative or interactive mismatch and repair. Keep in mind that successful communication can mean understanding infants' signals as well as sending messages to infants.

5. Discuss the confounded variables that make it difficult to compare programs with many children per caregiver to those with few children for each caregiver. Consider matters such as staff training and salary as well as parents' characteristics that might cause them to choose one program rather than another. How does the post hoc error interfere with thinking about these issues?

References

Freud, A., & Burlingham, D. T. (1973). *Infants without families and reports on the Hampshire Nurseries, 1939–1945*. New York: International Universities Press. (Note: If this book is not available, similar reports can be found in *Psychoanalytic Study of the Child*, volumes dated late 1940s–1950s. This publication is owned by many college and university libraries.)

Legendre, A. (2003). Environmental features influencing toddlers' bioemotional reactions in day care centers. *Environment and Behavior, 35*, 523–549.

National Association for the Education of Young Children. (2005). *NAEYC early childhood program standards and accreditation: The mark of quality in early childhood education*. Washington, DC: Author.

Whaley, S. E., Sigman, M., Beckwith, L., Cohen, S. E., & Espinosa, M. P. (2002). Infant-caregiver interaction in Kenya and the United States: The importance of multiple caregivers and adequate comparison samples. *Journal of Cross-Cultural Psychology, 33*, 236–247.

Claim 23

Screen devices provide excellent resources for encouraging infants' and toddlers' mental development.

Marie was looking for good toys for presents for her 12-month-old nephew. She was interested in finding some things that were genuinely educational. In a catalog, she came across the following statement: "Leave them to their own devices! Give little ones their very own cool electronic toys, and they'll stop reaching for yours! Toddler-friendly [brand name] toys engage kids with realistic designs and interactive content—each button or icon triggers fun sounds, speech and lights that encourage early learning!" Marie was not too sure that learning to press buttons or touch icons was any real step toward educational goals like reading or even increased vocabulary, although she could see the advantage of handing a toddler "his own cellphone" to keep him from grabbing his mother's. She was trying to decide whether one of these electronic toys would be a better gift than a book, but she was not at all sure.

Do screen devices contribute to young children's mental growth?

Although groups like the American Academy of Pediatrics (2011) have recommended against all use of screen devices by children under 2 years of age, and the Walt Disney organization several years ago offered refunds to those who had found that their "Baby Einstein" did not cause rapid intellectual growth (Lewin, 2009), parents and family friends continue to be influenced by advertising claims about the educational benefits of screen devices—and more such devices come on the market every day. Everyday nonscreen activities, talking, and reading are all known to have excellent educational benefits, but adults are still easily impressed by young children's rapid mastery of devices like cellphones that may seem challenging to the adults.

It does not seem likely that we can stop most infants and toddlers from experiencing a great deal of screen exposure. But what is the evidence for or against their ability to learn from screen devices? For example, can toddlers learn to imitate an action from seeing a model do the same thing on a screen? Families see every day that toddlers learn to imitate things they see done by parents, brothers, and sisters—both desirable things like brushing their teeth and undesirable things like using forbidden words. Is there clear evidence that they can also imitate what they see on a screen? Such evidence has actually been available for many years. Meltzoff (1988) showed that babies as young as 14 months could imitate what they saw someone do on television, both immediately and even 24 hours later. However, they did not do as well when imitating from television as they did when imitating a live model.

Why would there be a deficit in imitation of a video example? Why isn't the video situation just as good as the live situation? A major difference between the two is that a screen representation is two-dimensional, while the live model is seen in three dimensions. The real situation in which the toddler does the imitation is also 3-D, so when imitating the screen display, the child must make the cognitive jump from how things worked two-dimensionally to how they work in 3-D. He or she has to *transfer* what is learned from the screen to what is done in the real world, and this extra task makes imitation from the screen a step more difficult. But, as some authors have pointed out, this problem of transfer from 2-D to 3-D is no different for screen displays than it is for books (Barr, 2013; Golomb, 2007). And the same kinds of problems occur when the child is asked not to imitate but, for example, to use a name learned from a book or screen for a real-life object.

Given that adults continue to expose infants and toddlers to screen devices, the important question may not be how well young children learn from screen displays but whether we can make the displays work well with the different abilities of children of different ages. Like older children and adults—but even more than older people—babies remember better and can use information better if the information has been repeated more often.

In addition, if we want a toddler to be able to transfer information from a screen or book to the three-dimensional world, it will help if the 2-D picture has realistic details that give it a closer resemblance to the real-world object it represents. These details help the young child remember what was learned from the 2-D picture when he or she is faced with the 3-D object. In one study in which children of different ages were read to from books with different kinds of illustrations, 18-month-olds could imitate what they had seen in color photographs but not color drawings or line drawings. Not until 30 months did the children show the ability to imitate from line drawings as well as the two color representations (Simcock & DeLoache, 2006).

How about learning from sounds? One of the first claims made during arguments about screen learning is that toddlers learned Spanish words from watching "Sesame Street." But the effectiveness of learning words and sounds from screen devices seems to depend on what the sounds are. For example, having instrumental music accompany screen displays (a very common aspect of movie and television programming for adults) was shown to make 6-, 12-, and 18-month-olds less likely to imitate what they saw (Barr, Shuck, Salerno, Atkinson, & Linebarger, 2010). When the actions the children could imitate were accompanied by sound effects, their imitation was better, but it was not as good as what happened with live models to watch. As for learning vocabulary from the screen, some of the factors already mentioned, like repetition, seem to be important (Linebarger & Vaala, 2010).

In young children's language learning from real-world experience, an important question may be whether speech sounds from screen devices cause children to hear *less* speech from adults. For example, Kirkorian et al. (2009) found that parents' interactions with their young children were less frequent and poorer in quantity when television was on in the background than when no television was on. The presence or absence of the television sound was only one of the factors affecting the children's experience.

Conclusion

The research on infants' and toddlers' learning from screen devices suggests that such learning is very possible but that not all screen experiences are ideal ways of learning. Young children's cognitive ability is more challenged by screen displays of actions than it is by real-world experiences that look the same to adults. Learning from sounds can be lessened by added musical features. Essentially, early learning from screens can be effective if it is carefully planned and managed, but this does not mean that all screen devices provide a good learning situation. If Marie thinks her nephew's mother will read to him, a book might be a better present.

Critical Thinking

1. In the paper by Linebarger and Vaala (2010), the authors noted that in studies of babies learning language from screen devices, many researchers "have utilized simple stimuli created for the purpose of their study. This careful control of content comes at the expense of external applicability. . . . these simple videos, often devoid of fancy formal features and multiple simultaneous streams of information, do not resemble the commercially produced screen media that infants and toddlers watch in their homes." What does this comment suggest about the conclusions drawn from such studies? Do they support decisions about exposing infants and toddlers to screen displays?

2. In the Linebarger and Vaala (2010) paper, the authors noted that behaviors of adults toward children were altered while television or other screen displays were on. How would these changes potentially affect the children's learning from screen devices? What variables are confounded here?

3. Experimental studies using randomized designs are often considered the "gold standard" for research on child development. Could the study by Kirkorian et al. (2009) have been carried out as a randomized design? Why or why not? Can its findings be included as part of subsequent randomized designs about language learning from screen devices?

4. Look at some books intended for infants and toddlers. How do the illustrations compare with the conclusions drawn by Simcock and DeLoache (2006)? Comment on the reasons for this.

5. When researchers compare the mental development of babies whose parents say they watch a lot of screen displays with that of babies whose parents say they do not watch much, what variables are confounded? What factors may affect the parents' answers?

References

American Academy of Pediatrics. (2011). Media use by children younger than 2 years. *Pediatrics, 128,* 1040–1045.

Barr, R. (2013). Memory constraints on infant learning from picture books, television, and touchscreens. *Child Development Perspectives, 7,* 205–210.

Barr, R., Shuck, L. Salerno, K., Atkinson, E., & Linebarger, D. (2010). Music interferes with learning from television during infancy. *Infant and Child Development, 19,* 313–331.

Golomb, C. (2007). Representational conceptions in two- and three-dimensional media: A developmental perspective. *Psychology of Aesthetics, Creativity, and the Arts, 1,* 32–39.

Kirkorian, H. L., Pempek, T. A., Murphy, L. A., Schmidt, M. E., & Anderson, D. R. (2009).The impact of background television on parent-child interaction. *Child Development, 80,* 1350–1359.

Lewin, T. (2009, October 23). No Einstein in your crib? Get a refund. *New York Times.* Available at http://www.nytimes.com/2009/10/24/education/24baby.html.

Linebarger, D. L., & Vaala, S. E. (2010). Screen media and language development in infants and toddlers: An ecological perspective. *Developmental Review, 30,* 176–202.

Meltzoff, A. N. (1988). Imitation of televised models by infants. *Child Development, 59,* 1221–1229.

Simcock, G., & DeLoache, J. (2006). Get the picture? The effects of iconicity on infants' re-enactment from picture books. *Developmental Psychology, 42,* 1352–1357.

Claim 24

People who were abused as children are likely to abuse their own children.

Tamika and Brian had a little boy, Jared, who was about a year old. They had never married, but were discussing whether and when they should take that step. A lot of the hesitation came from their desire to save up and plan a really fine wedding, but there were other issues, too. Tamika worried that Brian was impatient with Jared and realized that if she wanted to break off with Brian, getting married would only make the situation more difficult to handle. Tamika confided her concerns to an older neighbor, Martha, who had known her and Brian since childhood. Martha agreed that Brian was sometimes pretty impatient and angry, and she told Tamika something that had never been mentioned before. "I used to live right next door to Brian's family," she said. "His father was hard to get along with. He used to beat on those kids sometimes, and somehow he always got maddest at Brian. You should think this wedding business over carefully, Tamika. You don't want to get stuck with a man who might abuse Jared, and you know it's the people who have been abused who turn into abusive parents."

Was Martha right in her advice? Is child abuse primarily a matter of repeating what people experienced in their own childhoods?

For some decades, people have puzzled over the causes of child abuse and neglect, in the hopes that it would be possible to prevent these disturbing events by striking directly at their causes. In the 1970s and 1980s,

Lenore Walker, an author concerned about domestic violence, introduced the idea of a "cycle of violence" in the battering of women and supported this idea with data from interviews. The idea of a cycle of violence was soon generalized to child abuse and the concept of intergenerational transmission, in which abusive behavior experienced in one generation was repeated when those abused children grew up and had their own children. This concept fit well with the developing view of social relationships as based on children's early attachment experiences with their parents.

But is there evidence to support the idea that child abusers are reenacting their own experiences? Such evidence is by no means easy to collect. Abusive and neglectful behavior often goes unreported, especially if no serious injury or death results from it. Neglect and abuse can be difficult to define and may even be categorized differently by researchers and by child protective services workers (Runyan, Cox, Dubowitz, Newton, Upadhyaya, et al., 2005). Definitions have been established and used in surveys like the National Incidence Study of Child Abuse and Neglect (Sedlak, Mettenburg, Schultz, & Cook, 2005), but are not necessarily adopted by everyone working in this area. When emotional abuse is added to the list of abusive behaviors, still more complications ensue. Sexual abuse is generally considered as a special topic but may go along with other types of abusive treatment.

In addition to these problems of definition, it is clear that no randomized, experimental work can be done when harm to children is the issue. The only research option is to collect information from individuals who have already had certain experiences in the natural course of their lives and to compare groups with different experiences or to look for correlations between experiences and outcomes. This situation means that confounding variables may play critical roles in determining the outcome of abusive experiences. Where there are strong possibilities of confounding variables at work, it is impossible to know whether the experience of abuse itself has caused an outcome; instead, we are forced to look at the impact of groups of factors that tend to occur together. For example, we might expect people who have experienced abuse also to be more likely than others to have grown up in poverty and to have histories of insecure emotional attachment. Their later tendency to abuse their own children could well be influenced by all of these factors.

One important problem of research on associations between childhood experience and adult behavior involves selection of a method. The events of interest occur many years apart rather than simultaneously. To deal with the time lapse, this kind of study can be either prospective or retrospective in design (Dixon, Browne, & Hamilton-Giachritsis, 2005). In a prospective study, the researchers will identify children who have recently been identified as experiencing abuse and will follow their development into their adulthood and record events of abusive behavior. Some work of this kind has followed children from the early years to adolescence, and the researchers have described the developmental pathway that may lead from maltreatment to later antisocial behavior (Egeland, Yates, Appleyard, & van Dulmen, 2002) but have not reported information specifically about later child abuse. Prospective studies are expensive and time-consuming, and it is easy for participants to be lost to the researchers' contacts.

In a retrospective study, adults who are known to have been abusive to children are studied and their early experiences of childhood abuse are investigated. This approach does not take as long as a prospective study, but it may be difficult or impossible to find out what early abuse was experienced. The abuse may never have been reported; it may have been forgotten by the individual or concealed by family informants; there may be differences between events the researcher considers abusive and the way the individual or the family thinks about these things. For example, hitting an infant with a switch or other object would be considered abusive by most researchers but is actually encouraged by some groups in the United States (Pearl & Pearl, n.d.).

Given the considerable difficulties of research on this topic, and the fact that much of the older research has not been done to a high standard (Ozturk Ertem, Leventhal, & Dobbs, 2000), what outcomes have been reported? There is general agreement that individuals who have experienced abuse in their early lives are more likely to commit acts of abuse against their own children. However, there is far from a one-to-one relationship between their early experiences and later behavior. By no means do all of those abused as children become abusive parents—and, importantly, some parents who do not report having been abused do commit abusive acts themselves. In one study, by the time they were 21 years old, 23% of sons of abused parents reported that they had been abused themselves. But the same report was made by 10% of the sons of parents who appeared not to have experienced abuse (Pears & Capaldi, 2001).

Not only did the great majority of previously-abused adults not behave abusively toward their children, but a substantial group of nonabused people did commit abusive acts. These facts suggest strongly that factors other than a history of child abuse played roles in abusive parenting. One important study reported that parents who had had multiple abusive experiences were more likely to be abusive than those with few such experiences. In addition, the researchers reported that abusive parents were more likely than others to be socially isolated and to have tendencies toward responding aggressively to other people (Berlin, Appleyard, & Dodge, 2011).

Conclusion

Martha's concerns about Brian are legitimate, and Tamika's own anxiety needs to be considered, but it would be a mistake to assume that his history of abuse locks Brian into abusive behavior toward Jared. Tamika should also pay attention to other known factors that she can easily observe. Is Brian not only impatient with Jared but inclined to respond aggressively in many social situations? Does he isolate himself socially, or does he have good relationships with a variety of friends, neighbors, and family members? Those characteristics may provide better predictions of Brian's behavior toward children than his own past experience of abuse.

Critical Thinking

1. Look at the document about the Fourth National Incidence Study of Child Abuse and Neglect at https://www.nis4.org/DOCS/Nis4Design_Method_Summary.pdf. Did the researchers have access to all reports of child abuse in the United States? How did they choose the materials they used?

2. Was the study by Pears and Capaldi (2001) a prospective or a retrospective study? What were the advantages and disadvantages of this choice?

3. When examining the connection between childhood abuse and adult potential for maltreatment, why is it important to know how many nonabused parents abused their own children? What problem of critical thinking can occur when people consider this topic?

4. Look at Michael and Debi Pearl's book, *To Train Up a Child* (n.d.). How would these authors' definition of child abuse probably differ from definitions given in the NIS-4 summary mentioned in question 1?

5. How might social isolation and aggressive behavior be intergenerationally transmitted? If this occurred, might it also appear that child abuse was transmitted in the same way?

References

Berlin, L., Appleyard, K., & Dodge, K. A. (2011). Intergenerational continuity in child maltreatment: Mediating mechanisms and implications for prevention. *Child Development, 82,* 162–176.

Dixon, L., Browne, K., & Hamilton-Giachritsis, C. (2005). Risk factors of parents abused as children: A mediational analysis of the intergenerational continuity of child maltreatment (Part I). *Journal of Child Psychology and Psychiatry, 46,* 47–57.

Egeland, B., Yates, T., Appleyard, K., & van Dulmen, M. (2002). The long-term consequences of maltreatment in the early years: A developmental pathway to antisocial behavior. *Children's Services, 5,* 249–260.

Ozturk Ertem, I., Leventhal, J. M., & Dobbs, S. (2000). Intergenerational continuity of child physical abuse: How good is the evidence? *Lancet, 356,* 814–819.

Pearl, M., & Pearl, D. (n.d.) *To train up a child.* Available at http://www.achristianhome.org/to_train_up_a_child.htm.

Pears, K. C., & Capaldi, D. M. (2001). Intergenerational transmission of abuse: A two-generational prospective study of an at-risk sample. *Child Abuse and Neglect, 25,* 1439–1461.

Runyan, D. K., Cox, C. E., Dubowitz, H., Newton, R. R., Upadhyaya, M., et al. (2005). Describing maltreatment: Do child protective services reports and research definitions agree? *Child Abuse and Neglect, 29,* 461–477.

Sedlak, A., Gragg, F., Mettenburg, J., Ciarico, J., Winglee, M., et al. (2008). *Fourth National Incidence Study of Child Abuse and Neglect (NIS-4). Design and Methods Summary.* Available at https://www.nis4.org/DOCS/Nis4Design_Method_Summary.pdf.

Sedlak, A., Mettenburg, J., Schultz, D., & Cook, D. (2005). *NIS definitions review.* Rockville, MD: Westat.

Part III

Preschoolers

Claim 25

Having kids listen to Mozart makes them smart.

Pam and Larry really wanted to do their best by their 2-month-old daughter, Molly. They monitored Pam's diet throughout her pregnancy and read and talked to their unborn child every day. Both parents were highly educated and had jobs that stressed mental abilities, so they wanted to be sure that Molly would grow up to be bright and academically successful. Posters and flash cards of French words surrounded Molly's crib. Only one thing seemed to be missing—the so-called Mozart effect. Pam and Larry had read in a parenting magazine that hearing the music of Mozart helps to "program" a baby's brain to work effectively. They bought some special recordings of Mozart's music that had been put together for just that purpose.

Were Pam and Larry right in what they were doing, or were they just victims of false advertising?

The idea that specific experiences with music can shape brain functioning and improve school performance has been around for some years now. This belief is an appealing one, suggesting as it does that a simple, inexpensive intervention can cut through the worrisome difficulties of intellectual and academic development. The reasoning behind the belief also has some real connection with known effects of experience on brain functioning. For example, flashing lights at different speeds can "drive" parts of brain wave patterns to alter their speeds. People who are good at mathematics are often interested in music, too, so it seems to make sense that experience with music might affect other abilities (Rauscher, Shaw, & Ky, 1993). The plausibility of this belief persuaded the governor of the state of Georgia to distribute classical music recordings to families of newborn babies in the hope that listening to the music would provide a good foundation for the children's mental development.

There is a connection between the belief in the effect of listening to Mozart and research about mental performance, but the association is rather distant and questionable. The original research, suggesting that hearing classical music such as Mozart's work could improve performance on spatial tasks, was conducted with adult participants rather than with children (Bangerter & Heath, 2004). In any case, researchers working with children have not replicated the effect found with adults. For example, in another study, preschoolers who listened to classical music showed no change in their tested spatial intelligence (McKelvie & Low, 2002). It would appear that the Mozart effect is a scientific legend, at least in the version that looks for an improvement in mathematical and spatial ability as a result of listening to classical music's repeated, predictable patterns of rhythms and tones.

But might there be other effects of music on mental functions? Spatial and mathematical skills are important, but they are not the only measurable intellectual abilities. More recent work examined the connection between music and language, an association that may not seem quite as obvious as the Mozart effect on quantitative abilities.

Why would musical experience have anything to do with understanding or using spoken language? All spoken languages depend on changes of pitch (i.e., perception of sound frequency) to convey meaning. The sound represented by one written letter is not just a single pitch but a pattern of extremely rapid pitch changes. Of course, music also involves a pattern of pitch changes, so a child's development of language ability might go hand in hand with the ability to recognize or carry a tune (Nagourney, 2007).

For certain languages, the ability to detect or create pitch changes is especially critical. These languages use *intonation*—a dramatic pitch change in part of a word, with the tone of the voice rising or falling—to indicate different meanings for the same basic sounds. The use of intonation to change meanings of words is common in Asian languages, but in English examples involve only certain actions, for example, using a higher pitch at the end of a sentence to indicate that a question is being asked. English-speaking people often have a lot of trouble learning to process the sounds of languages that use intonation.

Wong and colleagues (Wong, Skoe, Russo, Dees, & Kraus, 2007) compared 10 adult volunteers who had studied a musical instrument with

10 others who had no musical background. None of the adults spoke a Chinese language. All listened to a tape in which the Mandarin word *mi* was intoned in three different ways, which could make it mean "squint," "bewilder," or "rice." The researchers recorded the amount of brain activity devoted to processing the sounds and found that people with musical training showed more such activity than those without the training. In a later interview, one of the researchers speculated that schools should include music training as part of the curriculum because of the possible positive effect on language development.

A somewhat different research approach asked whether music changes mood and motivation, resulting in alterations in performance (Schellenberg, Nakata, Hunter, & Tamoto, 2007). This was reported to be the case for 5-year-olds, but this question would be much more difficult to answer for infants. And, of course, change of mood is temporary, so this evidence is not directly relevant to making kids smart.

Conclusion

Infants and young children do not seem to derive any special mental benefit from hearing classical music, particularly with respect to mathematical or spatial skills. It is possible that music training (rather than passive listening) can alter ways in which people pay attention to sounds, and this might affect language development. Pam and Larry may feel pleased and gratified if they play classical music for Molly, but it is doubtful that this listening experience alone will have much effect on her—although shared pleasure with her parents can help establish her interest in music, and possibly in language.

Critical Thinking

1. Consider the study by Wong et al. (2007). What would be two or three other possible differences between the music-trained and untrained groups and how might these confounding variables affect language development? Consult a child development textbook for further information about language development.

2. Read at least the abstract of the article by McKelvie and Low (2002). Did this study involve any of the confounding variables referred to in the last question? Explain your answer.

(Continued)

(Continued)

3. One research team (see Wong et al., 2007) speculated that musical training causes people to process speech sounds more effectively. What would be an alternative explanation of the results of the study? Remember that the participants in the study were volunteers who had made their own choices about whether to study music or possibly had those choices made for them by their parents.

4. Both the original Mozart effect study (see Rauscher et al., 1993) and the Wong et al. (2007) study tested adult participants, but the results were generalized to children. Is this an acceptable approach or not? Are conclusions from studies of children necessarily applicable to adults or vice versa? Explain your answer. Consult a child development textbook to locate information about the period of development in which basic language skills are most easily learned.

5. Using an Internet search engine, find websites about the Mozart Effect. Of the first 10 websites listed in your search, how many assume that the Mozart effect exists and how many find it questionable? What are two reasons given by Bangerter and Heath (2004) for this situation? (The Bangerter and Heath paper is also available online at www.si.umich .edu/ ICOS/Mozart%20Effect-final.pdf.) Are there problems of critical thinking that apply here?

References

Bangerter, A., & Heath, C. (2004). The Mozart effect: Tracking the evolution of a scientific legend. *British Journal of Social Psychology, 43*, 605–623.

McKelvie, P., & Low, J. (2002). Listening to Mozart does not improve children's spatial ability: Final curtains for the Mozart effect. *British Journal of Developmental Psychology, 20*(2), 241–258.

Nagourney, E. (2007, March 20). Skilled ear for music may help language. *New York Times*, p. F2.

Rauscher, F. H., Shaw, G. L., & Ky, K. N. (1993). Music and spatial task performance. *Nature, 365*, 611.

Schellenberg, E. G., Nakata, T., Hunter, P. G., & Tamoto, S. (2007). Exposure to music and cognitive performance: Tests of children and adults. *Psychology of Music, 35*, 5–19.

Wong, P. C. M., Skoe, E., Russo, N. M., Dees, T., & Kraus, N. (2007). Musical experience shapes human brainstem encoding of linguistic pitch patterns. *Nature Neuroscience, 10*(4), 420–422.

Claim 26

The time between birth and age 3 years is the most important period of development and learning in a person's life.

Two-and-a-half-year-old Emily lives a highly scheduled life. She goes with her mother to the gym, where they "work out" together in a class with other mothers and preschoolers. She attends nursery school for two hours, four mornings a week. She is about to start music lessons with a tiny violin. She has been taking dance lessons for six months. Her mother, Patricia, feels that she must help Emily pack as much as possible into the window of learning opportunity during Emily's first three years. Their 3-year-old neighbor, Rosie, goes to day care while her mother works 20 hours a week. She has no dance or music lessons, and although the family often goes to run around in the park, Rosie does not have any formal gym attendance. Rosie's mother, Ellen, says, "Oh, let her be a kid! There's plenty of time for that stuff when she goes to school. Anyway, she needs time to relax after hours at the child care center—and so do I."

Which mother has a better understanding of early development?

If it were shown to be true that the most important parts of development occur in the first three years of life, a critical step toward a solid theory of human development would be accomplished. Evidence about this issue would also have practical importance for education and for treatment of developmental problems. If the most important steps in development were to occur in the infant and toddler periods, then people would likely agree that most educational resources should be committed to infant education and to early intervention methods. On the other hand, if this early period is no more crucial than any other 3-year period in development, people may want to pour resources into the public schools, which are more cost-effective and easier to run than organizations that work with families and very young children.

When considering a variety of aspects of development, you will find that the claim about the importance of the first 3 years has different levels of support with respect to different types of developmental change. There is no question that brain development is rapid during this period, and it is also true that some problems that interfere with the brain's growth can be corrected if caught early and addressed with intervention. For instance, early brain growth depends in part on diet, with the consumption of high-quality proteins having a significant effect. Brain growth slows and complexity advances less if an infant or toddler is deprived of protein. The poorly nourished child's head circumference is abnormally small, compared with other, better-fed children of the same chronological age. During the first three years or so, the problematic development of the malnourished child can be corrected to some extent if the child is given a better diet, with milk, meat, eggs, or other good protein sources included. Catch-up growth can then help bring the brain closer to normal size, although the child's stature may always be short. However, delaying the improved diet until the child is 6 years old will not have the same effect. Although the formerly malnourished child will have better general health with more protein in the diet, brain size will remain small, and poor intellectual functions will be apparent. More specific studies of brain development were difficult to conduct until fairly recent times, when techniques for nonintrusive brain measurements were developed (Chugani, 1999; Papanicolaou et al., 2001).

Functions such as the development of spoken language also depend on both genetic factors and early experience. Newborns normally have good hearing at the time of birth, but they must learn from experience the important sounds of the language that will be their native tongue. Languages are different from each other in some of their basic sound patterns, but babies are not born with innate knowledge about the language their parents speak. Gradually, as a result of hearing older people speak, infants learn to pay attention to the sounds that are most important in their "cradle" language, and they also learn to ignore unimportant, accidental sounds that people make. (We aren't confused when a friend hiccups while talking because we learned long ago that a hiccup sound has no meaning.) By age 6 months—many months before a child can speak—a baby has made a great deal of progress in the task of learning which sounds contribute to meaning and which do not. Hearing impairment delays children's language progress, unless early help is made available. Help that does not arrive until children reach school age is much less effective than early help (Barinaga, 2000).

Development of visual functions has some similar time limitations. Some events need to happen in the first year, or development will not follow the normal pattern. Newborns are limited in their ability to coordinate the use of the left eye and the right eye, so they have poor skill at judging distances—a comparison of the picture seen by the left eye and the picture seen by the right. In the first months, better coordination develops, but good distance judgment requires good coordination and finely tuned brain processes. As a baby looks around and experiences many right-plus-left combined images, frequently used brain cells and connections strengthen; those that are rarely used gradually disappear. For most babies, this process works very well and results in a lifelong ability to judge distances accurately when performing tasks such as driving a car. However, a baby who has poor vision in one eye may lose that eye's function altogether. A baby who is cross-eyed may also have unusual problems if corrective surgery is performed after the brain's fine-tuning has already occurred. In this case, the new, normal-appearing positions of the eyes are not right for the brain functions that were already developed, and the individual sees double images—overlapping but separated pictures from the right and left side. The brain can no longer readjust after the early period of development is past (Chugani, 1999).

In this section, I presented several examples of development that depended on events in the early years. But what happens if young children are deprived of a good diet or experiences and there is no attempt to help them until they are older? This is obviously not a question that should be answered by experimentally subjecting children to deprivation or delayed help. It is difficult to reach a clear conclusion by comparing children who receive early help with those who do not because there are often confounding variables at work, such as family income or level of parental education. One approach to studying the effects of early or late intervention is to examine the effects of the Head Start program, a federally funded intervention program for preschool children that was established more than 40 years ago. According to some research, children who entered Head Start at age 3 years have experienced somewhat more positive effects than those who entered at age 4, but the 4-year-olds have shown some short-term benefits, such as improved vocabularies. Studies of Head Start have not made clear whether the first three years are of overwhelmingly powerful effect (Herrod, 2007) or whether later interventions can be useful. Unfortunately, children who do not receive early help do not just remain in a neutral state but are likely to be affected by negative aspects of their environments, such as neglect, abuse, and community violence, so it is quite difficult to read any effect of timing of an intervention.

With respect to personality and behavior problems, some important factors seem to arrive later rather than earlier in children's lives. For instance, Lorber and Egeland (2011) followed a group of children from birth and looked for events that appeared to make it more likely that the children would show behavior problems at school age. Rather than finding that children with behavior problems had been difficult from birth, these authors found that behavior problems were more likely when the mother was negative toward the child (incidentally, one of these mothers was only 12 years old) and when mother and child were unusually angry and uncooperative with each other when the child was $3\frac{1}{2}$. Two-year-olds and their mothers are often at odds, which is where the "terrible twos" get their name, but most of them soon settle down again; the mothers and their children who later had behavior problems continued to have difficulty.

Conclusion

Some aspects of children's development must take place in the first three years, or in an even shorter period of time, if they are to happen at all. But some other developmental changes may "catch up" if a later opportunity is offered. Generally speaking, however, the first few years need not be considered the only period of time to learn special skills, such as music and dance, or even to establish personality traits. Emily's and Rosie's mothers are making their decisions on the basis of their values and their convenience, which is a perfectly acceptable way for families to operate. Neither can appeal to clear research evidence to support her approach.

Critical Thinking

1. Use a child development textbook to define the term *critical period* (or *sensitive period*). Do any of the developmental processes discussed in this section indicate that one or more critical periods exist in the first three years of a child's development? Explain your answer.

2. Studies of "wild" children who did not talk have been used to support the view of a critical period for language development. Explain why

people might argue that such a critical period exists. What confounding variables make it more difficult to argue that children's social deprivation interfered with their language development?

3. Read the article by Cohn (2011). Does the article consider confounding variables? Support your answer with material from the article.

4. Using a child development textbook, define the term *plasticity*. Then briefly summarize the examples used in this section, using the terms *plastic* and *plasticity*.

5. Using the article by Barinaga (2000), create a list of aspects of language development that may have different critical periods. How many of the periods occur in the first three years? What problems of critical thinking would lead people to assume that all aspects of language develop together?

References

Barinaga, M. (2000). A critical issue for the brain. *Science, 288,* 216–219.

Chugani, H. T. (1999). Metabolic imaging: A window on brain development and plasticity. *The Neuroscientist, 5,* 29–40.

Cohn, J. (2011). The two year window. *New Republic, 242,* 10–13.

Herrod, H. G. (2007). Do first years really last a lifetime? *Clinical Pediatrics, 46,* 199–205.

Lorber, M. F., & Egeland, B. (2011). Parenting and infant difficulty: Testing a mutual exacerbation hypothesis to predict early onset conduct problems. *Child Development, 82,* 2006–2020.

Papanicolaou, A. C., Simos, P. G., Breier, J. I., Wheless, J. W., Mancias, P., et al. (2001). Brain plasticity for sensory and linguistic functions: A functional imaging study using magnetoencephalography with children and young adults. *Journal of Child Neurology, 16,* 241–252.

Claim 27

Children need to develop basic trust and show it by their confidence in other people.

Four-year-old Christopher was having a conflict with Sammy from next door. The two boys had been collecting different-colored leaves as they fell into their yards that October. They each had a bucketful, but Sammy didn't have many of the red ones, and he wanted to trade some of his yellow ones for some of Christopher's reds. Christopher was reluctant and finally stopped playing and went inside to sulk. His mother, Lisa, asked him what was wrong, and he said, "Sammy just wants to take my leaves." Later, Lisa told her husband, "I'm worried about Christopher. Why won't he trust Sammy? Aren't kids supposed to develop basic trust? Did we do something wrong that made him so suspicious?" Ed, Christopher's dad, wasn't sure what to think. He had read about basic trust, but he wasn't so sure that Sammy did mean to play fair.

Was Lisa right to be so concerned? Would an emotionally healthy 4-year-old be ready to trust playmates to this extent?

Erik Homberger Erikson, the great theorist of personality development, proposed that Freud's stages of psychosexual development should be reframed as stages of psychosocial development and understood as stages in the development of attitudes toward the self and other people. He suggested that the first year of life is a period in which a baby's experiences with other human beings help to establish a view of the world as a good place with some occasional bad experiences in it or as a bad and dangerous place in which there might occasionally be good things. The first view Erikson called "basic trust," and the second he named "basic mistrust." Although he would not have said that an individual's view of the social world was set in stone by his first birthday, he did suggest that general attitudes toward other people tended to build on early feelings of trust or distrust.

Ordinary experience tells us that even a person who is generally trusting will by adulthood have figured out that not everyone is to be trusted. Other people do not necessarily have our best interests at heart, nor do we necessarily care very much about theirs. It would be naïve or at best immature thinking that would make us believe that everyone is to be trusted. These facts have led to research on how realistic distrust or justified skepticism develops. The focus of that work has been on the preschool period, when much of the developmental change occurs.

Being distrustful is not always a matter of suspecting that someone wants to deceive you for purposes or advantages of their own. Another person may simply be mistaken in what she genuinely thinks, out of general inability or just out of the lack of opportunity to know something. As children develop the capacity to be aware of these facts, they may or may not change their acceptance of what people say—they may simultaneously state that a person is lying or mistaken, and act as if they believe what he says.

In a study by Vanderbilt, Liu, and Heyman (2011), preschool children watched a video in which an adult actor responded to other adult actors who pretended to be looking for an object in one of two boxes. Sometimes the first adult pointed to the right box and helped the others find the "prize," but at other times the first adult "tricked" the others by pointing to the wrong box. Later, the children were given boxes to look at to find a "prize," and a video was played in which the actor gave the children advice about the box to look in. (Whatever the children decide to do, they could open all the boxes and keep the "prizes.")

Because the distrust issue involves cognitive skills as well as the negative emotions we connect with distrusting a person, Vanderbilt et al. (2011) asked the preschoolers some questions. They asked whether the actor was trying to help or to trick the other adults, and also what the actor would do the next time. They also used questions that would rate the children's ability to use Theory of Mind to guess or predict what someone else was thinking or would decide to do.

The results of this study showed a distinct developmental change in trust and distrust of the "helping" actor and the "tricking" actor. Three-year-olds trusted the advice they got most of the time, no matter whether they had seen the actor in "helpful" or "tricky" mode. They trusted the "helpers" slightly more often. Four- and 5-year-olds were less trusting overall, but they trusted the "helpers" somewhat more than the "trickers." But when they were asked questions about the helper/tricker—whether he would help people or whether he was nice—only the 5-year-olds were able to connect the behavior they had seen with a general statement about the person.

The children's ability to treat "helpers" differently from "trickers" was correlated with their ability to use Theory of Mind. Once again, this is a matter of considering what other people know or want and thinking about its implications, a process sometimes called "belief-desire reasoning." Could the development of appropriate distrust have to do in part with this kind of reasoning, and could some beliefs and desires be harder to understand than others?

In one study on the speed and accuracy of belief-desire reasoning (Apperly, Warren, Andrews, Grant, & Todd, 2011), school-age children (6 to 11 years old) were asked to respond to stories where people had true beliefs, false beliefs (they thought they knew where something was, but they were wrong), positive desires (they wanted to have something), or negative desires (they disliked something and wanted to avoid it). These could be in several combinations: true beliefs about wanted items, true beliefs about disliked items, false beliefs about wanted items, or false beliefs about disliked items. In each case, the child was asked to respond as quickly as possible, decide what the person in the story would do, and press a key indicating what they thought would happen.

All the children took longer to respond when they had to deal with a false belief than with a true belief, and longer when there was a negative desire than when there was a positive desire. They also made many more errors when there were false beliefs than when there were true beliefs, and also more errors for negative desires than for positive desires. All the children also improved with age. The 6-year-olds took longer and made more mistakes than the 8-year-olds, who in turn did less well than the 10-year-olds. Understanding other people's thinking took a good deal of development, but even the adults who were included in this study took longer times and made more mistakes when they had to deal with false beliefs and negative desires.

Conclusion

Although Lisa was right in thinking that early trust and confidence in other people is a good foundation for personality development, Christopher's distrust of Sammy indicated a step forward in cognitive development. Christopher was able to realize that Sammy's wishes and his own might not coincide and that giving in to Sammy might not lead to an outcome he wanted. However,

Christopher was not old enough to be able to plan out or negotiate a trade that would be satisfactory to both sides; in frustration, he sulked and abandoned the play he had been enjoying. But his awareness of differences in beliefs and desires was a necessary development before he could arrive at more complicated social interactions including both cooperation and competition.

Critical Thinking

1. How does your textbook describe Erikson's (1950) concept of basic trust? How (if at all) does the idea of a justified distrust fit into Erikson's system?

2. Consider what was said above about the results of the Vanderbilt et al. (2011) study. Look at the study itself and read the last paragraph of the general discussion. Do the results of studies on children's understanding of deception depend in part on the measure chosen? Explain your answer by referring to details of this study.

3. Look at the article by Apperly et al. (2011). The graph in the results section shows response times and numbers of errors for all ages of children and all conditions. Which combination of conditions caused the slowest response times and the greatest number of errors for all ages?

4. Think about the Vanderbilt et al. (2011) study in terms of belief-desire reasoning as described by Apperly et al. (2011). Were the children in that study asked to deal with false beliefs? Why or why not? How about negative desires? Would the actor be demonstrating a negative desire in some situations? How would you expect that negative desire to affect the children's abilities to reason about whether they should trust the actor's advice or not?

5. Summarize what your textbook says about preschool children's social and emotional development and relationships. How would the development of reasonable distrust affect relationships with other children and with adults? How might that developmental change affect preschoolers' responses to teasing by older children or adults?

References

Apperly, I. A., Warren, F., Andrews, B. J., Grant, J., & Todd, S. (2011). Developmental continuity in theory of mind: Speed and accuracy of belief-desire reasoning in children and adults. *Child Development, 82,* 1691–1703.

Erikson, E. H. (1950). *Childhood and society.* New York: W.W. Norton.

Vanderbilt, K. E., Liu, D., & Heyman, G. D. (2011). The development of distrust. *Child Development, 82,* 1372–1380.

Claim 28

If a child is able to complete a task with an adult present, he or she is also able to do it alone.

Jack and his wife, Marian, were arguing about their 4-year-old, Tommy. Jack felt strongly that Tommy should be more independent, but Marian was inclined to help Tommy or even do things for him. She felt that Tommy liked being helped, and what's more, it was so much quicker to do things like button buttons than to wait for Tommy to get through the job. But Jack was very insistent that Tommy could and should put his shoes on alone before he came downstairs in the morning, even though Tommy called downstairs and said he couldn't do it. "I sat there with him every morning last week, and he did it by himself. He can put his shoes on, and you're just trying to baby him. If he can do it when I'm there, he can do it when we're down here."

Was Jack right about the evidence for Tommy's ability? (Never mind who was "right" in the parents' argument!)

When adults master a task, they can do it about as well alone as they do in company. If anything, they prefer to do a difficult job without having anyone watch or bother them. Plumbers are even said to charge more if a homeowner watches while they work!

Observation of children shows a very different kind of behavior pattern from infancy to adolescence. The child may do a task very well when with a familiar adult, even if the adult does not help directly or give advice but is simply present on the scene. But let the adult go away, or sometimes even *look* away from the child, and the skill may seem to evaporate. The child may seem discouraged or distressed by failure and seem unable to do the job that he or she did so well under other circumstances.

This kind of behavior is often seen in infants who have just learned to walk: The baby staggers around and around the living room, smiling and gazing toward the proud and attentive mother. Suppose someone comes into the room or the phone rings, and the mother gets up to respond to the new demand, perhaps even turning her back to the baby so as not to be distracted. Very soon, the baby, who was walking steadily, falls down—and begins to cry.

A similar situation, usually with fewer tears, can be seen among 4-year-olds: With much effort and guidance, the child has learned to put on and button a shirt or put on and fasten shoes with hook-and-loop fasteners (tying shoelaces usually comes later). A parent, who has been supervising this task every day, is finally convinced that the child can do it and one busy morning sends the child off to "do it all by yourself." An hour later, the parent checks to see what is happening and finds that the child is playing and has not made the slightest effort to get dressed. The child and parent may have had quite different ideas of their intentions—the parent assumed that they both shared the goal of getting the child dressed, but apparently this was not so. (Tollefson, 2005, discusses how young children manage to take part in shared actions even though they do not think clearly about what other people intend.)

Teachers may see the same type of behavior in older children: A particular sixth-grader seems to need some extra help in arithmetic, for example, and the teacher sits with the student, patiently guiding each step. Then the teacher says she will just watch: "You do the next one by yourself." The student completes the problem successfully, and the teacher is pleased that the student has learned the technique, thinking all the student needs now is reinforcement through practice and repetition. The teacher provides a problem set to practice alone and goes about other business. When the teacher checks back with the student, not a single problem is finished. "It's hard!" explains the student, on the verge of tears. In a case like this, the adult may have as much trouble as the child in understanding another's state of mind (Mason & Macrae, 2008).

Very little research has investigated this childhood behavior, which is so unusual in adults, so typical of children, and so frustrating to parents and teachers who see it as a deliberate refusal to cooperate. However, some ideas about early development can help people understand what these apparently reluctant children are doing. Not surprisingly, different factors may be at work for children of different ages.

Two factors are needed to try to explain the toddling baby's fall when the mother looks away. The first part has to do with the role of the mother's smile and approval of the baby's exploration of the world. As the baby approaches unfamiliar things (and of course everything is a bit unfamiliar when seen from the standing rather than the crawling position) or tries new actions, the baby uses *social referencing* to check whether the mother thinks the situation is frightening. If the mother's voice tone or facial expression shows concern, the baby is likely to back off from the activity. An expression of pleasure and happiness encourages the baby to go on, but in our example, as the mother turns away, her expression is abruptly removed and no longer supports the baby's actions.

A second factor in the baby's sudden failure to walk may involve a very specific way of maintaining balance. Adult dancers and figure skaters keep their balance when turning rapidly by fixing their gaze on an object. New walkers may do the same thing by keeping their gaze on the most interesting and attractive sight in the room, a smiling, familiar face. When this sight is no longer available, balance becomes much more difficult.

What about the older children? They are past the need for help with balance or with social referencing. Nevertheless, the adult's attention and orientation (physical and mental) toward the task may provide a form of *scaffolding* that helps maintain the child's concentration on steps leading to his or her goal. When getting dressed or solving an arithmetic problem, the child must remember the necessary actions and the order in which they have to be done. Distractions such as toys, classroom events, hunger, or anxiety may make this part of the task difficult, whereas the presence of an involved adult may help focus attention. Cultures that stress skills other than literacy make use of these ideas more than adults in the United States do, and these other cultures provide opportunities for children to be apprentices or to simply spend ample time watching what adults do (Rogoff, 1990).

When children do not seem to be doing a very good job of carrying out a task independently, it is probably best to withdraw adult help gradually (Skibbe, Behnke, & Justice, 2004). Responding with annoyance to the child's poor performance is likely to cause increased emotion and result in even less success in the task.

Parental concerns about children's independent performance usually focus on practical tasks. However, both teachers and parents may have to deal with problems about school performance. Should a child who has once shown mastery of a cognitive ability be expected to continue to do so? When thinking about stages of cognitive development, as suggested by

Piaget and others, people usually conclude that they can have this expectation. However, individual children's performances depend very much on the specific task, as well as on other events of the day, and under some circumstances children will not necessarily be able to solve a problem that they did well on another occasion (Willingham, 2008).

Conclusion

When children have not completely mastered a task, they may be able to do the job in the presence of a familiar adult but not when they are on their own. If children fail to complete a task independently, it's likely that they need more guidance and practice for complete mastery, not that the child wants to "boss" the adults or be a baby. Jack and Marian needed to think of Tommy's dressing competence as the learning of a useful skill rather than an interpersonal issue, but chances are that this disagreement was really about other family issues that would not be settled no matter how well Tommy put on his shoes.

Critical Thinking

1. Refer to a child development textbook to find information about the *zone of proximal development* (ZPD) as it was suggested decades ago by the Russian psychologist Lev Vygotsky. How is the ZPD related to the claim discussed in this section? What research approach would be needed to demonstrate the existence of the ZPD?

2. Find the definition of the term *scaffolding* in a child development textbook. Discuss why the teacher's actions with the sixth-grader described in this section can be considered scaffolding. Rogoff (1990) provides a number of examples of scaffolding from different cultures.

3. Use a child development textbook to find information about *parental style*. Which parental style would be most likely among parents who encourage a 4-year-old to stay near them when mastering dressing tasks? Explain your answer.

4. Consider a situation in which an adult believes that a child is deliberately refusing to do a task when left alone to do it. Use a child development textbook to read about Theory of Mind. At what age might a child first be capable of foreseeing the effect of his or her apparent refusal to perform a task that the adult thinks the child can do? Is the adult in this

(Continued)

(Continued)

situation using a mature level of theory of mind? Explain your answer, and include information about *adultomorphism*.

5. Use a child development textbook to find information about *social referencing*. If toddling babies need their mothers' attentive looks to maintain balance while walking, what would you expect to be the result of maternal depression or drug and alcohol use? Briefly state how researchers might look for evidence of the outcome you expect. Explain your answers.

References

Mason, M. F., & Macrae, C. N. (2008). Perspective-taking from a social neuroscience standpoint. *Group Process and Intergroup Relations, 11*, 215–232.

Rogoff, B. (1990). *Apprenticeship in learning: Cognitive development in a social context*. New York: Oxford University Press.

Skibbe, L., Behnke, M., & Justice, L. M. (2004). Parental scaffolding of children's phonological awareness skills: Interactions between mothers and their preschoolers with language difficulties. *Communication Disorders Quarterly, 25*, 189–203.

Tollefson, D. (2005). Let's pretend! Children and joint action. *Philosophy of the Social Sciences, 35*, 75–97.

Willingham, D. T. (2008). What is developmentally appropriate practice? *American Educator, 32*, 34–39.

Claim 29

Preschoolers who hold their breath when angry are trying to upset their parents and get their own way.

Four-year-old Marcus did it again. He was startled when his grandmother suddenly grabbed away a sharp knife he had picked up. (She was afraid he would cut himself.) Marcus took one breath and then stood there, not breathing. His lips turned blue, and after a moment he fell to the ground, apparently unconscious. Very quickly he began to breathe again and came to, sniffling a bit and surrounded by some frightened adults. Marcus's mother, Ayesha, rushed to call the doctor and report that Marcus had had another spell of breath holding. She was terrified that he would die during one of these incidents and wanted some preventive treatment. Marcus's grandmother was concerned too, but she commented, "That boy just does that when he's mad and wants to get back at people. I took the knife he wanted and he thought he'd punish me. But I wasn't born yesterday! Ayesha, don't bother the doctor anymore. We'll just ignore Marcus when he tries to get his way like this."

Were either Ayesha or her mother right about Marcus's breath-holding spells?

Breath-holding spells—more formally known as *cyanotic and pallid infantile syncope*—are frightening, frustrating, and even annoying to parents. These situations usually involve a preschooler who is surprised or suddenly angered by some event. Maybe another child grabbed a toy, or the preschooler's mother snatched the child away from a dangerous road. The child begins to cry loudly or just takes in a breath and holds it; in short order, the child turns pale or ashy or bluish, takes no other breaths, and loses consciousness. As one mother described it, "He went limp . . . his eyes had rolled back into his head. His face was covered with a sheen of sweat and had gone from pink to whitish-grey." A minute or so later, the child "opened his eyes. His pallor faded slowly. . . . His hair was wet from sweat" (Horn, 2007, p. F5).

Naturally, parents are scared by their child's apparent brush with death, especially the first time it happens. They are likely to seek assurance from medical professionals that there is no serious cause for the problem (as indeed they should, because not all loss of consciousness is the same; Stephenson, 2007). Repeat performances may receive a different reaction, especially if the parent forms the impression that the child is trying to manipulate or punish the adults or get his or her own way inappropriately. Parents who frame the situation as manipulative often respond with anger. They may act on advice to walk away and ignore the child or even to throw a bucket of cold water over the unconscious preschooler.

Does the breath-holding spell suggest that the child is trying to influence the adult? Sometimes breath holding accompanies anger, and sometimes that anger is directed at an adult caregiver. However, breath holding also can occur when a child is simply surprised, not angry, or when a child is angry at a pet or another child, who probably will not be much concerned at the apparently dangerous physical crisis. Whatever construction a parent may place on breath holding, the phenomenon is probably not an attempt to manipulate or punish anyone.

Can a preschooler understand adult thinking well enough to plan a show that will frighten a caregiver? This question deals not with a child's capacity to hold his or her breath for a long time but with the child's ability to contemplate the effects of the action. To make such a plan, the child would have to be able to imagine his or her own death or loss of consciousness, envision an adult's response to one of these events, anticipate the adult's deep emotional distress, and anticipate the practical consequences, such as calling an ambulance or doing CPR. Although adolescents and adults can have fantasies about "how they'll feel when I'm gone," preschoolers' limited understanding of others' mental states makes it unlikely that they could manage this complicated cognitive and emotional process. If a preschool child wished to punish or manipulate an adult by causing distress, the child would probably not be able to figure out how to do this. Even when dealing with other preschoolers, children do not usually manage psychological retaliation any more complex than the vague threat "I won't be your friend."

Given that preschoolers cannot plan to cause others emotional upset, questions remain about the actual events of breath holding. What is really happening when children suddenly lose consciousness? Can children voluntarily refrain from breathing until unconsciousness occurs? Although it is not always useful to examine adults' abilities to understand children's abilities, it seems significant that few adults can effectively hold their breath long enough to lose consciousness. The urge to breathe becomes irresistible, particularly as the person becomes faint and thinks less clearly about the goal. It seems most unlikely that young children could exert the will not to breathe more effectively than, or even as well as, adults. Even if a preschooler intended to cause emotional distress by losing consciousness, he or she could probably not manage to carry out the plan.

In fact, loss of consciousness following breath holding seems to be related to a reflex that is characteristic of preschool children and uncommon after 5 years of age. When blood flow to the brain is restricted—perhaps by pressure inside the chest due to loud crying—the child loses consciousness. Movement stops, and with this event the body's demand for oxygen is reduced, allowing the available supply to go to the vulnerable brain. Like other reflexes, this one is not under voluntary control, nor is it obvious what benefit the individual derives from the reflex, except for restoration of breathing. And, also like other reflexes, this one takes place when the right stimulus occurs, not when the individual wants it to happen (Stephenson, 2007).

What about throwing cold water on a child? Such a reaction might be gratifying to the perturbed adult, but it will not prevent another episode of breath holding. If children do not voluntarily hold their breath, then they cannot decide *not* to do this, even if it means they could avoid punishment. Waking up cold, wet, and confused will not be of any help. Children usually emerge from their loss of consciousness feeling exhausted and frightened, needing comfort rather than punishment. If breath-holding spells occur frequently in a child, the parents need to develop a good response plan. They also need to teach babysitters, relatives, and child care providers what to do when their child loses consciousness and to be sure that everyone understands that the child is not exhibiting "bad behavior." Everyone involved, including the child, can take some comfort in the problem being cured with time. However, some children go on for some years having breath-holding episodes (Goraya & Virdi, 2001).

Conclusion

Breath-holding spells are involuntary and are not a preschooler's way of intentionally distressing adults. Marcus's mother, Ayesha, was overly concerned and did not seem reassured that there was no serious medical problem; his grandmother's approach of ignoring Marcus was based on some incorrect assumptions about preschoolers' thinking and was probably not the best reaction.

Critical Thinking

1. Use a child development textbook to define the term *reflex*. What are some other examples of reflexes that change with age?

2. Horn (2007) described a way to test whether a child has the reflex involved in breath-holding spells. Stephenson (2007) mentions the same method to test the reflex. Under what circumstances would you think this test should be used? Would it be appropriate for most parents or teachers to perform the test?

3. Read about parental styles in a child development textbook. Explain how you would expect parents of each style to respond to a child's breath holding. What style would you expect to be associated with the assumption that children hold their breath to manipulate adults? Explain your answer. Consider the role of the fundamental attribution error in the parents' decisions.

4. Would you expect a preschooler to have more- or less-frequent breath-holding spells if given much care and comfort after each one? Explain your answer using the concept of positive reinforcement. Remember that breath-holding spells are not voluntary.

5. Would you expect a preschooler to have breath-holding spells less or more frequently if punished after each one? Explain your answer.

References

Goraya, J. S., & Virdi, V. S. (2001). Persistence of breath-holding spells into late childhood. *Journal of Child Neurology, 16*, 697–698.

Horn, J. (2007, July 10). Saving a child, scaring a parent: A fainting reflex. *New York Times*, p. F5.

Stephenson, J. B. P. (2007). Clinical diagnosis of syncopes (including so-called breath-holding spells) without electroencephalography or ocular compression. *Journal of Child Neurology, 22*, 502–508.

Claim 30

Vaccines and heavy metals cause autism.

Laurie and Joe had always thought autism was one of the worst things they could imagine happening to their children. They had seen several movies that featured autistic people, and Laurie and Joe found the images distressing. Even before their twins were born, Laurie and Joe became more concerned that something might happen to cause them to be autistic. Looking up autism on the Internet, they came across the idea that autism was caused by the administration of vaccines that contained mercury preservatives. Little Paula and Peter received their first immunizations on the normal schedule, but as they grew toward their first birthdays Laurie became terribly worried. She read accounts of babies who were perfectly normal, even beginning to talk, then had bad reactions to vaccines and were later diagnosed as autistic. She dreaded having something happen to her children, especially because she felt she knew enough to protect them. Laurie told her neighbor she was thinking about canceling the twins' pediatrician appointment and never going back. "But, Laurie," said her neighbor, "don't you realize what might happen if they got one of the diseases that are prevented by vaccines? They could be brain damaged or even die."

Was Laurie right to want to avoid exposing the twins to vaccines?

Although research has repeatedly disconfirmed the accuracy of the idea, people persist in believing that infants and toddlers who are immunized against childhood diseases may, as a result, be afflicted with autism or similar disorders. Gossip among parents, Internet chat groups, and published books and articles continue to blame vaccines for the existence of autism. Most often, the responsible factor is said to be not the vaccine itself but a mercury-containing preservative, thimerosal, which has not been used for some years.

Although no evidence supports vaccines as the cause of autism (Caplan, 2006), the idea is not without logic. Many immunizations are scheduled in the first months and years of life, and babies usually respond to them with distress—most notably crying and sometimes a slight fever and restlessness. The early toddler period is also the point at which many parents of autistic children notice for the first time that something is unusual about their child's behavior and development, particularly the beginnings of speech (Young, Brewer, & Pattison, 2003). Parents typically seek help for their children when the children reach about 3 years of age and still do not talk or communicate in other ways. The shared timing of immunizations and noticeably unusual behavior makes it easy to assume that one causes the other, even though no evidence supports that conclusion. Some researchers have suggested that variant forms of autism exist: a form that shows symptoms in very early infancy and another that results in developmental regression in the toddler period (Ozonoff, Williams, & Landa, 2005; Woo et al., 2007). The regressive type of disorder obviously raises the question of causation by a recent, preceding event.

There is also a certain logic in placing blame on mercury. This toxic substance has been associated with brain damage in both children and adults. The old expression "mad as a hatter" refers to brain damage sustained by people who were exposed to manufacturing chemicals, including mercury, while making felt hats. It is not unreasonable to speculate that such a dangerous substance can change the pattern of development in a young child's vulnerable brain. However, the use of mercury-containing thimerosal as a preservative was discontinued some years ago, so the idea that recent cases of autistic disorders are caused by mercury in vaccines defies logic.

It is not surprising that families with autistic children seek desperately for an environmental factor causing this pervasive mental and social disturbance. If experts could identify an environmental cause for autism, they could prevent and perhaps cure this very serious disabling condition. So far, though, only weak evidence exists to support environmental factors as the cause of autism. If environmental causes exist, the responsible events must be quite complex or it would be unlikely that four times as many boys as girls would be diagnosed as autistic; boys and girls have different experiences, but perhaps not that different during the first 3 years of life.

In 1998, the British physician Andrew Wakefield announced his conclusion that vaccination for measles, mumps, and rubella was a major cause of autism. He associated autism with intestinal problems and suggested that the measles virus continued to live in the children's digestive tracts. This paper caused much interest and concern among parents on both sides of the Atlantic and created both resistance to childhood vaccination and claims that vaccination had caused autism, views that were supported and encouraged by celebrities. In 2010, after years of discussion and investigation, the British medical journal that had published Wakefield's paper retracted the publication on the grounds that it was fraudulent (Harris, 2010). Subsequently, following a review of undesirable side effects of vaccination the U.S. Institute of Medicine issued a report indicating that no evidence supported the idea that vaccination causes autism (Institute of Medicine Report, 2011).

It seems likely that even if environmental factors have an effect on the development of autism, no single factor causes all cases, and it may even be that no single case is caused by a single factor. Ongoing research is looking at a wide range of environmental factors that may play roles in the development of autism (probably in combination with genetic factors). Prenatal exposure (through the mother) and exposure in early infancy to thimerosal have not been linked with increased occurrence of autism (Price et al., 2010). Neither has experience of ultrasound during gestation (Grether et al., 2010). However, there has been a report of a "modest" increase in autism among children whose mothers used certain antidepressants during pregnancy, as compared to a control group who were not exposed (Croen et al., 2011). Also, children of older mothers and older fathers have a somewhat increased chance of autism, especially if they are the firstborn (Grether et al., 2009).

It has already been mentioned that misunderstanding of the connection between vaccines and autism has led to potentially dangerous failures to immunize. When people mistakenly believe that heavy metals cause autism, they may seek medical treatments that may be harmful, even though there is little evidence that autistic children have heavy metals in their bodies (Soden, Lowry, Garrison, & Wasserman, 2007). Chelation, a treatment aimed at removing metals from the body, may be appropriate in cases of actual poisoning, but it may be harmful if no such metals are present; in one study of rats, chelation was helpful to their behavior when they had been exposed to lead, but caused cognitive impairment in animals that had no lead exposure (Stangle et al., 2007). In addition, when chelation therapy is performed on autistic children (or others who do not have excessive amounts of metals in their bodies), the result may be the child's death ("Pennsylvania," 2007).

Conclusion

Vaccines have not been shown to be causes of autism, which is probably largely genetic in origin, and the diseases the immunizations prevent are very serious. Laurie would do well to follow her neighbor's advice and follow a regular immunization schedule for her twins.

Critical Thinking

1. Boys are much more likely than girls to be diagnosed with autism. What does this fact suggest about the causes of autism? Argue for and against the idea that genetic factors are the primary cause.

2. In the study by Wakefield referred to in this essay, the term "pervasive developmental disorder" is used in the title rather than "autism." Use your textbook and other sources to find information about these two terms and what they mean. What are autism spectrum disorders?

3. Look at the "Table: Summary of Causality Conclusions" in the Institute of Medicine Report (2011). State in different words what is meant by "rejection" on the line referring to the association between the MMR (measles, mumps, rubella) vaccine and autism.

4. In the Institute of Medicine Report (2011), the Report Brief section says the following: "The committee did not use a category to designate evidence that supports no causal relationship, because it is virtually impossible to prove the absence of a very rare relationship with the same certainty that is possible to establish the presence of one." Restate this in different words, and include in your statement the idea of "reversed burden of proof," which you may find defined in various sources.

5. Is the absence of heavy metals from the bodies of autistic children clear evidence that autism was not caused by heavy metals? Why or why not? Use the idea of irrelevant conclusions in your answer.

References

Caplan, A. (2006, Feb. 6). Fact: No link of vaccine, autism. *Philadelphia Inquirer*, p. A11.

Croen, L. A., Grether, J. K., Yoshida, C. K., Odouli, R., & Hendrick, V. (2011). Antidepressant use during pregnancy and childhood autism spectrum disorders. *Archives of General Psychiatry*. Available at http://archpsyc.ama-assn.org/cgi/content/short/archgenpsychiatry.2011.73.

Grether, J. K., Anderson, M. C., Croen, L. A., Smith, D., & Windham, G. C. (2009). Risk of autism and increasing maternal and paternal age in a large North American population. *American Journal of Epidemiology, 170,* 1118–1126.

Grether, J. K., Li, S. X., Yoshida, C. K., & Croen, L. A. (2010). Antenatal ultrasound and the risk of autism spectrum disorders. *Journal of Autism and Developmental Disorders, 40,* 238–245.

Harris, G. (2010, Feb. 2). Journal retracts 1998 paper linking autism to vaccines. *New York Times.* Available at http://www.nytimes.com/2010/02/03/health/research/03lancet.html.

Institute of Medicine Report. (2011). *Adverse effects of vaccines: Evidence and causality.* Available at http://www.iom.edu/Reports/2011/Adverse-Effects-of-Vaccines-Evidence-and-Causality.aspx.

Ozonoff, S., Williams, B. J., & Landa, R. (2005). Parental report of the early development of children with regressive autism. *Autism, 9,* 461–486.

"Pennsylvania: Charge in death after chelation treatment." (2007, August 23). *New York Times,* p. A17.

Price, C. S., Thompson, W. W., Goodson, B., Weintraub, E. S., Croen, L. A., et al. (2010). Prenatal and infant exposure to thimerosal from vaccines and immunoglobulins and risk of autism. *Pediatrics, 126,* 656–664.

Soden, S. E., Lowry, J. A., Garrison, C. B., & Wasserman, G. S. (2007). 24-hour provoked urine excretion test for heavy metals in children with autism and typically developing controls, a pilot study. *Clinical Toxicology, 45,* 476–481.

Stangle, D. E., Smith, D. R., Beaudin, S. A., Strawderman, M. S., Levitsky, D. A., & Strupp, B. J. (2007). Succimer chelation improves learning, attention, and arousal regulation in lead-exposed rats but produces lasting cognitive impairment in the absence of lead exposure. *Environmental Health Perspectives, 115,* 201–209.

Wakefield, A. J., Murch, S. H. , Linnell, J., Casson, D. M., et al. (1998). Ileal-lymphoid-nodular hyperplasia, a non-specific colitis, and pervasive developmental disorder in children. *Lancet, 351,* 637–641. Available at http://briandeer.com/mmr/lancet-paper.pdf.

Woo, E. J., Ball, R., Landa, R., Zimmerman, A. W., Braun, M. M., & VAERS Working Group. (2007). Developmental regression and autism reported to the Vaccine Adverse Event Reporting System. *Autism, 11,* 301–310.

Young, R. L., Brewer, N., & Pattison, C. (2003). Parental identification of early behavioral abnormalities in children with autistic disorder. *Autism, 7,* 125–143.

Claim 31

Autism rates are rising rapidly, especially in certain parts of the country, so something must be happening to cause more cases of this serious developmental problem.

The Becker family had one child, a 5-year-old boy, and a second baby was on the way. Sherry Becker and her husband, Alan, had discussed many times how much they'd like to have a summer house by the shore, and it seemed that it would be so nice to be able to spend part of each hot East Coast summer at the beach. Sherry mentioned this to her sister, naming the coastal community where they were considering buying. To Sherry's great surprise, her sister was horrified. "You're not going to go there while you're pregnant or when the baby's little, are you? Haven't you read the papers about all the cases of autism they've found in that place? The rates are getting higher and higher. There has to be something dangerous there that gets into the babies' brains. Please promise me you won't do this." Sherry didn't know what to think.

Was it wise for the family to move to such an area at this point in their lives? Are there places where "something happens" that causes autism?

O f all mental disorders of early life, autism is the one most likely to receive frightening treatment in the headlines. References to autistic disorders in the movies and on TV have made the diagnosis familiar to most people but have not provided them much real information about its symptoms or treatment. It is certainly true that autistic children suffer from a number of problems of development and that the lives of their families can be much disrupted by the demands of the children's mental and emotional states. It is also true that although children with autism continue to develop toward adulthood, the chances are small that they will manage to attain a fully mature and independent way of life. A small number of high-functioning autistic individuals, such as the noted author Temple Grandin, achieve a great deal of competence, but most autistic people need a good deal of support and protection.

Autism is no picnic for anyone, and it is not surprising that parents are easily alarmed about it. However, some frightening ideas about the disorder may be less disturbing with explanation. Two of these ideas are that rates of autism are increasing rapidly and that an environmental event is causing the problem.

To analyze these ideas, one must first consider the changing rates of autism. It is easy to forget that *rates* are not measures of absolute numbers. In other words, if the number of new cases of autism in a state are cited, the numbers do not refer to a rate. The term *rate* refers to a proportion and is related to the word *ratio*. Information about a rate must state the number of cases of a disorder for a total number of people, both those with and those without the disorder. The more people in an area, the more cases of autism; likewise, the fewer people, the fewer cases. But the actual *rate* (proportion of autistic individuals out of the entire population) could be the same in both situations.

A second important point involves reported rates of diagnosed disorders (Steuernagel, 2005). The reported rates are not based on a magical method of instantly counting how many people have a disorder. Instead, the determination of diagnosed cases involves the process of examining each individual, making the decision about the diagnosis, and collating that information for a given area. If a diagnosis is difficult to make, and few people have received the diagnosis, the rate of a disorder in an area will appear low, even if there are many undetected cases. If the authorities become more aware of a disorder and if practitioners develop more accurate diagnostic techniques, the rate will appear to rise, even though there are no real changes in the underlying facts. The number of diagnosed cases of autism in an area is related to the actual number of cases, but the number of diagnosed cases can rise or fall without any changes in the actual number. The rate of diagnosed cases of autism can vary a great deal from one area of the country to another, without any real difference in children's conditions in different states or towns.

A recent study by the Centers for Disease Control and Prevention (CDC) compared the number of children diagnosed with autism in 14 states, in each state's case comparing the proportion of autistic 8-year-olds to the entire 8-year-old population of the state (Kelley, 2007). Researchers noted large differences among the states. For example, New Jersey had the highest proportion of children diagnosed with autism, with 16.8 boys identified out of every 1,000 boys of this age. Alabama had the lowest rate, with only 5 boys diagnosed as autistic out of every 1,000 boys. The same state difference held for girls, with 4 out of every 1,000 New Jersey girls assessed as autistic, and only 1.4 of every 1,000 Alabama girls receiving this diagnosis.

After reading these data, you may be thinking, what is going on here? Is there a problem in New Jersey? Does the industrial background of parts of this state expose children to lead and mercury, toxic substances whose contribution to autistic disorders has been hypothesized? This might make some sense in comparison with Alabama, a much more rural and agricultural area, where one might expect children to be exposed less to toxic manufacturing materials. But looking back at the data provided by the CDC, readers would see that Utah has a high rate of autism reported for boys and a rather low rate for girls. Now what do readers do with the idea that toxic materials are causing autism? Can it be that in Utah boys are exposed to toxic substances and girls are not?

The CDC data do not explain the causes of autism; however, inspecting differences between states may help readers to detect certain important factors related to reported autism rates as well as the actual number of autistic children, both diagnosed and undiagnosed. It's true that there will probably not be many cases of autism reported if there are not many autistic children present, but it is also true that there can be few cases reported when there actually are many children with the disorder. Before a case is reported to CDC and entered into the records, one or more adults must have been aware of symptoms of autism, ready to take a child to be evaluated, and able to make and communicate the diagnosis and file the record in a state data system. The presence or absence of adults able to do these tasks may be one of the essential factors that determine the reported rate of autism in a state. Autistic symptoms are both subtle (Jones, Carr, & Feeley, 2006) and pervasive (Herbert, 2005). Paradoxical as it may seem, larger numbers of educated and competent adults in a state may cause the reported rate of autism in the state to rise. (But few people would argue that autism is caused by exposure to educated adults.)

One issue about counting numbers of autistic children is that such children may be identified as having a different diagnosis, such as mental retardation, for instance. They may also have more than one diagnosis and be identified as both autistic and mentally retarded, or autistic and suffering from problems of language development. Because of this, some researchers have looked back at old and recent records to see whether there have been changes in identification of children as autistic or mentally retarded or both; the records show whether a given child was evaluated for particular problems. In a study done in California, there did not seem to have been any changes due to shifts in the way problems were classified, but more recently there have been fewer autistic children who also had a diagnosis of mental retardation and more autistic children who were never evaluated for mental retardation (Grether, Rosen, Smith, & Croen, 2009).

A distressing issue about autism involves clusters of cases in specific geographical areas. Reports of clusters lead people to think that an unidentified characteristic of an area is making children autistic. Parents who are aware of clusters may also think that if they stay away from the implicated areas, their children will not become autistic. However, the real cause of a cluster may be chance. Random distribution of cases, which is expected for natural disorders, does not mean absolute uniformity of occurrence in all places. It would be surprising if there were no natural variation—the phenomenon that causes some areas to have higher and some to have lower numbers of cases of autism (or any other disorder). In addition, mistakes in identifying a cluster may be made if the expected number is not accurately determined or even if the definition of autistic symptoms has changed (Baron-Cohen, Saunders, & Chakrabarti, 1999).

Experts seem to have a much better understanding of how autistic children receive a diagnosis, and what statistical factors are at work, than of how children become autistic. However, one thing is clear: When people see an increase in rates of autism and want to make related decisions for their families, they need to consider whether the increase results from better reporting or from real changes in children's conditions.

Conclusion

Changes in reported rates of autism are influenced by many factors other than the actual proportion of autistic children in the population, so people cannot use information about only those changed rates to determine causes of autism. Sherry's sister has misinterpreted the significance of high reported rates of autism in a geographical area.

Critical Thinking

1. Use a child development textbook to find a description of autism. Basing your answer on this description, explain why 8-year-old children were chosen for the CDC study. Isn't it possible to diagnose the disorder in much younger children?

2. If no autistic children were in a group, would none be diagnosed? If several autistic children were in a group, would any or all be diagnosed? Read a textbook description of autism and use it to explain your answer to this question. Be sure to consider whether all autistic individuals behave in the same way or whether there are individual differences. Don't forget that autism can be confused with mental retardation or other problems.

3. Why is it important to compare proportions of children diagnosed with autism (e.g., 16.8 boys per 1,000 in New Jersey and 5 per 1,000 in Alabama) rather than absolute numbers (e.g., 722 in one state and 135 in another)?

4. Read the article by Kelley (2007). Why does the author think it is significant that a state diagnoses many autistic children while they are still very young? Provide more than one reason that supports this attitude.

5. Each state in the CDC study reported that the number of boys diagnosed with autism was at least three or four times more than the number of girls diagnosed with autism. Comment on two possible causes of autism that might explain this fact.

References

Baron-Cohen, S., Saunders, K., & Chakrabarti, S. (1999). Does autism cluster geographically? A research note. *Autism, 3,* 39–43.

Grether, J. K., Rosen, N. J., Smith, K. S., & Croen, L. A. (2009). Investigation of shifts in autism reporting in the California Department of Developmental Services. *Journal of Autism and Developmental Disorders, 39,* 1412–1419.

Herbert, M. R. (2005). Large brains in autism: The challenge of pervasive abnormality. *The Neuroscientist, 11,* 417–440.

Jones, E. A., Carr, E. G., & Feeley, K. M. (2006). Multiple effects of joint attention intervention for children with autism. *Behavior Modification, 30,* 782–834.

Kelley, T. (2007, February 18). An autism anomaly, partly explained. *New York Times,* p. WK2.

Steuernagel, T. (2005). Increases in identified cases of autism spectrum disorders. *Journal of Disability Policy Studies, 16,* 138–146.

Claim 32

Preschool children who lie are developing along dangerous lines and need to be corrected severely in order to stop this bad behavior.

Three-and-a-half-year-old Marco grabbed his little sister's cookie when no one was watching. The little girl naturally howled, and Marco's mother turned around to see him with half the cookie in his mouth. "Marco!" she demanded. "Did you just take Dina's cookie?" But Marco just said, "No!" Raina and Rick, Marco's parents, were confused and disturbed by this event. Marco had never lied to them before. They scolded him both for taking the cookie and for the lie but thought that perhaps this was not such an unusual thing for a preschool child to do. However, when Raina mentioned this to their neighbor, the neighbor had a much different reaction. "You have to punish the boy, and do it hard enough so he knows not to tell lies! If you don't teach him right from wrong now, he'll grow up to do a lot of other bad things, too. What he did was 'crazy lying' because he knew you could see he had the cookie. Kids who do that will steal and even worse things." Rick did not take this very seriously because he remembered fibs he and his brothers had told, but Raina was worried.

Was the neighbor right? Is lying a symptom of serious disturbance in preschool children?

Lying is the act of intentionally stating something that the liar does not believe, with the intention of creating a mistaken belief in a listener. This definition sounds pretty clear until we realize that in order to study lying, we have to be able to tell whether a person actually does not believe his or her own statement, as well as whether there is an intention to "fool" the listener. It's easy enough to know whether a statement is correct but more difficult to know whether a speaker also knows whether it is correct; we assume that if the speaker saw or experienced an event, he or she must know whether a statement about it is true, but this might not be the case (as we can see in some "eyewitness" evidence). With respect to the intention of creating a mistaken belief, we also assume that a person who lies does so with a desire to be believed—perhaps in order to get a reward or avoid a punishment, but perhaps not. It's possible that an adult could lie while knowing that the listener is not deceived but do so in order to establish a comfortable social situation, but this is not as likely for children.

How do we study lying in children? Although it's useful to hear stories like the one about Marco, these do not provide any way to look systematically at children's lies—especially if they involve complicated circumstances in which a child might expect to be punished. One systematic method was used by Evans and Lee (2013). They used a guessing game with 2- and 3-year-olds. The experimenter began the "game" by holding a toy behind the child's back and squeezing it to produce a noise—for example, a duck toy made a quacking noise. The child was asked to guess what the toy was, which of course she could do easily. Then the experimenter told the child she was going to put the next toy on the table while she went to get something from the toy box, but the child was not to turn around and peek at it. A hidden camera recorded whether the child did peek. The experimenter subsequently asked the child whether he or she had peeked and also what the toy was.

In the Evans and Lee (2013) study, 80% of the children peeked, but the older children were less likely to peek than the younger ones, and the older children also waited longer before peeking. When asked if they had peeked, 40% of the peekers lied, and older children were more likely to lie than younger ones. According to this evidence, 2-year-olds are sometimes able to lie, but this ability increases with age.

The apparent honesty of the younger children may not be a matter of moral virtue but of a lack of the cognitive skills that make lying possible. This idea is confirmed by evidence that children with autistic spectrum disorders, although they do lie sometimes, are less likely to lie than typically developing children matched for mental age (Talwar et al., 2012).

What kinds of lies do children tell? Do children think all lies equally bad? Are there even some lies both children and adults consider to be socially desirable? False denials of transgressions are probably the most highly motivated lies for young children and tend to be the first lies to be observed (Talwar et al., 2012), even though the children agree that these lies are morally wrong. During the preschool period, children already know that there are "white lies" that help them act politely in challenging social situations, such as receiving a present they don't like. They think those lies are wrong but not as bad as lies that are told maliciously to "get somebody in trouble" or without any good reason except to get something the child wants. Both preschool and older children are often instructed by their parents to tell "white lies" about liking presents they actually dislike or about enjoying foods they do not care for. In a study by Talwar, Murphy, and Lee (2007), children between ages 3 and 11 were given uninteresting presents and asked whether they liked them. A majority of all the children lied that they liked the present even without being coached, but older children lied more and even made up reasons why they liked the object (the present was soap, and some of the children explained untruthfully that they had run out of soap at home, or gave other reasons). When they were coached by their parents to say politely that they liked the gift, the children were even more likely to tell "white lies."

Even preschoolers have begun to learn the social conventions that guide us to lie rather than hurt someone's feelings. In real life, as well as in experiments, parents instruct the children how and when to do this but also tell them not to lie in other situations. Parents also lie to their children for many reasons—to protect the adults' privacy, to avoid explaining "grown-up" information like where babies come from, to try to discipline children by threatening them with unlikely consequences for misbehavior (a policeman coming to take them away, etc.), or simply to simplify life by evading endless questions. Do parents' lies affect their preschool children's tendency to lie? In a study by Hays and Carver (2014), children were tested on the "peeking" game described earlier. Preschoolers whose parents had lied to them were no different in peeking or lying than preschoolers whose parents had not lied, but older children were more likely to peek and to lie if they had been lied to.

Conclusion

Rick was right in thinking of lying as a typical part of children's development rather than the beginning of social and emotional disturbances.

Children of Marco's age are quite likely to lie about breaking rules. Fortunately, they are also starting to be able to tell appropriate and effective "white lies" so they do not hurt other people's feelings. Rather than punishing preschool "liars" severely, their honesty can be encouraged by parents who are truthful with them. Threats or use of severe punishment are likely to encourage children to lie in the hope of avoiding discomfort.

Critical Thinking

1. Use a child development textbook to read about Theory of Mind and its development in preschool children. What possible connection is there between Theory of Mind and lying?

2. When Raina asked Marco whether he had taken the cookie (which she knew he had), what did her question suggest to him about what she actually knew? Would his capacity for Theory of Mind make him think that perhaps she did not know?

3. Use a child development textbook to read about executive functions and their development in preschool children. What are the possible connections between executive functioning and lying as discussed by Evans and Lee (2013), especially with respect to the delayed peeking of the older children?

4. Read the discussion section of the paper by Leach et al. (2004). Were the adults in this study able to detect whether children were lying?

5. Use the Internet or other sources to find information about eyewitness testimony by young children. What conclusions about eyewitness testimony by children of different ages can be drawn from the material about lying that you have just read?

References

Evans, A. D., & Lee, K. (2013). Emergence of lying in very young children. *Developmental Psychology, 49*,1958–1963.

Hays, C., & Carver, L. J. (2014). Follow the liar: The effects of adult lies on children's honesty. *Developmental Science, 17*, 977–983.

Leach, A. M., Talwar, V., Lee, K., Bala, N., & Lindsey, R. C. L. (2004). Intuitive lie detection by law enforcement officials and university students. *Law & Human Behavior, 28*, 661–685.

Lee, K. (2013). Little liars: Development of verbal deception in children. *Child Development Perspectives, 7*, 91–96.

Talwar, V., Murphy, S. M., & Lee, K. (2007). White lie-telling in children for politeness purposes. *International Journal of Behavioral Development, 31,* 1–11.

Talwar, V., Zwaigenbaum, L., Goulden, K. J., Manji, S., Loomes, C., & Rasmussen, C. (2012). Lie-telling behavior in children with autism and its relation to false-belief understanding. *Focus on Developmental Disabilities, 27,* 122–129.

Xu, F., Bao, X., Fu, G., Talwar, V., & Lee, K. (2010). Lying and truth-telling in children: From concept to action. *Child Development, 81,* 581–596.

Claim 33

Preschoolers who try to bargain with their parents really want to manipulate and control adults, and they should not be allowed to negotiate.

"Oh, Mom! I want to play some more. Can't I have one more game? Can I wait until the long hand is on the six?" One more game, one more minute, one more hug, one more drink of water, one less spoonful of green beans—these were the requests 4-year-old Hamid made of his mother, many times every day and on into the night. Hamid's mother found life much simpler if she gave in and agreed to some of these bargains, although she usually drew the line at some point. Hamid generally did what she asked him to after a little negotiation had taken place. But Hamid's grandfather did not approve. "You're just letting him get his own way all the time. You've already spoiled him. Otherwise, he wouldn't be trying to control you so much. You'd better insist he does things your way, whether he cries and begs or not! He'll become a monster if you don't!"

Is Hamid's grandfather right? Are all of Hamid's requests aimed at taking command of the adults, who ought to be in charge?

Like human beings of any age, preschoolers want what they want (it would be pretty silly for them to want what they don't want). In that sense, bargaining with parents is an attempt to be in control of their own lives. But parents of preschool children often feel that some bargaining goes far beyond matters that the child actually wants or needs. It seems to some parents that bargaining is a way of life for their preschooler, and many parents become concerned that their child wants to take control of everything in the household. Could this be true? Is a child's wish to be in control for the sake of control itself? Is the preschooler's goal to exploit adults and to win a secret game that is being played without the adults' knowledge? These questions are probably most accurately answered in the negative. Bargaining and negotiating over bedtime, meals, and departure for child care are most likely normal steps in a preschooler's development of social skills and close relationships.

Late toddlerhood has been labeled "the terrible twos," in part because of children's strenuous efforts to get their own way in matters that sometimes seem ridiculous to their parents. Exactly why preschoolers behave in this sometimes very trying way is difficult to explore through empirical research, unfortunately. Children of this age group are not able—and might not be willing—to explain their motives. Indeed, even if researchers waited until the children were older to investigate this issue, and perhaps tried to link parent reports of toddler argumentativeness with later attitudes toward other people, they would find their research embroiled with multiple confounding variables.

Because research approaches are difficult, attempts to explain early childhood bargaining have usually been in the form of theoretical statements based on clinical observation and have sometimes stemmed from the study of working relationships between parents and children. The famous attachment theorist John Bowlby (1982) and some of his successors consider negotiation and bargaining to be a natural and desirable stage in the growth of an internal working model of social relationships. An internal working model is a set of thoughts and feelings, in this case the ideas and emotions that help to determine how a person behaves toward others and expects them to behave toward him or her. In Bowlby's view, negotiation with parents follows a child's establishment of an emotional attachment to a few preferred, familiar people, and such negotiation is part of a child's efforts to handle separation. The young child cannot avoid all experiences of separation from familiar adults, but the child can have some sense of security, control, and confidence as a result of negotiating about separation.

The ability to delay the parent's departure from the day care center by asking for five more kisses or to put off saying "good night" by arguing over the exact amount the door is to be left open is sufficient to help buffer the young child against the fear of separation and possible loss.

Bowlby's (1982) view of bargaining stresses the comfort the preschooler can derive from negotiating with adults. Such comfort and security can provide a good context for exploring and learning about the world, much like the secure base a toddler needs for exploring the world. A child who cannot bargain and negotiate may experience anxiety that interferes with learning and thinking. In addition, the experience of bargaining with adults is an excellent way to practice negotiation and compromise skills that will be beneficial in the future. Children can also work on such skills with peers, but an adult's ability to bargain provides a more advanced model from which a child can learn.

Because negotiation and bargaining involve at least two participants, they can be considered from a transactional point of view, with the assumption that each person affects and is affected by the other. Modern research on this topic studies the contributions of both the parent and the child to their conflict and its resolution.

Although it may seem most important to study what the children do, parents play a powerful role in a child's learning about negotiation. Parents frequently introduce their own strategies of bargaining and reasoning to a preschool child's resistance or expression of distaste (e.g., rejection of a food item) (Crockenberg & Litman, 1991). Experience with these parental strategies is a factor in developing a child's later willingness to cooperate and compromise. Parents who respond to conflict with coercion, and stress their authority, may be setting the stage for their children to be poor and reluctant negotiators.

Why does parental negotiation have a positive effect on a child's cooperativeness and social skills? One reason may be the use of language and reasoning modeled by the parent, learned by the child, and later employed by the child in interactions with other children and adults. Language of some sort is essential to bargaining. Parents who react coercively to children's behavior may model little useful language because they may remain silent or shout in ways that convey little except their anger.

The process of negotiation also requires some knowledge of what another person might know or want and how that knowledge or motivation may be different from one's own. A child who offers a teddy bear as an incentive for a parent to forget about bedtime will probably be unsuccessful, but one who promises to stay quietly on the sofa wrapped in a blanket may succeed, especially if the parent's real wish is for a little peace rather than for the child actually to be asleep. Similarly, a parent who is trying to say good night may find the promise of a distant trip to Disneyland unsuccessful, but a child who really wishes to postpone separation might accept a promise to come back in 10 minutes and look in the door. Parents' and children's negotiations help children learn how other people's needs and wishes are different from their own, knowledge that will contribute greatly to later abilities to compromise and cooperate. For example, both preschoolers and older children frequently find themselves in conflict with their peers (David, Murphy, Naylor, & Stonecipher, 2004), and negotiating skills that were learned earlier can be helpful in these situations.

Adults who lack the ability to understand a child's needs may find negotiation a demanding and frustrating task, as may those who find it hard to articulate a compromise position between their wishes and their child's. The same difficulties can occur when parents feel anxiety about the outcome of negotiation and believe, as it has traditionally been claimed, that "either you rule your child or your child rules you." These parents' beliefs about human relationships can lead children to avoid compromise rather than encourage children's negotiating skills. Parents who have better empathic abilities, on the other hand, may both foster secure attachment in their children and negotiate with them more successfully (Gini, Oppenheim, & Sagi-Schwartz, 2007).

Conclusion

Difficult as it may be to deal with a preschooler's bargaining demands at times, negotiations between parents and young children have real advantages for social development. Children who have healthy bargaining experiences, where both sides compromise, can develop useful social skills. Hamid's mother is right in negotiating with him, but of course she is also right in stopping when a reasonable compromise has been achieved.

Critical Thinking

1. Use a child development textbook to find a description of a parental style that avoids negotiation with young children and relies on exertion of the parent's authority. Explain your choice.

2. Read the study by Crockenberg and Litman (1991). Why do you think the authors chose to study this particular group of mothers and children?

(Continued)

(Continued)

Do you think the findings would be different if this study were done again today? Explain your answer.

3. Studies of family interactions often have difficulty in separating the effects of variables such as mothers' styles and child gender or age. What confounding variables were present in the Crockenberg and Litman (1991) study? Explain your choice.

4. What relationship do you see between the use of physical punishment, such as spanking, for preschoolers and the encouragement of compromise and cooperation? Can parents use physical punishment regularly and still have opportunities for bargaining? Explain your answer.

5. List and describe several situations in middle childhood in which the ability to bargain and compromise would be useful. Consider events at home, in school, and in play or sports. Use information from a child development textbook to support your view.

References

Bowlby, J. (1982). *Attachment*. New York: Basic.

Crockenberg, S., & Litman, C. (1991). Effects of maternal employment on maternal and two-year-old child behavior. *Child Development*, *62*, 930–953.

David, K. M., Murphy, B. C., Naylor, J. M., & Stonecipher, K. M. (2004). The effects of conflict role and intensity on preschoolers' expectations about peer conflict. *International Journal of Behavioral Development*, *28*, 508–517.

Gini, M., Oppenheim, D., & Sagi-Schwartz, A. (2007). Negotiation styles in mother-child narrative co-construction in middle childhood: Associations with early attachment. *International Journal of Behavioral Development*, *31*, 149–160.

Claim 34

A young child can tell when someone is just teasing.

Four-year-old Michael's grandmother had a game she really enjoyed playing with him when he was in a bad mood. If Michael sulked or acted angry, she would say "Oh! I hear something at the window! It might be the bear that eats bad boys." She would go to the window and peek out cautiously, telling Michael, "I'm not sure, but I think I see him out there. There's something furry just around the corner." The grandmother thought this was a funny way to put Michael back in a good humor, and would elaborate on her story at length. But to her surprise and annoyance Michael did not think it was funny, became even more distressed, and would run to his father if possible. The grandmother was disgusted with this behavior and said to Tom, Michael's father, "He knows perfectly well that I'm just teasing. He just likes to put on a drama and get your attention." Tom knew Michael's moods pretty well and thought the child was really upset, but at the same time he couldn't imagine that Michael thought his grandmother was serious about bears in an urban neighborhood.

Could Michael tell that his grandmother was teasing him when she talked about bears?

Teasing is a form of social interaction in which one individual, the teaser, makes statements to another, the teasee, which the teaser represents as true although he or she knows they are false. These statements may refer to events that the teasee would like, but which are actually not going

.appen, or to events the teasee fears or dislikes, but which again are not .ng to happen. The teasee's confusion and concern provide amusement .o. the teaser, and mild and familiar forms of teasing may be amusing for the teasee as well. However, teasing about serious matters may be distressing for the teasee. Adults generally tease children rather than the other way around, and an adult may be offended or annoyed by a child's display of distress when teased, rather than sympathetic or apologetic. Adult teasing of children may be a form of veiled hostility in response to a child's bad mood, as in the case of Michael's grandmother.

It would be impossible to tease a normal adolescent or an adult by talking about bears in an urban setting. The older individual knows not only that bears are rarely found in residential areas, but that it is possible for people knowingly to make false statements with intentions other than to communicate information. The older person has mastered Theory of Mind, a way of thinking about others' behavior that interprets the behavior in terms of what the other person knows, wants, and intends. Although toddlers understand to some extent that people's actions are affected by their beliefs (Onishi & Baillargeon, 2005), they are far from having a complete understanding of what others want or believe.

Even preschool children are only beginning to understand that behavior is shaped not only by what another person wants, but by what they know or do not know, and that false statements can be made intentionally even though the speaker knows they are false. Because that understanding is not yet well-developed, preschool children are easily teased to the point of distress. They only gradually develop the ability to understand others' intentions and knowledge.

One important study devised a scale that assessed how well a child's theory of mind had developed (Wellman, Fang, & Peterson, 2011). The authors considered skills that a preschool child had to attain before being able to interpret others' intentions reasonably well. The skills developed in a predictable order. First, children became capable of understanding diverse desires—that different people might want different things with respect to the same object, for example something to eat that one liked and the other did not. Second, they come to understand that people may believe different things about something—for instance, thinking that something is good to eat or not good to eat—even though the child does not know which one is right. Third, they learn that a person who does not have access to knowledge (for example, not being able to see what is in a box) does not know for sure what someone else can know if he or she has access to knowledge. Fourth, preschool children come to be able to judge whether another person does or does not know something that the child does know. The final step in this progression is that the child knows that people can hide their emotions and that their behavior does not necessarily indicate what they really feel or want.

How is this theory of mind scale related to teasing? Children who do not understand diverse desires will be confused by the apparent attitudes of a teaser toward events the child either wants or fears and dislikes. The teaser's apparent nonchalance about these emotionally colored events will be in particular contrast to the sensitivity and responsiveness of caregivers that are an important part of early relationships. Children who do not understand diverse beliefs would not be able to interpret a teasing statement that contradicts their own beliefs. Children who have not yet grasped the roles of lack of knowledge or of false beliefs will not be able to understand that an adult could accidentally or intentionally make an inaccurate statement. And children who do not understand that emotion can be hidden or simulated will not understand the apparent blandness or cheerful manner of an adult who is talking about what should be a distressing subject.

A further step in the development of theory of mind seems necessary for an explanation of preschooler's responses to teasing. When do young children learn that people can want to trick or fool others, for reasons of their own? A study by Vanderbilt, Liu, and Heyman (2011) looked at children's ability to learn from experiences of seeing an actor pretend that he or she did not know where something was and mislead another person who was looking for the object. Three-year-olds in this study were trusting of the information they got from adults, and it did not matter very much to them whether they had seen the actor trick people by giving them false information, or help them by giving correct information. Both 4-year-olds and 5-year-olds trusted the "helpers" a bit more than the "trickers," but only the 5-year-olds could correctly describe as "nice" the helpful people rather than the tricking people. That individuals may be trustworthy or untrustworthy as a rule is a concept that comes into play only toward the end of the preschool period, so it is not until that time that children are likely to understand that one person characteristically teases and should not be taken seriously.

Does the gradual development of theory of mind mean that nobody should ever tease preschoolers? Can children learn anything from experiences of teasing? There seems to be little that is positive in a situation where adults get angry when a child they have teased is upset, and a child who experiences this may learn to distrust the teasing adult in general, or to imitate that adult by teasing younger children. However, mild teasing is not very far from pretending, and pretend play is an important achievement of the preschool years. Pretending and mild teasing may be ways to practice theory of mind and to develop greater empathy with others' thoughts and feelings.

Conclusion

Preschoolers have only limited abilities to understand what other people know, want, or believe. Michael cannot yet take his grandmother's perspective and understand that when she talks teasingly about scary things, her conscious intention is to amuse him and cheer him up. Although he may know that he has never seen a bear in their neighborhood, he also knows that adults can know things he does not know, and the occasional presence of wandering bears may be among those things. Michael's continued distress, and his wish to be near his father, are clear evidence that he does not understand the "pretend" nature of his grandmother's comments and that he needs some respite from her teasing approach.

Critical Thinking

1. One important question in the study of theory of mind has been whether longitudinal studies gave the same results about development of these skills as cross-sectional studies do. Using your textbook or other sources, define each of these research approaches. What might be some reasons why the two could give different answers to the same research question?

2. Use your textbook or other sources to define a Guttman scale. Why is the scale of theory of mind development described by Wellman, Fang, & Peterson (2011) considered to be a Guttman scale? You may need to read the introduction to the article in order to be able to answer this question.

3. Wellman and his co-authors (2011) reported that children with hearing impairments were much slower in developing theory of mind than hearing children. Using your textbook and other sources, find information about language development that might help to explain this fact. How would a child's level of language development affect her response to teasing?

4. Look at the article by Vanderbilt, Liu, and Heyman (2011), referenced below. Was its design longitudinal or cross-sectional? Why would the authors have chosen one approach rather than another?

5. Use your textbook or other sources to describe the development of pretend play in the toddler and preschool years. Could these developmental changes help predict a child's response to teasing?

References

Onishi, K. H., & Baillargeon, R. (2005). Do 15-month-olds understand false beliefs? *Science, 308,* 255–258.

Vanderbilt, K. E., Liu, D., & Heyman, G. D. (2011). The development of distrust. *Child Development, 82,* 1372–1380.

Wellman, H. M., Fang, F., & Peterson, C. C. (2011). Sequential progressions in a theory of mind scale: Longitudinal perspectives. *Child Development, 82,* 780–792.

Claim 35

Children with attachment disorders must be treated very sternly and differently from typically developing children— even in ways that are ordinarily considered abusive.

Six-year-old Alisha came home from her after-school baby-sitter's with big eyes. "Mom!" she said. "On the TV there was a lady who got arrested and they said she did mean things to her little boy. She put hot sauce in his mouth and pushed him into a real cold shower. Is that true? Why did she do that?" Sally, Alisha's mother, was taken aback. "I wish Mrs. Abbott wouldn't let you kids watch things like that," she replied. "I don't know what it's all about." Thirteen-year-old Liz interrupted. "I know all about it," she said. "That kid had a thing called Reactive Attachment Disorder and it makes them really bad. The mother said she had to punish him like that or he'd be terrible." Sally thought that might be reasonable, but she didn't want to encourage the girls to think that abusive treatment of children was all right. Later, she heard that the mother in that case had been convicted of child abuse.

Is it appropriate to use methods that are usually thought of as abusive to discipline children who have attachment disorders?

A number of child abuse or even murder trials have used the "RAD defense"—the claim that abusive treatment was appropriate, even desirable, as a disciplinary method for children thought to suffer from the emotional disturbance Reactive Attachment Disorder. The earliest uses of this defense appear to have been with the trials of the parents of Lucas Ciambrone in Florida in 1995 and of the mother of David Polreis in Colorado in 1996. Both of these murdered children had been adopted, and the defenses claimed that their early experiences had caused them emotional disturbances that made them uncontrollable, forcing the parents to use harsh methods. Juries convicted the parents in both cases, however.

More recently, an adoptive mother in Alaska, Jessica Beagley, was tried on charges of child abuse after participating in a television program in which she was shown using hot sauce and icy showers as punishment techniques for her 7-year-old Russian adoptee son. Ms. Beagley's attorney argued that the child's emotional disturbance made it necessary for the parents to control him with severe punishment (Goodell, 2011). The jury did not accept this position.

There are two issues that we need to examine as we consider whether the "RAD defense" is based on good evidence. The first question is simply "What is Reactive Attachment Disorder?" Does this disorder, in and of itself, involve uncontrollable and violent or dangerous behavior? The second question is "Is harsh punishment effective when mild forms of discipline are not?" The combined answers to these questions will help to refute or support the "RAD defense" and the general idea that some childhood emotional disturbances make harsh discipline necessary.

To answer the question about the nature of Reactive Attachment Disorder, we can turn to the *Diagnostic and Statistical Manual of Mental Disorders* of the American Psychiatric Association, usually called just *DSM* and often referred to with its edition number (e.g., *DSM-5*, the most recent [2013] version). *DSM* contains the "official" definitions of types of mental health diagnoses, as well as lists of criteria which a person must meet in order to be diagnosed with a particular disorder.

In describing Reactive Attachment Disorder, *DSM-5* gives the following description: There is a consistent pattern of inhibited, emotionally withdrawn behavior toward adult caregivers, manifested by rarely seeking or responding to comfort when distressed. Children show persistent social or emotional disturbance with at least two of the following: minimal social and emotional responsiveness; limited positive emotion; and episodes of unexplained irritability, sadness, or fearfulness when in nonthreatening situations with adult caregivers. The child's background is a history of extremes of insufficient care, with at least one of the following: social neglect or deprivation by caregivers, repeated changes of caregivers, or rearing in unusual settings that make attachment difficult because of high ratios of children to caregivers. In addition, the child is not autistic, and the disturbance appears between a developmental age of 9 months and 5 years.

There is nothing in this description about uncontrollable, aggressive, or violent behavior on the child's part. There are other diagnostic categories in *DSM* that list such behaviors as part of their criteria, but these have nothing specific to do with attachment or any form of disorders of attachment.

It appears that whatever the "uncontrollable" child behaviors were in the cases mentioned above, they were not related to Reactive Attachment Disorder. But, just for the sake of argument, let's suppose these children had behaved in ways that were dangerous to others or to themselves. Let's suppose that their parents had spanked or scolded them in ways that are common in the United States and are not ordinarily considered abusive. And, to continue supposing, let's consider the possibility that the children's behavior continued to be problematic, in spite of the unpleasant consequences that followed it. Would it then be advisable for the parents to move on to harsher alternatives like "hot sauce-ing," even though those are generally considered abusive? Should a parent who does this be acquitted of child abuse charges?

Unusual and disturbing punishments, often known as "aversives," and including electric shock, have been used with children who are genuinely dangerous to others or themselves. In many cases, aversives have been used to prevent severely disturbed or developmentally delayed children from biting their tongues or poking fingers into their eyes, and they can be effective if used properly (Foxx, 2005).

However, the effectiveness of aversives (which would include hot sauce and icy showers) depends not on their severity, unpleasantness, or unusualness, but on the timing of their administration. Ideally, aversive treatments occur simultaneously with the unwanted behavior, or even slightly ahead of it, as the child prepares for the forbidden action. The longer the delay after an unwanted behavior, the less effective is any punishment in preventing the behavior—although a delayed punishment may be effective in making a child anxious or wary of a punishing adult. So, for example, if Ms. Beagley discovered that her son had punched another child yesterday, and followed her discovery by putting hot sauce on his tongue, she would find no effect on his probability of violence toward other children, but might well find that he avoided her or was tense and watchful when she approached him. If she felt it was necessary or appropriate to use punishment as discipline, she would have more success in using mild punishments soon after the problem behavior than abusive treatment later on.

Some Internet discussions and popular books have claimed that children with Reactive Attachment Disorder are unable to associate causes with effects and therefore do not learn from rewards. But it is almost inconceivable that a child who could deal with advanced cognitive skills like language would not be able to understand the nature of cause and effect—a connection that is made at a simple level by babies in the first days of life as well as by dogs, mice, and even worms. Presumably, if this assumption about cause-and-effect thinking were correct, it would also apply to learning from punishment and would be the case whether the punishment was extremely harsh or not; severe punishments would be pointless rather than necessary.

Conclusion

Juries that have evaluated the "RAD defense" have rejected the idea that unusually harsh punishments are necessary for children who may have attachment disorders, and systematic evidence shows that such children are not necessarily either aggressive, or limited in their ability to learn from ordinary disciplinary methods. Unfortunately (and in line with Sally's concerns), material in the media and on the Internet may encourage beliefs about these matters that encourage people both to tolerate and to use abusive techniques in child-rearing.

Critical Thinking

1. Use your library or the Internet to read the part of the *DSM-5* material on Reactive Attachment Disorder that is not quoted in this book. Compare the description to one or two other descriptions of childhood mental health problems in *DSM-5*. What single feature of the Reactive Attachment Disorder description is not found in the other descriptions?

2. Use the Internet to find four or five other descriptions of Reactive Attachment Disorder. Look especially at any "checklists" of characteristics of children with the disorder. How do these descriptions and lists compare to the *DSM* description? How does your textbook define Reactive Attachment Disorder, and how does the definition compare to the *DSM* description?

3. If a parent chooses child mental health treatments that include methods that are usually considered abusive, is he or she guilty of child abuse?

(Continued)

(Continued)

Some proponents of such treatments have argued that treatment for cancer, for example, may be very painful and distressing for a child but is not considered abusive. Does overgeneralization play a role in conclusions about this issue?

4. Google "Reactive Attachment Disorder cause and effect thinking" and find several websites that comment on this topic. Compare that material to your textbook's discussion of cause-and-effect thinking in infants and toddlers. Are the two sources (text and websites) talking about the same kind of thinking? Explain.

5. Search the Internet for several cases in which the "RAD defense" was used when children had been injured or killed by their caregivers. What did the cases you found have in common with respect to characteristics of the children? Did the defense arguments share anything other than the "RAD defense"? Did you find other cases in which children were blamed for their own injuries or deaths, but the parents were not said to have been forced to use harsh punishment?

References

American Psychiatric Association. (2013). *Diagnostic and statistical manual of mental disorders* (5th ed.). Washington, DC: American Psychiatric Association.

Foxx, R. M. (2005). Severe aggressive and self-destructive behavior: The myth of the nonaversive treatment of severe behavior. In J. W. Jacobson, R. M. Foxx, & J. A. Mulick (Eds.), *Controversial therapies for developmental disabilities* (pp. 295–310). Mahwah, NJ: Erlbaum.

Goodell, A. (2011, Aug. 17). *Beagley hot sauce abuse trial begins.* Retrieved from http://articles.ktuu.com/2011-08-17/hot-sauce_29898507.

Claim 36

Spanking should never be used to discipline a child because it is ineffective and causes children to model the aggression they experience.

Two second-grade teachers, Sheri and Keisha, were discussing a child who was a discipline problem on the playground. Sheri was very annoyed at having to deal with the boy's rambunctiousness. "That Kegan!" she sighed. "There he went again this morning, pushing the girls who were trying to jump rope. One fell down and I had to take her to the office for first aid. Then all Kegan got was a timeout. If I could just smack his rear! Or if his mother would do it, it would be even better. Then he'd straighten out." Keisha was sympathetic, because she too had to cope with Kegan on the playground. But she felt Sheri was wrong in proposing physical punishment as a way to change the boy's behavior. "No, I really don't think that would work," Keisha said. "I was reading that spanking really doesn't work very well, and besides, it teaches kids that aggression is the way to get what you want. When they see a grownup act aggressive they think that's the right thing to do . . . but, I really don't know what else to do, either."

Is Sheri's proposal to spank Kegan a good idea, or is Keisha right in saying that such punishment is ineffective and perhaps makes behavior more aggressive instead of less?

we consider the pros and cons of this argument, let's make abso-
sure that everyone knows what is being discussed. Both Sheri
.eisha are talking about *spanking*, a form of punishment that involves
one to several blows with an adult's bare open hand, generally on a child's
bare or clothed buttocks but possibly on the legs or hands. Spanking does
not include blows with the fist or kicks, nor does it include striking with
any type of object—belt, paddle, switch, plastic plumbing supply line, or
ruler. It is difficult to say whether more than a few blows with the bare
hand would move the action to some category other than spanking. Blows
to the face and head are generally not considered spanking even if delivered
with the open hand. Both spanking and physical punishment other than
spanking are illegal in Europe, and some forms may or may not be considered abusive in parts of the United States. Initiatives that would make
spanking illegal (see www.nospank.org) have led to much discussion of the
scientific evidence for and against spanking.

As a general rule, research on the effects of spanking has been of a correlational nature, or has compared nonrandomized groups. It is not likely
that parents who reject spanking would agree to be randomly assigned to
an experimental group that would spank their children, and similarly those
who approve of spanking would not participate if assigned to a group that
used nonphysical methods of discipline. Looking at children's development
in families who spank or don't spank because of their own beliefs, lets us
see how punishment methods correlate with outcomes but do not show us
whether the outcome is caused by the punishment method or whether both
have a cause in some additional factor. Comparing the children of spanking
parents with those of nonspanking parents can cause confusion between
associated factors; for example, we cannot tell whether the children whose
parents spanked them began as more impulsive or difficult than the children
whose parents did not spank, or whether any problematic behavior emerged
from the parents' methods. Confounded variables like these are always a
problem in correlational studies or comparisons of nonrandomized groups
to each other.

There were one or two experimental studies involving spanking that
were carried out at a time when ethical standards for research were less
strict than they presently are, but even those focused on special issues in
spanking rather than on its general use by parents of ordinary children.
Roberts (1988; Roberts & Powers, 1990) was interested in helping mothers of oppositional preschoolers become able to use timeout methods as
discipline. The mothers and children were being treated for relationship
problems including the children's disobedience. As is not uncommon, the
children sometimes refused to stay in the timeout chair, creating a second
problem in addition to whatever they had originally been given a timeout

for. Roberts assigned the mothers of nine children to spank a child when he or she got up from the timeout chair without permission. The mothers of the other nine children were taught to place the disobedient child in a room where a barrier prevented escape until the mother decided to let the child come back out. Both spanking and confinement to the room with barrier were effective in teaching the child not to leave the timeout chair, but there was more disruption associated with spanking.

The body of nonexperimental work on the effects of corporal punishment has been examined by several authors. This can be done by means of a systematic research synthesis, which looks at the characteristics and research designs of a group of studies and considers their conclusions, or through a meta-analysis, which focuses on issues like effect size as well as whether there were statistically significant correlations or differences between groups. A systematic research synthesis can point out whether some studies were weak in their research designs, and a meta-analysis can draw overall conclusions rather than being confined to conclusions from the small number of participants that may have been studied in individual investigations.

Gershoff's reviews (2002, 2010) reported that, although corporal punishment was effective in stopping unwanted behavior in the short-term, it was associated with greater child aggression and emotional disturbance in later years. But a commentary on this work pointed out that Gershoff had combined in her review reports on the effects of more serious and intense forms of physical punishment, not just studies of spanking (Larzelere & Baumrind, 2010). The commentary authors argued that spanking could form a part of the authoritative parenting style so often reported to have excellent outcomes in terms of behavior and school achievement.

One important question about the effects of physical punishment is the age of the child being punished. The research that shows spanking (but not other forms of corporal punishment) as having a positive effect over the long term generally focuses on spanking during the preschool period, and looks at outcomes as measured during adolescence. Although a small number of authors recommend spanking or whipping infants as young as six months of age, such practices are generally considered abusive, and no empirical investigations have examined their outcomes. Physical punishment of teenagers is potentially abusive, in part because the adolescent may fight back and serious injury to both combatants may result. In one study related to physical punishment of teenagers, such punishment was seen as a risk factor for aggression toward mothers (Pagani et al., 2004), but there was also a background of aggressive behavior that contributed to the situation; physical punishment was only one of the factors that led to aggressive behavior. It also seems very likely that the child's age is associated with different effects of physical punishment, and of course research reports state the ages of the children studied—but in spite of this, there is a tendency for people to want to generalize from preschoolers (for example) to children of all ages.

Conclusion

Keisha is mistaken in thinking that spanking is ineffective in the short run, although questions remain about its long-term effect. If spanking were administered immediately after Kegan's misbehavior, chances are good that he would stop the specific action that led to the spanking (although pushing the girls might be replaced by starting a fight with someone). Kegan is a couple of years older than the children for whom spanking has been shown to have positive outcomes in later years, and most research on spanking alone (not other physical punishment) has not looked systematically at effects on school-age children. Whether being spanked at school would cause Kegan to learn to be more aggressive would probably depend on other factors in his life. Once again, of course, these comments apply to spanking as properly defined, not to blows with a paddle or other physical punishments.

Critical Thinking

1. Use the Internet to find one or two organizations that propose to make all physical punishment of children illegal. What evidence do they offer to support their viewpoints?

2. Adults who were themselves spanked as children sometimes argue that they are okay now, therefore spanking is good for children. What errors of critical thinking may interfere with understanding this issue when people depend on their own experience for evidence?

3. What are the problems associated with comparing such small groups of children as those in the Roberts (1988; Roberts & Powers, 1990) studies? What problem of bias exists in these studies and makes it difficult to generalize from the research to more common concerns about spanking? The article by Larzelere, Kuhn, and Johnson (2004) may help you on this.

4. Use information from your textbook or other sources to discuss how the use of meta-analysis or of a systematic research synthesis can contribute to understanding of the effects of spanking. Do these approaches consider effect sizes?

5. Use the Internet to find one or more authors who *recommend* physical punishment of infants. What are the behaviors these authors seek to control? What is their reasoning?

References

Baumrind, D., Larzelere, R. E., & Owens, E. B. (2010). Effects of preschool parents' power assertive patterns and practices on adolescent development. *Parenting: Science and Practice, 10*, 157–201.

Gershoff, E. T. (2002). Corporal punishment by parents and associated child behaviors and experiences: A meta-analytic and theoretical review. *Psychological Bulletin, 128*, 539–579.

Gershoff, E. T. (2010). More harm than good: A summary of scientific research on the intended and unintended effects of corporal punishment on children. *Law and Contemporary Problems, 73*, 31–56.

Larzelere, R. E., & Baumrind, D. (2010). Are spanking injunctions scientifically supported? *Law and Contemporary Problems, 73*, 57–87.

Larzelere, R. E., Kuhn, B. R., & Johnson, B. (2004). The intervention selection bias: An underrecognized confound in intervention research. *Psychological Bulletin, 130*, 289–303.

Pagani, L., Tremblay, R., Nagin, D., Zoccolillo, M., Vitaro, F., & McDuff, P. (2004). Risk factor models for adolescent verbal and physical aggression toward mothers. *International Journal of Behavioral Development, 28*, 528–537.

Roberts, M. W. (1988). Enforcing chair timeouts with room timeouts. *Behavior Modification, 12*, 353–370.

Roberts, M. W., & Powers, S. W. (1990). Adjusting chair timeout enforcement procedures for oppositional children. *Behavior Therapy, 21*, 257–271.

Part IV

School-Age Children

Claim 37

Girls who get their first period early are also likely to mature quickly in other ways.

Sophie got her first period four months before her eleventh birthday. Fortunately, this happened in the summertime and she did not have to deal with changing sanitary napkins at her school, which only had fourth, fifth, and sixth grades and did not have restroom supplies the way a high school would. Sophie's mother, Angie, mentioned this event to her mother-in-law, Judy. Angie was worried that Sophie might have a hard time with the practical demands of menstruation. Angie had not expected Sophie to get her period so soon and had not really tried to prepare her for it. But Judy said not to worry, that the hormones that brought on Sophie's first period would help her mature mentally, too. "Besides," Judy said, "she'll feel like a young lady now and I think she'll act more like one."

Is early menarche associated with more mature thinking and behavior?

In fact, it has been known for a long time that girls who get their first periods on their eleventh birthdays or earlier are *more* likely to show behavior problems, substance abuse, and delinquency than girls who mature later. The same thing is true of boys, in the sense that early pubertal changes are associated with behavior problems, although perhaps to a lesser extent (Mendle & Ferrero, 2012; Mendle, Turkheimer, & Emery, 2007)—and of course, boys' puberty is on the average two years later than girls'. The preponderance of the research on this topic shows the same conclusions (Skoog & Stattin, 2014).

Yet, as so often happens in psychological research, it's clear that there must be more than one factor at work here. Not all girls with early pubertal timing display behavioral or psychological problems, and some whose puberty is at an average age or late do have behavior problems. Whatever is going on, it is not just a matter of hormones at work.

Like many other important real-world problems, this one cannot be approached by research using a randomized design. We depend on correlational studies or nonrandomized comparisons of existing groups for information about the effects of early menarche, and that means that we must deal with the possibility of confounded variables. We can study a single factor like social pressures on early-maturing girls, but that kind of investigation does not readily tell us whether there are other important variables that influence the one we are studying and that are themselves indirect or direct causes either of early menarche or of problem behavior. The hormonal factor mentioned by Sophie's grandmother is one of those, but so are social pressures from parents and from peers; personality characteristics of the girls that lead to depressive reactions; genetic factors that may be responsible for timing of menarche or for social behavior or for both; and interactions between genetic factors and environmental stresses like social demands from parents, teachers, girl peers, and boys. In addition, research on behavior problems of adolescents has to take into account that "bad behaviors" of girls often include *status offenses*—actions like running away from home or breaking curfew that would not be considered crimes if an older person did them. Early-timing girls' problem behaviors are not necessarily matters of violence or theft, although these are possible, too.

There have been several suggestions about how early menarche might cause girls to develop psychological and behavioral problems. One of these, the *maturational deviance hypothesis*, describes the possibility that being "out of step" with peers is stressful. A girl who has a very early menarche may find she is embarrassed to tell her less-mature friends about this or to explain why she has cramps and does not want to play a game. A late-maturing girl may feel left out of confidences and may even wonder what is wrong with her and whether she will ever catch up. But this hypothesis is not well-supported because the evidence is that the early-timing girls have the most problems. A second idea, the *stage-termination* hypothesis, places the causes of distress in undeveloped cognitive and behavior skills that make it difficult for early-timing girls to understand or deal with other people's responses to them—whether these are older women who want a girl to be more "lady-like" or slightly older boys who find a girl physically attractive. (See Skoog & Stattin, 2014, for further discussion of similar attempts to explain the effects of early puberty.)

Other investigators have asked why it is that some girls experience early menarche. Could it be that causes of early menarche could also be causes of delinquency and other behavioral problems? One possibility is that early-maturing girls have already experienced more environmental stress than others; for example, research has implicated maltreatment, harsh parenting, and poverty as factors related to early puberty (Harden & Mendle, 2012). Early experiences of excessive stress may have interfered with a girl's ability to tolerate the stresses associated with puberty, and thus have made her more prone to behavioral and psychological problems. A second possibility is that genetic factors that encourage early puberty also make delinquent behavior more likely. (These are not mutually exclusive explanations because genetic and environmental factors can function separately and can also interact with each other.)

An intriguing aspect of the connection between early puberty and delinquency has to do with girls' contacts with boys. In one study, early-timing girls became delinquent if they went to mixed-sex schools, but not if they went to single-sex schools (Caspi, Lynam, Moffitt, & Silva, 1993). A more recent study (Skoog, Stattin, Ruiselova, & Ozdemir, 2013) compared behavioral outcomes for girls with early menarche in two countries: Sweden, which is quite permissive about adolescent sexuality, and Slovakia, where girls are allowed limited contacts with boys. In Sweden, early puberty was associated with behavior problems, and these problems resulted from involvement with boys. In Slovakia, there was much less connection between early menarche and problem behavior, except when girls did have contacts with boys, in which case a link was seen.

Conclusion

Unfortunately, Judy's belief that early menarche means early psychological maturation does not seem to be correct, but this does not necessarily mean that Sophie is bound to become delinquent or to suffer from psychological problems. How Sophie's life will progress depends in part on her previous experiences; if she has had a stressful life and previous problem behaviors, her early menarche may be more likely to be followed by behavior problems. If Sophie has these factors in her background, her contacts with boys may be an important factor in determining delinquent or nondelinquent behavior. In any case, her parents and teachers would do well to offer her as much support as they can as this fifth-grader deals with practical and emotional issues for which she is not completely prepared.

Critical Thinking

1. Use a child development textbook or other sources to learn about precocious puberty. How is this phenomenon different from the early menarche discussed in this section?

2. Is the variable of single-sex versus coeducational schools likely to be confounded with other relevant variables that could influence girls' delinquent behavior? Are single-sex schools more likely to be attractive to certain religious or ethnic communities? Explain the possible connections. (The paper by Skoog et al. [2013] can help you on this.)

3. Use a child development textbook to identify three types of gene-environment interactions. How would each of these types apply to the connection between early menarche and problem behavior?

4. Using a child development textbook or other sources, what evidence do you find that genetic factors are at work in behavior problems?

5. State a hypothesis that would explain how the influence of boys may lead early-maturing girls into delinquent behavior, and describe how you would test the hypothesis. (You can assume that you have all the resources you need to carry out the investigation you propose.)

References

Caspi, A., Lynam, D., Moffitt, T. E., & Silva, P. A. (1993). Unraveling girls' delinquency: Biological, dispositional, and contextual contributions to adolescent misbehavior. *Developmental Psychology, 45,*1164–1176.

Harden, K. P., & Mendle, J. (2012). Gene-environment interplay in the association between pubertal timing and delinquency in adolescent girls. *Journal of Abnormal Psychology, 121,* 73–87.

Mendle, J., & Ferrero, J. (2012). Detrimental psychological outcomes associated with pubertal timing in adolescent boys. *Developmental Review, 32,* 49–66.

Mendle, J., Turkheimer, E., & Emery, R. E. (2007). Detrimental psychological outcomes associated with early pubertal timing in adolescent girls. *Developmental Review, 27,* 151–171.

Skoog, T., & Stattin, H. (2014). Why and under what contextual conditions do early-maturing girls develop problem behaviors? *Child Development Perspectives, 8,* 158–162.

Skoog, T., Stattin, H., Ruiselova, Z., & Ozdemir, M. (2013). Female pubertal timing and problem behavior: The role of culture. *International Journal of Behavioral Development, 37,* 357–365.

Claim 38

Children have different learning styles, depending on whether they are left brained or right brained.

Melody's teacher was concerned about 10-year-old Melody's poor math skills, and she said so at a parent-teacher conference with Melody's mother, Tasha. But Tasha was not concerned or even very impressed by the teacher's statements. "Melody has always liked to draw and sing and dance. She's one of those right-brained people who isn't good at schoolwork like reading and arithmetic. She's more intuitive, like her daddy. I'm not going to worry about this, because I know she has talent and will be a great performer someday."

Was Tasha right to think that people who are good at the arts are not good at schoolwork? Can Melody's teacher use other special methods to teach her in a "right-brained" way?

The idea that human beings have learning styles that depend on their tendency to use one side of the brain more than the other became popular about 40 years ago and has remained a common assumption. Generally, this belief includes the idea that left-brained activities are analytical, whereas right-brained activities are creative, holistic, and intuitive. Some educators find this point of view very appealing; others take a more general view of individual learning styles that contribute to academic achievement (Hadfield, 2006).

Most children and adults are right-handed, and only about 10% use their left hands for fine movements, such as writing. Right-handed people fairly consistently use their two hands in predictable ways, using the right hand for skilled small muscle tasks and the left for less delicate movements, such as holding the top of a sheet of paper or steadying an object by gripping it. Left-handed people do things the other way around, although they are usually a bit more skillful with their right hands than "righties" are with their left.

The brain's control over motor skills follows a predictable pattern, too. The left side of the brain sends the signals that control the right hand's movements, and the right side of the brain controls the left hand. So, in that sense, people are left brained if they are right-handed and right brained if they are left-handed.

So far, so reasonable. But what about learning styles? Why have some people associated the dominant activity of one side of the brain with particular ways to learn, or even particular skills other than movements such as hand use? In fact, the idea of being right brained or left brained in learning style is a big jump in reasoning from studies of brain surgery. Surgical treatment of brain-damaged patients, beginning in the 1940s, was the source of the idea that one or the other cortical hemisphere could do much of people's brainwork. Patients who had epileptic seizures because of an injury to one side of the brain (e.g., a man who was clubbed in the head while a prisoner during World War II) were treated by surgery that cut many of the neural connections between the right and left brain halves. This procedure allowed the healthy side of the brain to take more control over the body and to prevent the seizures caused by the injured side.

After surgical treatment, the health of these patients improved, but they had some other interesting changes, too. Because communication between the two sides of the brain was interrupted, each side was much more isolated from the other. Normally, much of the information about something seen with one eye is communicated to both sides of the brain, but following split-brain surgery, only one side of the brain received information from one eye. The same held for hearing. In a person with normal auditory functioning, sounds that come into one ear are signaled to both sides of the brain, but after the split, sounds entering the left ear were communicated only to the left half of the brain.

This unusual isolation of left and right cortical hemispheres allowed researchers to observe whether each side of the brain had specialties or tasks that it could perform especially well. Researchers had long known that the left hemisphere of a right-handed individual had a special connection to spoken language and that injury to the left side of the brain was more likely than right-side injury to damage language ability. The split-brain research confirmed this fact and suggested other differences between the two sides—information that quickly spun into the claim that brain preferences somehow determine preferred tasks and ways of learning.

However, there were some problems with the left-brain, right-brain idea. First, an intact brain—with the hemispheres normally connected—does not work like a split brain. The two sides of the brain ordinarily function together, in coordination, although one may do a bit more of some tasks (especially language) than the other. To look at one hemisphere alone gives an inaccurate view of normal functioning—as inaccurate as studying how a person's right leg would be used after the left had been amputated, as a way of understanding normal walking. Brain imaging studies, which were not available in the early split-brain research, showed that both sides of the brain act together under normal circumstances.

Many important tasks require something from each hemisphere, so, for example, in an emotional conversation between two right-handed people, the right hemispheres work to comprehend emotion in speech, and the left sides work to understand and remember stories that have emotional meaning. A person who had one of these abilities, "right" or "left," and not the other would not be an effective sender or receiver of emotional information. Similarly, in carrying out tasks in school, children use both sides of the brain to deal with cognitive tasks and the emotional—and motivating—aspects of their assignments (Willingham, 2006).

Abilities in the arts and in academic subjects are not necessarily connected to specific sides of the brain, nor are they mutually exclusive. Research in particular topics supports this idea. For example, a small number of musicians have absolute pitch, the ability to identify or sing a note in isolation from other notes (rather than as part of a tune). They are reported to be more likely to have this ability if they had musical instruction before school age and if they also have an analytical, cognitive learning style (Chin, 2003). In light of this evidence, people should reject the simple claim that artistic ability is a right-brain characteristic because this aspect of musical skill was partly dependent on training and not innate. In addition, it seems that people should reject the idea that ability in the arts is associated with a nonanalytical cognitive style or with a particular personality.

A new and possibly fruitful approach to thinking about skills "belonging to" brain parts is consideration of the dorsal and ventral connections within the brain rather than the left and right sides. The dorsal, or "top," system has been described as analyzing where a perceived object is and the ventral, or "bottom," system as deciding what the thing is. Some authors have argued and shown evidence that the dorsal system is strongly influenced by expectations about what might be seen or heard, and that the ventral system deals with individual events and characteristics like shape, color, or pitch (Borst, Thompson, & Kosslyn, 2011). Others have noted the connections between dysfunctions of the dorsal system and cognitive functioning, diagnosis of problematic development such as autistic behavior, and even appropriate treatment of problems (Macintyre-Beon, et al., 2010; Santos, Duret, Mancini, Gire, & Deruelle, 2009). So far, however, the dorsal-ventral difference has not been popularized into teaching suggestions as the "right brain/left brain" concept has been.

Conclusion

Individual children can prefer certain school tasks and have preferred ways of learning, but these are not solely the result of dominance of one side of the brain or of specialized abilities that belong to the left or to the right cortical hemisphere. Being skilled in the arts does not mean a child cannot be good at math or vice versa. It would be good for Tasha not to suggest to Melody that she is not the kind of person who does math; instead, Tasha should encourage Melody to practice her math skills and see them as abilities all adults need, no matter how talented they are in other ways.

Critical Thinking

1. Refer to a child development textbook to find information about the connection between handedness and hemispheric dominance. What proportion of people would you expect to be right brained, considering the proportion of left-handed people? How does this proportion relate to the proportion of U.S. children who perform poorly in math?

2. Search the Internet to locate a popular (nonscholarly) book or article that explains how people can use a particular side of the brain. How does the publication's approach to brain functioning compare to the comments in this section?

3. Explain the role that temperament might play in preferences for particular learning activities or topics. Choose several temperamental factors for examination. Refer to evidence from your child development textbook in your explanation.

4. Read the section on autism of the article by Macintyre-Beon et al. (2010), referenced below. What do these authors suggest about teaching autistic children, and how is their thinking related to the idea of dorsal and

ventral brain functions? How is this idea different from the right-brain/left-brain distinction?

5. Read the article by Willingham (2006). Describe the parts of the brain surgeons cut during split-brain surgery. Search the Internet or print sources to find information about people who never had one or both of these brain structures (this situation will be described as *agenesis* of the structures). Would you expect the abilities of these people to be similar to those of people in the surgical cases? Explain your answer, watching out for the problem of overgeneralization.

References

Chin, C. S. (2003). The development of absolute pitch: A theory concerning the roles of music training at an early developmental age and individual cognitive style. *Psychology of Music, 31*, 155–171.

Hadfield, J. (2006). Teacher education and trainee learning style. *RELC Journal, 37*, 367–386.

Macintyre-Beon, C., Hussein, I., Hay, I., Cockburn, D., Calvert, J., Dutton, G. N., & Bowman, R. (2010). Dorsal stream dysfunction in children: A review and an approach to diagnosis and management. *Current Pediatric Reviews, 6*, 166–182.

Santos, A., Duret, M., Mancini, J., Gire, C., & Deruelle, C. (2009). Preterm birth affects dorsal-stream functioning even after age 6. *Brain & Cognition, 69*, 490–494.

Willingham, D. T. (2006). "Brain-based" learning: More fiction than fact. *American Educator, 30*(3), 27–33, 40–41.

Claim 39

It's healthy for children to be a little on the chubby side.

Jess was feeling pretty aggravated when she left the pediatrician's office. At 6-year-old Ella's well-child visit, the doctor had said that the little girl was overweight and that even though she was not actually obese, that was a problem. What's more, he pointed out that he had told Jess about this when Ella was only 3. When Jess talked to her friend Jennifer, she had a few pointed remarks to make about the doctor. "I'd like to know what he expects me to do! Ella eats the same things as the rest of us, and she's a little chubby like the rest of us, too. Am I supposed to put her on a different diet than the whole family? Besides, I don't really see the problem. My mother always said that it was good for kids to have a little extra weight in case they got sick and didn't eat much for a while. That makes sense to me, too. Anyway, what difference does it make what she weighed when she was 3? He just seems to be saying that I'm not a good mother and I never have been." Jennifer thought that it seemed a shame to put a child on a diet and deprive her of birthday cake and other things that are part of childhood. But she wondered whether there really was some reason to be concerned with Ella's weight. She had seen a lot in the news lately about rising obesity rates in children.

Was it a problem for Ella to be overweight? Why did the doctor refer to her weight at age 3 when she was 6 years old?

For all of us at any age, it's true that we gain or lose weight when the number of calories we take in is not the same as the number we use for energy when we move or grow. The difference between children and adults is that children need about 2% more calories per pound than adults do, to provide for normal and healthy growth in size (Skinner et al., 2004). Surprisingly, the caloric intake of children in the United States declined between 1999 and 2010 (Jones-Smith et al., 2014).

Normally developing babies up to about a year of age look chubby, and if their diets are good this is usually not a problem. They are still expending a lot of energy on movement and growth. But as they enter the toddler period, their weight gain slows and they become more "leggy" as their proportions change. For a period, their body mass index (BMI; a measure that compares height and weight) will be at its lowest. But within the next several years, they will not only grow taller but will begin to add more weight in proportion to height, so the BMI increases. This increase in body mass involves both fat and fat-free mass and is called the *adiposity rebound.* Children who have an early adiposity rebound (by about age 3) are likely to have a higher BMI in later childhood, adolescence, and even adulthood than those whose adiposity rebound does not come until age 5 (Chivers et al., 2010). Unfortunately, those with the early adiposity rebound and higher BMI are also more likely to develop diabetes and other health problems, which may have very serious effects over the long run.

Being too heavy in childhood has more ill effects than these obvious medical problems. Not only do obese children experience rejection by playmates, they actually have academic problems such as poor math achievement, compared with children who have never been overweight (Gable, Krull, & Chang, 2014). Their teachers also rate them as having poor interpersonal skills and feeling anxiety, loneliness, and sadness. These difficulties put obese children in a difficult position as they approach adolescence, a time when they will need both math and interpersonal skills for success in school and will be exposed to many new experiences that may make them feel especially anxious or lonely.

One possible outcome of childhood obesity is unusually early puberty for both boys and girls. Some reports on this possibility have stated that there are hormonal and other factors that might cause early puberty to occur, but that there are so many problems in measurement of events other than first menstruation that the real effects are not clear (Ahmed, Ong, & Dunger, 2009). However, at least one longitudinal study has concluded that heavier children reach and complete puberty earlier than others, and that they are of shorter stature when they complete puberty (De Leonibus et al., 2014). Early puberty can also cause problems with peers and make adolescents prefer to spend time with older persons, who may take advantage of the younger individuals' naiveté with respect to sexuality or other matters.

Why do some children have an early adiposity rebound and continue to have a high body mass index? Both genetic characteristics and eating habits shared with family members can play strong roles, but less obvious factors are also important. For whites, Hispanics, and Asians, overweight has been shown to be negatively correlated with socioeconomic status (Jones-Smith et al., 2014), although this was not shown for Native Americans and African Americans.

What causes early adiposity rebound and later overweight or obesity? Breastfeeding exclusively until age 4 months or later seems to be preventive of later overweight (Chivers et al., 2010), but it is still not very common for infants to have this feeding pattern. Mothers who smoke are more likely to have obese children, as are families that have few rules about behavior and little engagement of parents with children (e.g., eating dinner together or going on outings together; Huang, Lanza, & Anglin, 2014). But one of the most important factors in creating obesity may be television watching (Janz et al., 2002; Taylor et al., 2011). It's possible not only that watching television interferes with children's active play but that periods of time spent with very little activity reduce the benefit of periods when high activity is burning many calories. What is especially notable is that spending time watching TV, as opposed to playing actively, seems to have an especially strong effect during the adiposity rebound period (ages 2 to 8).

Clearly, being overweight has ill effects on developing children. But can it be that other existing problems cause or are related to increased body mass index? Children with Down syndrome tend to be overweight or obese in comparison with their non-Down siblings, and this may be because they spend less time in vigorous play (Whitt-Glover, O'Neill, & Stettler, 2006). Children diagnosed with autism spectrum disorder are also inclined to be overweight or obese, with 35% of one sample falling into those categories (Zuckerman et al., 2014). For both disorders, high body mass index may cause additional problems with social interactions, sleep, and learning.

Conclusion

It may have been true many years ago that a few extra pounds could help a child survive a serious infectious disease, but with modern medical treatment this is certainly not correct. On the contrary, extra weight can mean ongoing problems of health, social interactions, and school achievement. The timing of the adiposity rebound is a good predictor of overweight in later childhood, so it's possible to have effective early intervention, which may need to take the form of family behavior changes as well as increased active play for the child. Jess may find it difficult to make the changes that Ella needs for a more normal weight gain pattern, but making these changes now could prevent many problems later. For parents of younger children, it can be easier to get food preferences off to a better start in the first year by avoiding sugar-sweetened beverages—including fruit juices with extra sugar (Saint Louis, 2014).

Critical Thinking

1. The Chivers et al. (2010) article discusses the role of breastfeeding in preventing obesity at school age. How is the conclusion that an early event causes a later one vulnerable to the post hoc fallacy? State one way that researchers might try to avoid the post hoc problem.

2. Most of the studies discussed in this section were longitudinal studies. How do longitudinal studies help to avoid confounded variables?

3. Read the discussion section of the Jones-Smith et al. (2014) paper. Do the authors conclude that socioeconomic status is directly responsible for childhood obesity, or do they suggest obesity-causing factors that are more likely to occur in low status than in high status families? (The paper is pretty complicated, so begin by skimming the discussion section for a few paragraphs that are relevant to this question.)

4. Find on the Internet one or two websites that claim that autism is caused by gastrointestinal problems. What does the paper by Zuckerman et al. (2014) suggest might be the actual cause of such problems in autistic children? Look at the introduction to the paper for a discussion of this.

5. In the paper by Janz et al. (2002), the authors say they are not sure whether fatness causes inactivity or inactivity causes fatness. Can a correlational study answer this question? Why or why not?

References

Ahmed, M. L., Ong, K. K., & Dunger, D. B. (2009). Childhood obesity and the timing of puberty. *Trends in Endocrinology & Metabolism, 20*(5), 237–242.

Chivers, P., Hands, B., Parker, A., Bulsard, M., Beilin, L. J., Kendall, G. E., & Oddy, W. H. (2010). Body mass index, adiposity rebound, and early feeding in a longitudinal cohort (Raine Study). *International Journal of Obesity, 34,* 1169–1176.

De Leonibus, C., Marcovecchio, M. L., Chiavaroli, V., Giorgis, T., Chiarelli, F., & Mohn, A. (2014). Timing of puberty and physical growth in obese children: A longitudinal study in boys and girls. *Pediatric Obesity, 9*(4), 292–299.

Gable, S., Krull, J., & Chang, Y. (2014). Boys' and girls' weight status and math performance from kindergarten entry through fifth grade: A mediated analysis. *Child Development, 83*(5), 1822–1839.

Huang, D. Y. C., Lanza, H. I., & Anglin, M. D. (2014). Trajectory of adolescent obesity: Exploring the impact of prenatal to childhood experiences. *Journal of Child and Family Studies, 23*, 1090–1101.

Janz, K. F., Levy, S. M., Burns, T. L., Torner, J. C., Willing, M. C., & Warren, J. J. (2002). Fatness, physical activity, and television viewing in children during the adiposity rebound period: The Iowa Bone Development Study. *Preventive Medicine, 35*, 563–571.

Jones-Smith, J. C., Dieckmann, M. G., Gottlieb, L., Chow, J., & Fernald, L. C. H. (2014). Socioeconomic status and trajectory of overweight from birth to mid-childhood: The Early Childhood Longitudinal Study Birth Cohort. *PLoS ONE, 9*(6), 1–10.

Saint Louis, C. (2014, September 2). Childhood diet habits set in infancy, studies suggest. *New York Times*, A13.

Skinner, J. D., Bounds, W., Carruth, B. R., Morris, M., & Ziegler, P. (2004). Predictors of children's body mass index: A longitudinal study of diet and growth in children aged 2–8 years. *International Journal of Obesity, 28*, 476–482.

Taylor, R. W., Williams, S. M., Carter, P. J., Goulding, A., Gerrard, D. F., & Taylor, B. J. (2011). Changes in fat mass and fat-free mass during the adiposity rebound: FLAME study. *International Journal of Pediatric Obesity, 6*, e243–e251.

Whitt-Glover, M.C., O'Neill, K., & Stettler, N. (2006). Physical activity patterns in children with and without Down syndrome. *Pediatric Rehabilitation, 9*(2),158–164.

Zuckerman, K. E., Hill, A. P., Guion, K., Voltolina, L., Fombone, E. (2014). Overweight and obesity: Prevalence and correlates of a large clinical sample of children with autism spectrum disorder. *Journal of Autism and Developmental Disorders,44*(7), 1708–1719.

Claim 40

Birth order is an important factor that determines children's intelligence and personality.

Justin was doing moderately well in fifth grade, but he was certainly not the academic leader of his class. He was much more interested in art and music than in math and science, and the subjects that interested him did not contribute to his grade average. Justin's parents were convinced that he could do much better, especially because his second-grade sister was reading far above her grade level. Justin's mother told her friend, "I know he could do much better if he just decided to. I don't know what makes him so stubborn. But I read that firstborn kids have higher intelligence than the later ones, so there's no question in my mind that Justin ought to do better in school than his sister does."

Is Justin's mother right? Should his position as firstborn make him more intelligent and therefore more academically successful? Or are there other reasons that help determine both tested intelligence and academic achievement?

"She's a typical middle child; she doesn't care a bit about school"; "he's an oldest child, always worried and trying to manage things, studying all the time"; "she's so selfish—what an only child!" Popular beliefs about the effects of birth order involve some clear statements about personality

225

and school achievement, and those beliefs stand to reason—that is, most people think they make some kind of intuitive sense and some research evidence confirms them (Sulloway, 2007). However, other factors, such as temperament and experiences outside the family, may be able to override any effects of birth order. That multiple factors determine a child's development provides a strong hint that the situation cannot be a simple one.

In examining the effects of any factor that influences development, one task researchers must do is consider the possible *mechanisms* at work— the series of measurable events that links the cause to the outcome. Any effects of birth order, for instance, might be based on biological events. An illustration of this mechanism would be changes in a mother's reproductive system caused by events during each pregnancy, changes that result in a different prenatal environment for a later-born than for an earlier-born child. A different mechanism might involve social and emotional change: Parents may be more skillful in the care of but less excited about the birth of later-born babies, resulting in caregiving differences between firstborn and later-born children. Another factor that might cause birth order effects involves experiences with younger or older siblings—a firstborn child has no older siblings by definition, whereas a later child has at least one older sibling and sometimes several older and several younger. All of these possible mechanisms may be involved in the effect of birth order on any aspect of development. These mechanisms can work separately, together, or in different ways at different periods in an individual's life, so simply naming mechanisms is only the beginning of understanding birth order effects. However, to figure out which questions to ask about birth order, researchers first need to identify various important factors and mechanisms.

Whether birth order affects personality is one of the most intriguing questions for most readers, who even in old age may still be trying to understand how they differ from their brothers and sisters. But studying personality factors can be difficult because personality is not easy to measure. Many different personality characteristics can be considered. A somewhat simpler approach is to try to determine how birth order affects tested intelligence. This is the approach taken by many researchers of birth order effects.

A good deal of the empirical research conducted on birth order and IQ focuses on the very slightly higher intelligence test scores of adults who were firstborn children. But not all research reports the same relationships of IQ and birth order. Some studies found no difference between firstborn and later-born adults, and some studies of children showed that later-born children actually have higher IQ scores than their older brothers and sisters (Kristensen & Bjerkedal, 2007). (This does not mean that the younger children answered more questions correctly than the older ones but that the *intelligence quotients* calculated on the basis of age were higher for the later-born children.)

It is confusing that the research findings for children seem to be the opposite of those for adults, but this is actually not unusual. This situation is an example of an important concept in the study of development: that differences between groups or measurements commonly seen among children may not hold up as the individuals grow into adulthood, and they may even be reversed in later life. Characteristics of groups of adults may not explain what they were like as children, and, discouragingly, characteristics of children may or may not predict who they will be in the future. Of course, it is possible that some early events will positively correlate with later ones, but researchers know this only by careful evaluation and comparison of people at different times in their lives. It would be very unwise to assume that people do not change.

Why might birth order influence IQ? What mechanisms would make firstborns slightly superior in adulthood or later-borns superior in childhood? A biological explanation might make sense for the adult comparison but cannot simultaneously explain what happens in childhood. No simple biological cause seems capable of creating superior performance in adulthood but lower performance in childhood.

Can a social cause account for the higher intelligence test scores of adults who were firstborn? The usual explanation is that firstborn children are provided with undiluted parental interest, attention, and stimulation and model themselves on competent and affectionate adult behavior. This situation applies particularly to the learning of speech. Firstborns are primarily around adults, who demonstrate large vocabularies and complicated grammar, whereas later-born children are primarily around other children, which can limit the scope of speech that they hear. Firstborn children thus receive a head start on development and are able to stay ahead of others as they grow into adulthood—experiencing many successes, being expected to do well, and possibly also striving to be like competent adults.

This explanation stands to reason. But how can researchers explain the evidence that, during childhood, later-born children score higher on intelligence tests? This phenomenon seems to indicate that older siblings promote the development of later-born children, that older children are hindered by having toddlers in the house, or possibly that both of these situations are true. It may be true that older brothers and sisters help to educate their younger siblings, offering them models that are not too difficult for them to follow (as adults' models might be). It is also a possibility that having younger children to care for removes parents' attention from their older children and temporarily slows the older ones' development. Again, however, empirical research, not simply speculation, is needed to help understand these possibilities.

A recent study in Norway compared IQ scores for men of different birth order positions, including some whose older siblings had died (Kristensen & Bjerkedal, 2007). This study examined both the real birth order, based on the number of children previously born to a mother, and the *social order*, or number of older children living in a household with a given child. The social order was reported to be the more significant factor, and second-born sons whose older sibling had died were equal in adult IQ to firstborn sons. This study seems to indicate that experience is the mechanism by which birth order affects adult IQ. But differences as they seem to exist in childhood are still difficult to explain—and it is possible that different mechanisms are at work at different times of life. For example, birth order seems to influence the behavior of parents toward young children (Keller & Zach, 2002), but this effect may not persist for long and of course will no longer be present after the parents die and the children are middle-aged or older.

An important issue in the study of birth order effects involves method. Most birth order studies have used a cross-sectional approach, in which individuals from various families are grouped according to their birth order within their families (e.g., all firstborns together). However, a preferable method may be to study individuals within their own families, comparing firstborns to their own later-born siblings. When this method is used, the birth order effect on intelligence is no longer apparent (Wichman, Rodgers, & McCallum, 2006). Are the differences previously reported for birth order just a matter of differences between families, not differences in birth order? This is possible, but the best way to study this question has not yet been determined.

Conclusion

Information about the effects of birth order on development indicates that adults born early in the family sequence may have slightly higher tested intelligence than those born later, and the children's different experiences may be responsible for this. However, comparisons during childhood give different results. Justin's mother is mistaken in thinking that he should do better academically than his little sister—and she is forgetting that school achievement depends on interest, motivation, and effort as well as intelligence.

Critical Thinking

1. Read the Sulloway article (2007) to find the average IQ difference between firstborn and later-born adults. Using information from a child development textbook as evidence, compare this difference with the measurement error associated with standardized intelligence tests. Would you expect the intelligence difference to have any practical effect? Explain your answer.

2. Kristensen and Bjerkedal (2007) concluded that individuals whose siblings died are disadvantaged on some factors associated with intelligence. Locate several such factors in a child development textbook and summarize the statements in the article, using more specific terms.

3. Read about intelligence tests in a child development textbook. Find out how the tests for younger children are different from those for older children. How would you connect those differences with the reports of higher IQ for later-born children during childhood? Are early-developing aspects of intelligence encouraged by the presence of older children?

4. Identify some personality factors that have a strong genetic basis, referring to a child development textbook for information. Do genetic factors override the effect of birth order on personality? Explain your answer.

5. What did Kristensen and Bjerkedal (2007) mean when they said that birth order effects might be an artifact? In your explanation, focus on their references to the lower IQ of children from larger families.

References

Keller, H., & Zach, U. (2002). Gender and birth order as determinants of parental behaviour. *International Journal of Behavioral Development*, 26, 177–184.

Kristensen, P., & Bjerkedal, T. (2007). Explaining the relation between birth order and intelligence. *Science*, 316, 1717.

Sulloway, F. J. (2007). Birth order and intelligence. *Science*, 316, 1711–1712.

Wichman, A. L., Rodgers, J. L., & McCallum, R. C. (2006). A multilevel approach to the relationship between birth order and intelligence. *Personality and Social Psychology Bulletin*, 32, 117–127.

Claim 41

When a child is mentally ill, any psychological treatment is better than no treatment.

Eight-year-old Kevin's mother, Marcia, was worried about her son's mental health and was telling her friend Lupe about the situation. "I'm afraid he really might be crazy," she confided. "I keep finding him playing with matches. The cat won't let him near her—like he's been doing things to her that I don't know about. The other day I heard him talking, like he was talking to somebody, but when I went to look there was nobody else there." Lupe put in her contribution: "I know your family doesn't like to mention this, but there was that uncle of yours who ended up in the state hospital. These things can run in families. Don't you think you need to get him some help?" "Sure," said Marcia, "but what kind? Who do I go to?" Lupe didn't think that mattered. "It's good to get therapy," she said. "How's it going to hurt? It can only help."

Was Lupe right? Are all psychotherapies for children helpful?

Do all child psychotherapies help? Is it possible that they can be harmful? These are somewhat separate questions. A treatment could fail to be helpful while simultaneously failing to do any direct harm, but indirect harm would come about if a family invested its resources in an ineffective treatment and later could not pay for an intervention that could actually help. But, disturbingly, it also appears that some psychotherapies used for children can be directly harmful.

Although child psychotherapies have been available for almost a hundred years now, a long time had passed before serious questions were asked about the effectiveness of psychological treatments in general and of those for children in particular. In the late 1990s, psychologists began to focus on some of the concerns brought up by the evidence-based medicine movement (Sackett et al., 1996), a way of thinking about medical treatment that used only treatments for which systematic evidence indicated that they were helpful and not harmful. A similar evidence-based practice movement in psychology and social work set up rules for making decisions about the effectiveness of psychosocial treatments (Chambless & Hollon, 1998).

More recently, psychologists began to discuss whether some treatments that are in use are potentially harmful (Lilienfeld, 2007). It seems unlikely that a psychotherapy that did predictable physical harm would continue to be used, but it would be of concern if a treatment was only probably harmful for some individuals. At least one form of treatment for children has been associated with a number of deaths—one actually occurring at the hands of the therapists, others through misunderstandings or inappropriate behavior of parents (Mercer, Sarner, & Rosa, 2003). Other treatments have been shown to have less serious but real negative effects such as worsening the condition for which the person was originally treated. It has been suggested that awareness of such problems should form part of the training of clinical psychologists (Castonguay et al., 2010).

Of the 10 treatments listed as probably harmful for some individuals by Lilienfeld (2007), 5 are primarily intended for children or adolescents (Scared Straight interventions, Facilitated Communication, Attachment Therapy, boot camps for conduct disorder, and the DARE program). One other therapy, oriented toward Dissociative Identity Disorder, may also be used with children.

These facts suggest that children are even more likely than adults to be placed in treatments that have the potential to do harm. Another important issue for treatment of children is that, of course, children do not choose their own treatments, but are placed in treatment according to decisions made by parents or school or court officials. Adolescents may have more of a voice in the selection of treatment by their parents than younger children do, but are also more likely to have committed offenses such that their treatment is court-ordered. It's usually expected that adolescents as well as their parents will give "informed consent" to their treatment after being provided with information about the intervention, but this is rarely done with younger children.

Even if parents and adolescents are given information about a mental health treatment before they give their consent to be treated, most people are far from clear on what makes a psychotherapy effective, ineffective, or harmful. The information they would need to be given on these points is lengthy and complex in most cases, and chances are that few parents or adolescents will make the effort to read it all. They may already have had great difficulty in finding a therapist near their home or one who takes their particular type of health insurance, so it is unlikely that they will decline a treatment on the basis of challenging information.

Ideally, parents would look for information showing that systematic research has supported the idea that a treatment is effective for the problems their child appears to have. In many cases, though, that research is difficult to do and may exist only in simplified form. Some authors have talked about research on psychotherapies as yielding different levels of evidence (Mercer & Pignotti, 2007). The highest level would involve randomizing the study by assigning some patients to one treatment, others to a different or (less desirably) no treatment. At the highest level of evidence, research designs will have made sure that children, parents, and teachers were unaware what sort of treatment a child was receiving. Highest-level evidence would also involve studies that had been replicated, or repeated with similar outcomes, by different researchers. At the lowest level—a level that should not be acceptable—none of those requirements would be met, and in addition there would be evidence that the treatment had sometimes had a harmful outcome. But, again, very few parents bringing their children for psychotherapy have the background necessary for exploring the evidence for a treatment.

If a treatment is followed by actual harm to a child, is it correct to say that it involved child abuse? Why aren't such things illegal? This is a more difficult point than it may appear. For one thing, it is conceivable that one child has characteristics that make him vulnerable to certain treatment in a way that would rarely or never occur for other children. For another, it is possible that a therapist could make a mistake and cause an outcome that is not ordinarily part of a treatment's effects. A parent following a therapist's instructions might accidentally or through misunderstanding cause harm to a child, as in the case of one father who suffocated his adopted daughter while using a method he had been taught (Mercer, Sarner, & Rosa, 2003). Whether a child psychotherapy is in itself abusive may not be clear from a small number of cases where harm was done. It is possible that some treatments that have been harmful to children would not have done as much harm if the therapists involved had not pressed the treatment beyond what common sense would dictate (Shermer, 2004). These facts make it difficult for laws to prohibit the use of certain techniques, but some professional organizations have spoken out against child psychotherapies that they regard as abusive (Chaffin et al., 2006). One psychologist has argued that even treatments that create "emotional burdens" by making patients feel sad or distressed are undesirable unless there are no alternatives (Linden, 2013).

Conclusion

The evidence is that not all treatments offered as child psychotherapies are helpful, and some have even been shown to present a risk of harm. Unfortunately, the chances are that it would be difficult for Marcia or her friend to get together the evidence about an intervention or to understand it easily if they had it. Even if they could do this, constraints on their time and resources may make parents likely to go with whatever treatment is readily available rather than to seek an intervention that is well supported by research evidence.

Critical Thinking

1. Use the Internet or other sources to find a definition of the "Dodo Bird verdict" as it applies to psychotherapy. What does the existence of potentially harmful treatments have to do with this concept? In your answer, refer to iatrogenic effects.

2. What is Facilitated Communication? What evidence for its effectiveness is described by Mostert (2010)? Find evidence for its potential harmfulness in Mostert's or others' published papers or in Internet sources; the Lilienfeld (2007) article will also provide some evidence.

3. Look at several websites that advertise psychotherapies for children. Do they present research evidence for the interventions, or do they provide testimonials from clients to support their work's effectiveness? Do they state specific claims of effectiveness, such as "Backrub Therapy works!"?

4. What are "adverse events" in medicine? How are they reported? Look at www.apa.org to see whether the American Psychological Association has a way to report such events resulting from psychotherapy. Are "emotional burdens" (Linden, 2013) usually included as adverse events?

5. Read the discussion and conclusion of the article by Chaffin et al. (2006). What kinds of information do the authors use to support their decision to reject the child psychotherapy under consideration?

References

Castonguay, L. G., Boswell, J. F., Constantino, M .J., Goldfried, M. R., & Hill, C. E. (2010). Training implications of harmful effects of psychological treatments. *American Psychologist, 65*, 34–49.

Chaffin, M., Hanson, R., Saunders, B. E., Nichols, T., et al. (2006). Report of the Task Force on Attachment Therapy, Reactive Attachment Disorder, and Attachment Problems. *Child Maltreatment, 11*, 76–89.

Chambless, D. L., & Hollon, S. D. (1998). Defining empirically supported therapies. *Journal of Consulting and Clinical Psychology, 66*, 7–18.

Lilienfeld, S. O. (2007). Psychological treatments that cause harm. *Perspectives on Psychological Science, 2*, 53–70.

Linden, M. (2013). How to define, find, and classify side effects in psychotherapy: From unwanted events to adverse treatment reactions. *Clinical Psychology and Psychotherapy, 20*(4), 286–296.

Mercer, J., & Pignotti, M. (2007). Shortcuts cause errors in systematic research syntheses: Rethinking evaluation of mental health interventions. *Scientific Review of Mental Health Practice, 5*, 59–77.

Mercer, J., Sarner, L., & Rosa, L. (2003). *Attachment therapy on trial.* Westport, CT: Praeger.

Mostert, M. P. (2010). Facilitated Communication and its legitimacy—Twenty-first century developments. *Exceptionality, 18*, 31–41.

Sackett, D. L., Rosenberg, W. M. C., Gray, J. A. M., Haynes, R., & Richardson, W. S. (1996). Evidence-based medicine: What it is and what it isn't. *British Medical Journal, 312*, 71–72.

Shermer, M. (2004). Death by theory. *Scientific American, 290*(6), 48.

Claim 42

Bullying is a natural behavior for children, and there's nothing you can do to stop it.

Will was a stocky, strong 12-year-old, but his size and muscles did not keep him from getting pushed around by older kids at school. On the playground or at the bus stop, someone was always threatening him, shoving him, or tearing up a few pages of his homework. Taking his lunch money was a regular thing, of course. Will became depressed and anxious and dreaded Monday mornings when he would have to go to school after a peaceful weekend. His grades were suffering, and he was waking up everyone in the house with nightmares. Finally, he told his father everything and begged for help. Will's father said he would talk to the teacher and the principal, and even though Will was reluctant about this, he accepted the idea that it might be the only way to get help. Both members of the school staff were sympathetic and friendly, but the principal said, "Look, there's not a thing we can do about this. That's just the way kids are. It's human nature. If I tell them not to bully Will, they'll bully him more. Why don't you get him boxing lessons? Then maybe they'll respect him."

Was the principal right? Is there nothing schools can do to help children who are bullied?

Oddly, behaviors that people attribute to human nature always seem to be unpleasant. No one seems to include compassion, empathy, or charity as part of human nature. Calling a behavior natural usually implies

235

that the behavior is undesirable and cannot be modified or altered. Even teachers often take this point of view about bullying or feel that a teacher who is good at dealing with bullying has a "natural" ability to deal with the "natural" behavior (Crothers & Kolbert, 2008).

There is no doubt that bullying in schools is highly undesirable. At its worst, bullying causes physical injury or even death. Long-term bullying and rejection are associated with suicide. In the short term, bullying affects school attendance because bullied children often avoid attending school as often as they can, resulting in missed academic work and fewer positive social interactions with other children. Unfortunately, there is also no doubt that bullying and intimidation of children is widespread.

Is it possible to reduce bullying in schools? Personnel who implement antibullying programs have a difficult job to do because the act of bullying is presumably gratifying to the bully, who experiences a sense of power and may also gain material items, such as money extorted from victims. Children who bully or are bullied may have personality characteristics that are related to their actions or at least a long history of related behaviors (Pellegrini & Bartini, 2000; Tani, Greenman, Schneider, & Fregoso, 2003). Programs need to have sufficiently powerful components to deal with actions that have been punished many times but are consistently rewarding to the bully.

Since the 1990s, a variety of antibullying programs have been developed. Application and testing of these programs help determine whether bullying behavior can be modified, at least by the approaches that are now available. Studies of the outcomes of antibullying programs are especially helpful if they show whether programs have both initial effects and long-term influence in reducing bullying in school.

Some antibullying programs assume that bullies turn to inappropriate behavior because of a lack of skills for positive social interaction. For example, one program, studied some years ago, focused on school aggression in general, rather than specific bullying behavior, and attempted to guide elementary school boys to think about the causes of other people's behavior. Considering that aggressive boys were likely to interpret others' actions as hostile when they were actually accidental, this program, BrainPower, provided lessons in interpreting others' intentions and responding to the motive rather than the behavior. Four schools were studied, and some children in each school were randomly assigned either to the BrainPower program or to one of two control conditions, either a problem-solving program or a no-attention condition. The researchers reported that the BrainPower program reduced aggression by a small amount, but the effect disappeared within 12 months (Hudley et al., 1998).

More recent antibullying programs tend to be much more complicated than the BrainPower approach. For example, in the Steps to Respect program, teachers present classroom lessons about empathy to elementary school children and provide instruction in how children should act when someone tries to bully them (the suggestion is to make eye contact and use a strong voice). In addition, when teachers observe bullying among children, the teachers provide on-the-spot coaching in more appropriate behavior for both the bully and the victim. To test the effects of the Steps to Respect program, one study (Hirschstein, Van Schoiack Edstrom, Frey, Snell, & MacKenzie, 2007) randomly assigned schools, not children, to either the antibullying program or a comparison condition. Both children and teachers were asked to rate children's social skills and playground behavior. A reduction in bullying was reported for the Steps to Respect schools.

The study raised an interesting question: In the Steps to Respect program, the best results occurred when the teachers provided the lessons as they had been instructed. Why might teachers not follow instructions? Sometimes teachers preferred teacher-led activities to the program's required role-plays. Another problem may have involved the difficulties teachers experience in carrying out one-to-one coaching while involved in other important activities. Success or failure of a program may depend on teachers' ability and willingness to follow through with the program, inside and outside of the classroom. The teachers' involvement may in turn depend on the quality of the instruction they received in the program, the commitment of the school administration, and the number of bullying problems the teachers address each day. Teachers who must contend with a high turnover of students or with poor and unpredictable attendance may become discouraged because they have to repeat lessons children have missed or provide repeated instruction to children who enter the school later in the year.

Related research (Menon, Tobin, Corby, Menon, & Hodges, 2007) suggests that it would be unwise for antibullying programs to try to raise bullies' self-esteem in an effort to improve their social behavior. Longitudinal studies showed that aggressive children with high self-esteem become more, not less, aggressive over time; they increasingly enjoy aggression and its rewards; they become less concerned about the harm they do to their victims.

Conclusion

It seems to be possible for some programs to reduce the amount of bullying in schools, but not all programs are successful, and some programs work only in good situations. Effective programs may need to focus on changing victims', as well as bullies', behavior. Will's principal could take some action to help reduce bullying, but he would have to have financial resources and high-quality teacher training to accomplish this goal.

Critical Thinking

1. Review a child development textbook and federal websites, such as the National Institutes of Mental Health site, to find information about consent to research. Explain the rationale for parental consent and the consent of older school-age children for playground observations. What rules govern this kind of research?

2. One of the studies discussed in this section (Hudley et al., 1998) randomly assigned children to programs; the other study (Hirschstein et al., 2007) assigned schools to programs. What unwanted factors might affect the outcome of the first study but not the second? Explain your answer.

3. Imagine a study in which the participating teachers who present antibullying information are also the observers who report changes in bullying behavior. What factors might affect the outcome of this study? Explain your answer.

4. The BrainPower study excluded girls. In the Steps to Respect study, about half of the child participants were girls. Explain how this difference might affect reports of bullying behavior in school-age children. Consider both cognitive and physical gender differences and the changes that occur between third grade and the end of sixth grade. Refer to a child development textbook for information to support your explanation.

5. Why wouldn't researchers simply measure children's social skills at the beginning of a school year, then compare them to measures of the same children after a year's exposure to an antibullying program? What problem might result from this method? Would the problem be more serious in a study of sixth-graders or a study of third-graders? Explain your answers.

References

Crothers, L. M., & Kolbert, J. B. (2008). Tackling a problematic behavior management issue: Teachers' intervention in childhood bullying problems. *Intervention in School and Clinic, 43*, 132–139.

Hirschstein, M. W., Van Schoiack Edstrom, L., Frey, K. S., Snell, J. L., & MacKenzie, E. P. (2007). Walking the talk in bullying prevention: Teacher implementation variables related to initial impact of the Steps to Respect program. *School Psychology Review, 36*, 3–21.

Hudley, C., Britsch, B., Wakefield, W. D., Smith, T., Demorat, M., & Cho, S.-J. (1998). An attribution retraining program to reduce aggression in elementary school students. *Psychology in the Schools, 35*, 271–282.

Menon, M., Tobin, D. D., Corby, B. C., Menon, M., & Hodges, E. V. E. (2007). The developmental costs of high self-esteem for antisocial children. *Child Development, 78*, 1627–1639.

Pellegrini, A. D., & Bartini, M. (2000). A longitudinal study of bullying, victimization, and peer affiliation during the transition from primary school to middle school. *American Educational Research Journal, 37*, 699–725.

Tani, F., Greenman, P. S., Schneider, B. H., & Fregoso, M. (2003). Bullying and the Big 5: A study of childhood personality and participant roles in bullying incidents. *School Psychology International, 24*, 131–146.

Claim 43

Sugar is a major cause of hyperactive behavior.

It was Sally's first year as a second-grade teacher, so of course she kept her ears open to hear the opinions of more experienced teaching staff. In the teachers' lounge, several people expressed their dread of the first of November. "Oh, boy, is that going to be the day from hell!" exclaimed one experienced teacher. "It's like this every year—fighting, crying, nobody can stay in their seats. The whole day is ruined. They go out for Halloween and then it's just sugar, sugar, sugar until they finally go to bed. The parents always say they'll limit the candy, but they don't—and I don't blame them because my kids are exactly the same way!" Sally listened carefully and was not surprised when her classroom was chaotic on the first day of November.

Were Sally and her colleagues right in thinking that Halloween candy was the cause of the disruption?

Since at least the 1950s, parents and teachers have been assuring one another that sugar causes children to become overactive and inattentive, with symptoms characteristic of ADHD (attention-deficit/hyperactivity disorder). As evidence, believers in this connection often point to the day after Halloween, an occasion when adults anticipate seeing, and often do see, children behaving disruptively, especially in the classroom. Many of these children went out trick-or-treating on Halloween night, received large amounts of candy, and undoubtedly ate a good deal of it, even though their parents tried to set limits. Reports of candy consumption and observation of hyperactive and inattentive behavior are interpreted to mean that sugar consumption causes a behavior change.

Parents who limit sugar and food additives in their children's diets often report improvement in child behavior and conclude that past undesirable behavior was caused by an unsuitable diet (Smucker & Hedayat, 2001). Although the food additive factor complicates this conclusion, these parent reports are also taken as evidence that ADHD and related problems are caused by ingestion of sugar, especially refined sugar.

Some people who accept the sugar-ADHD link argue for a commonsense connection: Sugar is easily digested and converted to energy, hyperactive children seem to have too much energy; therefore, limiting children's sugar intake will make them less energetic.

Considering the difficulties created by impulsiveness and hyperactive behavior, it is too bad that these claimed connections do not seem to be correct (Lilienfeld, 2005). Contrary to the reasoning stated in the last paragraph, all food must be converted to the sugar glucose before it is used to fuel cell functions, so dietary sugar has no more direct connection to energy than any other food. Of course, children who are actually starving become lethargic, but this is because of a lack of nutrients and calories, not because they are calmed by their candy-free diet. In addition, scientifically controlled studies show no association between sugar in the diet and undesirable behavior.

Although parents seem to have more accurate information about the facts of ADHD than teachers do (West, Taylor, Houghton, & Hudyma, 2005), some groups of parents hold mistaken beliefs about certain issues, such as the links between diet and hyperactivity (Bussing, Gary, Mills, & Garvan, 2007). In the absence of much systematic research, it is all too easy for teachers and parents to forget that most human behaviors have multiple causes rather than a single simple factor at work. It is also easy to forget that multiple causes are often confused with one another in ways that make it difficult to know the effects of a specific cause. More confusion comes from letting personal experiences influence one's understanding of complex matters.

If sugar does not cause hyperactivity, why, then, do teachers and parents commonly report disruptive behavior on November 1? For an explanation, the confounding variables contributed by the noncandy aspects of Halloween need to be examined, and there are many to consider. Features of Halloween experience and behavior include children's reluctance to eat dinner when more exciting things are happening; scary stories and costumes; activities outside after dark, which parents usually discourage in the colder fall weather; the perceived dangers and delights of visiting strangers' homes, which is usually forbidden, even for fundraising sales (e.g., Girl Scout cookies); and a lack of sleep caused by the extension of bedtime and difficulty falling asleep after an exciting night. Alterations of normal diet and sleep patterns, added to exciting or even frightening experiences, are enough to change mood and behavior in adults as well as children. (In fact, both parents and teachers may be affected by Halloween events and eat sweets and lose sleep.) Although this logical analysis cannot rule out the contributions of sugar ingestion, it does show that alternative explanations can be made, suggesting confounding variables that may influence teacher and parent reports of post-Halloween disruption. Systematic research is needed before claims can be made about the causes of children's behavior changes.

How can systematic research be carried out to test the assumptions often made about sugar and behavior? A reliable study of this issue requires that neither adults nor children know whether the children's diets contain components that might affect their mood and behavior. Adult expectations about the effect of diet can cause parents or teachers to notice and report children's behavior in ways that match the adult expectations—or even to act toward children in ways that contribute to behavior alterations. Children who expect sugar to make them excited and impulsive may feel justified after Halloween if they abandon their usual efforts to behave calmly. Just as adults may excuse inappropriate drunken behavior as "the alcohol talking," children may believe that candy bars make them jump up and down or push in line.

Of course, in everyday situations, both adults and children know when children have consumed extra candy. The same holds when parents use special diets for children. The parents obviously know what they are doing, especially because some diets are rather demanding and effortful for the cook, and the children are likely to recognize from the appearance and taste of the food that their meals are not ordinary. Children may also hear their parents discuss their expectations about the diet, or the parents may tell the children directly that they will be able to behave better after they eat different foods.

Can the effects of beliefs about diet and ADHD be limited by research designs? To do this, researchers need to make sure that neither the children nor the adults who assess children's behavior know the diet a child is receiving (i.e., both groups must be blind to the children's diets). Obviously, an adult must decide which child receives which diet, but that adult should not be in contact with the children. How can this be accomplished? Certainly, this research must be done in a restricted environment, such as a residential camp or boarding school, where the children are limited to the food provided by adults (e.g., children should not be allowed birthday cupcakes sent from home). In addition, the children's basic diet needs to be made from scratch, without the flavor or appearance of a food cooked with refined sugar. All of the children in the study must receive the same diet (even though they may not like it), but a randomly selected half should receive daily capsules containing sugar or any other dietary additives to be tested. The other half of the group should receive capsules of identical appearance but without potentially active ingredients. A comparison of behavior changes in the two groups will reveal any connections between diet and behavior, without any effect of beliefs and expectations. Past research that met these requirements did not show a connection between sugar in the diet and inappropriate behavior.

It is possible for some children to have sensitivities to sugar or to other dietary components, and parents' reports can provide hints about this. Nevertheless, for real understanding of diet as a cause of impulsive behavior, researchers always need to control parents' and children's expectations and prevent these confounded variables from confusing the outcomes.

Evidence and logical argument about the effect of sugar say nothing about the possible effect of food additives on children's attention, mood, and behavior. Each type of food additive needs to be tested individually, following the same rules discussed earlier, and some researchers have conducted well-designed studies suggesting that some food additives have the effects once ascribed to sugar (Rosenthal, 2007).

Conclusion

Well-controlled research does not show that sugar consumption is a cause of ADHD or other impulsive or inappropriate behaviors. Confounded variables usually accompany children's eating of extra candy, especially at parties or on holidays, including the expectations of teachers, parents, and children that bad behavior will follow. It may be that Sally's own attitude and behavior contribute to the disruption she expects and finds in her second-grade classroom.

Critical Thinking

1. Using a child development textbook, find information about the effects of parental styles. Describe the ways parents' behavior can influence children's behavior, making the children more, or less, inattentive and hyperactive.

(Continued)

(Continued)

2. What problems of critical thinking may be involved in the belief that sugar cause hyperactivity?

3. How would you expect impulsive children to influence a parent's or teacher's behavior toward them? Would it make any difference if the adult were impulsive as well?

4. Review information about temperament in a child development text-book. Explain how temperamental differences between a child and a parent might cause the parent to describe their child as impulsive and inattentive.

5. What confounded variables are removed by having children randomly assigned to Sugar or No sugar groups? How might the research outcomes in this design differ from those where parents select their children's diets? Read the article by Rosenthal (2007) for other ideas about design of this kind of research. Explain how the designs discussed in the article can be applied to the study of dietary sugar effects.

References

Bussing, R., Gary, F. A., Mills, T. L., & Garvan, C. W. (2007). Cultural variations in parental health beliefs, knowledge, and information sources related to attention-deficit/hyperactivity disorder. *Journal of Family Issues, 28,* 291–318.

Lilienfeld, S. O. (2005). Scientifically unsupported and supported interventions for childhood psychopathology: A summary. *Pediatrics, 115,* 761–764.

Rosenthal, E. (2007, September 6). Some food additives raise hyperactivity, study finds. *New York Times,* p. A3.

Smucker, W. D., & Hedayat, M. (2001). Evaluation and treatment of ADHD. *American Family Physician, 64,* 817–829, 831–832.

West, J., Taylor, M., Houghton, S., & Hudyma, S. (2005). A comparison of teachers' and parents' knowledge and beliefs about attention-deficit/hyperactivity disorder (ADHD). *School Psychology International, 26,* 192–208.

Claim 44

Adopted children have many more social and emotional development problems than do nonadopted children.

Sixteen-year-old Jazzmin was delighted when a new neighbor asked her to babysit 8-year-old Terence one weekend. Terence seemed like a nice enough kid, and Jazzmin definitely needed some money for prom expenses. Jazzmin was very surprised when her mother hesitated about the job. "But Mom— they live right down the street! What could happen? And I really, really need some money to get my nails done!" Jazzmin's mother said, "You're young yet. Maybe you don't understand this. I heard that that boy is adopted . . . adopted kids can really have problems. Some people even say they can be killers. I don't want you to have to deal with any craziness. We'd better see if you can find another way to earn your nail money."

Was Jazzmin's mother right about the problems of adopted children, if not necessarily about Terence?

Like many other myths and misunderstandings about child development, the claim that adopted children are emotionally disturbed involves a tiny portion of reality and logic, mixed with a large dose of fantasy (Demick,

2007). Knowing some facts about early social development, and knowing the impact of early separation and loss, people might guess that adoption is a disturbing experience. But guesses are not necessarily accurate because individual experiences involve differences in timing, conditions, personality, and family characteristics as well as the experience of separation.

Adopted children, by definition, have experienced separation from their birth parents and may have been separated from later caregivers as well. Studies of toddlers who experience abrupt, long-term separations from familiar adults show that these children respond with intense and long-lasting grief. Separated toddlers go through a lengthy mourning period, withdraw from social contact, become uninterested in play, and eat and sleep poorly. With sensitive, responsive care from new adults, the children gradually recover and form new emotional connections, returning to their normal developmental pathways. Lack of sensitive care, or repeated separations, may make it difficult for toddlers to recover completely from their losses, and, possibly, their social behavior and capacity for relationships may be negatively affected.

So far, it seems that evidence supports the claim about adopted children. Some children are greatly distressed as they proceed through the adoption process. However, it would be a mistake to assume that all children and all adoptions are alike. The effects of adoption depend on three highly significant factors that may be quite different for different adopted children: the child's age at separation, the circumstances surrounding the adoption, and the caregiving abilities of the adoptive parents. (These factors may be related to each other, as, for example, the age of a child at adoption is often related to the circumstances under which the adoption occurred.)

The child's *age at adoption* helps to predict the developmental outcome of the experience. Toddlers, as explained earlier, respond with severe distress to abrupt separations and need help to recover. But what about children of other ages? Are there developmental differences in children's reactions to adoption? In fact, infants who are adopted in the first months of life show very few differences in development compared with nonadopted children. Children who are older than 5 or 6 years of age when moved from their familiar families to other homes are likely to be sad and confused, but they do not grieve inconsolably. In fact, the period between about 6 months and 3 years of age seems to be the time when children are most intensely affected by adoption events. Children in this age group are not able to understand what is happening, but they are old enough to have formed an attachment to familiar people; as a result, they are more likely than children in other age groups to have behavioral or mood disorders that require professional help. However, resilient children even of this vulnerable group may recover well with the support of responsive caregivers.

What about the *circumstances* of adoption? Children adopted immediately following birth have no more problems than nonadopted children. There are more difficulties among those who remained with birth parents, were abused or neglected, and then finally placed for foster care or adoption. Children adopted from foreign orphanages may have experienced severe neglect and often show physical and cognitive delays when placed in the care of their adoptive families (Pomerleau et al., 2005). However, most foreign-adopted children do very well and catch up developmentally within several years of adoption (Rutter, 2002).

Discussion of circumstances of adoption should also include individual characteristics of children. Some infants are placed in foster care (and later adopted) because they tested positive for drugs at the time of birth. Others are separated from their birth parents because the children have actual or potential disabling conditions that are challenging to the birth parents. Birth parents who have disabilities, such as mental retardation, may be persuaded or even forced to give up their child, who may or may not share or be affected by the parents' conditions. Toddlers with emotional disorders may be mistreated or abandoned by immature or incompetent parents, placed in long-term foster care, and possibly later adopted. In all of these cases, developmental risks are present before the child is adopted—problems that may not be cured by adoption but were certainly not caused by adoption, either.

The third factor, adoptive parents' *caregiving abilities*, involves the adoptive parents' understanding of developmental changes in emotional needs and their capacity and willingness to respond to those changes. Some adoptive parents do well with young infants because the parents expect and want to cuddle and comfort a baby; however, they do less well with older children, who need a sense of autonomy and may be concerned with school and friends. In this situation, the adopted infants progress well, but the older children may be more likely to display emotional or behavioral problems. The reverse can also occur if the adoptive parents have different preferences and skills. It seems, too, that adoptive parents are anxious and concerned about the children's needs and are more likely to seek services for adopted rather than for nonadopted children (Le Mare, Audet, & Kurytnik, 2007).

One issue that confuses people's understanding of adoption is the periodic change in adoption rules and standards. Experiences of children adopted today may be very different from those of children adopted 20 or 30 years ago, and future adoptees may have different experiences from adoptees of previous periods. For example, today's adoptions involve "falsified" birth certificates that conceal children's actual parentage, so children grow up without knowing about their biological backgrounds and may not be able to find this information when they are adults. A number of states are considering altering this arrangement (Raymond, 2007). Some families, of course, participate in *open adoptions*, which encourage a connection between the biological parents and the adoptive family. How these changed circumstances influence adopted children is still unknown.

It appears that most adopted children do very well and that differences between adopted and nonadopted groups are small. Social and emotional problems in adopted children are caused by a combination of risk factors, not by adoption alone (Rutter, 2002). And, of course, children who are not adopted may have serious problems, too. People should not expect all adopted children to be completely without mental health difficulties, but neither should they assume that serious emotional problems are characteristic of all adoptees. Some adopted children may experience difficulties resulting from a combination of factors, such as the adoptive parents' lack of readiness for their parenting tasks and past sexual abuse or neglect of the children (Simmel, 2007). Most will do well in a family environment that provides what they need.

Conclusion

Adoption alone does not cause social and emotional problems, although some problems may exist before adoption. The differences between adopted and nonadopted children are small, especially if adoption took place in the first months of a child's life. Serious mental illness and violent behavior are not particularly associated with adoption. Jazzmin's mother was naturally concerned about her daughter's safety at the neighbor's house, but she need not worry that adoption alone makes Terence dangerous.

Critical Thinking

1. Read about social reactions in a child development textbook. Present a description of reactions common in children between birth and 6 months of age and those common in children about 18 months old. In which period of time would adoption cause less stress? Explain your answer.

2. Describe three confounded variables that make it difficult to interpret comparisons of adopted and nonadopted children. You can find some further information about this in Rutter (2002). (This is a lengthy and complex article, and you will probably find the discussion section most helpful.)

3. In a child development textbook, find information about genetic factors in behavior. Discuss the accuracy or inaccuracy of the old belief that adopted children might be "bad seeds." Review the article by Demick (2007) for other mistaken beliefs about adoption. What evidence does Demick offer to refute such beliefs?

4. Describe three confounded variables that might make it difficult to compare the results of international and domestic adoptions (variables that are characteristics of either international or domestic adoptions, not variables shared by both groups). Be sure to include characteristics of the adopting family. Search the Internet to find what foreign adoption websites tell prospective parents about adoption and include this information in your description.

5. Read about adolescents' emotional needs in a child development textbook. Explain why parents might be challenged by these needs after adopting a school-age child. Keep in mind the amount of time that may pass between the adoption and the child's entry into adolescence.

References

Demick, K. (2007). Challenging the common myths about adoption. *Brown University Child and Adolescent Behavior Letter, 23*(4), 8.

Le Mare, L., Audet, K., & Kurytnik, K. (2007). A longitudinal study of service use in families of children adopted from Romanian orphanages. *International Journal of Behavioral Development, 31*, 242–251.

Pomerleau, A., Malcuit, G., Chicoine, J.-F., Seguin, R., Belhumeur, C., et al. (2005). Health status, cognitive and motor development of young children adopted from China, East Asia, and Russia across the first 6 months after adoption. *International Journal of Behavioral Development, 29*, 445–457.

Raymond, B. B. (2007, July 29). Mystery-free adoption. *New York Times*, p. NJ15.

Rutter, M. (2002). Nature, nurture, and development: From evangelism through science toward policy and practice. *Child Development, 73*, 1–21.

Simmel, C. (2007). Risk and protective factors contributing to the longitudinal psychosocial well-being of adopted foster children. *Journal of Emotional and Behavioral Disorders, 15*, 237–249.

Claim 45

If a child is sexually molested, he or she will probably repress the memory.

Becky and Imani were discussing an unfortunate incident at the school their children both attended. A young male teacher had been accused of inappropriately touching a boy in the same fourth-grade class as Imani's son Jake. Imani said she had questioned Jake closely, but he said nothing had happened to him—in fact, he didn't remember ever having talked to the teacher. Becky argued that Jake's not remembering could indicate that something so serious had taken place that he had responded by repressing the memory. "You should take him to a therapist and see if they can recover the memory," she said. "That might be just the kind of evidence we need to lock that guy up and throw away the key." Imani did not feel comfortable with the idea of taking Jake to a therapist, and she wasn't sure she wanted to know about something that didn't seem to be troubling her son. Besides, she thought to herself, it could be that the man didn't really do anything, and it would be awful to send him to jail if he was innocent.

Was Becky right? Do children repress their memories of frightening or painful events like sexual abuse?

The idea of repression of memories—a type of forgetting motivated by the pain and anxiety of remembering—dates back to the late 19th century and Freud's formulation of psychoanalysis. The repression concept is associated with the fact of "amnesia" for the events of early life and the ordinary failure to recall significant events like one's own birth. In recent years, authors like the Swiss psychotherapist Alice Miller have stressed the idea that cruel treatment of children is responsible for much later emotional disturbance, but that the capacity for repression means that few will recall the repressed material without special help (Miller, 2006). The psychiatrist Judith Herman (1981/2000) was among the first to emphasize repression of child sexual abuse memories as an important cause of women's emotional problems. These beliefs, both the older and the more recent ones, led to the suggestion that if a person recalled and re-experienced traumatic memories, he or she would be freed from the influence of the repressed material. Recovering a memory would cure any problems it had caused.

An important question to ask about the repression concept is whether there are any reasons other than repression why a memory might be lost and then reappear. This certainly happens in ordinary forgetting; we can't remember that milk was on the list while we're at the grocery store, but clap our hands to our foreheads as we walk in the front door without the one thing that was really needed. In addition, when something unpleasant occurs, we may make an effort *not* to remember or think about it. Clancy and McNally (2005) studied a group of 27 people who reported that they had forgotten about an experience of sexual abuse in childhood and later remembered it. About half of the participants felt they had forgotten the abuse because they had actively tried not to think about it.

A second question has to do with the nature of distressing events. Ordinarily, we would expect that vivid, intense experiences are especially easy to remember, particularly if they have been repeated. Can pain or fear associated with a vivid experience actually interfere with remembering it? If that were the case, we would expect that injuries in serious accidents, experiences with painful or frightening medical treatment, or childhood experiences of war or domestic violence would all be difficult to remember. On the contrary, descriptions of Post-Traumatic Stress Disorder indicate that intense, disturbing experiences are excessively difficult to forget, and their memories intrude into consciousness even when an individual works hard to avoid thinking of them.

Does memory function in special ways, including repression, when an experience was sexual in nature? Adults might assume this, because of their awareness of the special position of sexuality in social and moral thinking. But the issue is more complicated than it may appear when the focus is on childhood sexual experiences. The actual event may vary from simply seeing exposed genitals to fondling to physical penetration with or without violence, and the perpetrator may be familiar or unfamiliar, a large adult or a slightly older child. In addition, the term "childhood sexual abuse" could be applied to a victim who is a tiny infant, an almost-full-grown adolescent, or at any age in between. Along with differences in age, victims will differ in their understanding of or interest in sexuality. School-age and younger children may not think of an activity as sexual, although as they get older they are likely to realize the sexual intent of the perpetrator and recognize the real nature of "mysterious" events like ejaculation. It is possible that a sex-related experience could cause memory to operate differently than other types of experiences do, even if the victim did not think at the time that sexuality was involved, but it is hard to understand why that might happen.

Is it possible that many experiences of childhood sexual abuse were not actually perceived as traumatic at the time but were only later interpreted as a bad thing to have happen? This question does not apply, of course, to brutal penetrative rapes or beatings with sexual involvement on the attacker's part; it would be foolish and cruel to dismiss these dreadful experiences as nontraumatic. As soon as force or even implied threats come into the picture, an element of trauma must be considered. But fondling or rubbing against a child may be sexual acts that are no more than confusing for the child, and that could even be pleasurable. It is difficult to imagine how parents could miss so many cases of molestation if every sexually abused child came home or arrived at school crying, flushed, and agitated, as we would expect from a traumatic experience. In fact some research suggests that many adults who recall childhood sexual abuse report that they did not experience the event as traumatic (McNally & Geraerts, 2009)—which would explain why they forgot it for periods of time, without the explanation having to resort to the concept of repression.

Conclusion

There seems to be no reason to argue that a special form of forgetting called repression is needed to explain why people forget childhood sexual abuse, or why they remember it later. Certainly, it's inappropriate to conclude that a lack of memory for an event means that the event must have happened and been repressed. If Jake says he doesn't remember ever talking to the teacher, the most likely explanation is that he did not ever talk to him; a second possibility is that he did talk to the teacher casually and has forgotten about it through ordinary memory processes; the next most likely explanation is that there have been events that he remembers but prefers not to tell his mother about, for any of a variety of reasons.

Critical Thinking

1. Who were the participants in the study by Clancy and McNally (2005)? How were they located? Would it be possible to create a control group of persons who had experienced childhood sexual abuse and never remembered it?

2. How does the error of affirming the consequent affect discussion of repression of childhood sexual abuse?

3. Use your textbook or other sources to find information about memory loss due to central nervous system damage, like concussion during a football game. What kinds of childhood experiences might be followed by memory loss of this kind? Would such experiences be remembered later?

4. Use Internet sources to find several cases in which the idea of repressed memories was used in court proceedings about accusations of past sexual abuse. Read the discussion section of the paper by McNally and Geraerts (2009). How do those authors suggest that courts should use information about repression and recovered memories?

5. Find several published papers that contradict the conclusions of Clancy and McNally (2005) about repression of memories of abuse. Summarize their arguments in support of repression as a special type of forgetting.

References

Clancy, S. A., & McNally, R. J. (2005). Who needs repression? Normal memory processes can explain "forgetting" of childhood sexual abuse. *Scientific Review of Mental Health Practice, 4,* 66–73.

Geraerts, E., Raymaekers, L., & Merckelbach, H. (2008). Recovered memories of childhood sexual abuse: Current findings and their legal implications. *Legal and Criminological Psychology, 13,* 165–176.

Herman, J. (1981/2000). *Father-daughter incest.* Cambridge, MA: Harvard University Press.

McNally, R. J., & Geraerts, E. (2009). A new solution to the recovered memory debate. *Perspectives on Psychological Science, 4,* 126–134.

Miller, A. (2006). *The body never lies.* New York: W.W. Norton.

Part V

Adolescents

Claim 46

Regular experience of shared family meals is critical for children's academic and behavioral development.

Qwanisha Jackson had three children who were all doing well. The eldest, 12-year-old Michael, had been playing baseball in community leagues for a while and was just starting in a league that had night games and practices that started at about 5:30. Michael was very excited about this, but it certainly made for confusion at supper time when Qwanisha was trying to get him to eat something before he played, while getting her own meal and those of the younger children at a more normal time. To complicate matters, Qwanisha's mother criticized her for letting Michael eat by himself. She had seen on TV a news story about the importance of family meals and the risks of poor schoolwork and behavior when children did not eat with the family. Qwanisha had also heard those warnings, but she did not see why family meals were so magical or how else she was to handle the situation.

Was it important for Qwanisha to rearrange the family mealtimes so Michael did not eat alone?

Research on everyday factors influencing child development is always complicated and difficult to do. It's not generally possible to persuade or pay families to treat their children in some prescribed fashion, especially not over the period of years that might be needed before an experience had a measurable effect. The ideal randomized design is just not practical, whether we're talking about the effects of spanking, of church attendance, of a gluten-free diet, or any other aspect of daily life.

What research methods can address an issue like the effect of the frequency of shared family meals, then? This kind of problem can be approached by nonrandomized methods like correlational studies that examine mathematical relationships between variables such as family meals and school success, or by methods that compare groups of children whose families have different mealtime practices. In either case, large data sets are needed in order to extract meaningful statistical information about the issues of concern. Small groups of measurements are more likely to yield erroneous results than large ones, so even data drawn from all the children in a single school would not be adequate for our purposes (look at any elementary statistics book for an explanation of this point). Data from many thousands of children are needed. Even then, there may be confounded variables that confuse the results.

An additional complication of this type of research has to do with the power of developmental change. The basic question about the effect of frequent family meals is whether children who often share meals will *at some later point* do better academically and behaviorally than those who do not. This means that measurements need to be made at several points during childhood and that each child's performance must be compared to the same child's performance at various times. The only way to do this is by means of a longitudinal study—research that follows each child over a period of development and collects a series of measures. Longitudinal studies are obviously time consuming because they cannot be completed until the participants reach the age that is the end point of the study, and the clerical and professional work involved in them is quite expensive.

In spite of these difficulties, there have been a number of studies about the effects on children of frequently sharing family meals. For example, Eisenberg and her colleagues (2008) asked about 800 high school students about the number of times they had a meal with their families during a week and also questioned them about their use of tobacco, alcohol, and marijuana. The authors concluded that frequent family meals helped protect adolescents against substance abuse. One review and discussion article (Larson, Branscomb, & Wiley, 2006) listed a wide range of benefits reported to accrue from frequent family meals, including improvements in both nutrition and literacy.

But a much larger, more complex study (Miller, Waldfogel, & Han, 2012) has found no significant effects of family meal frequency on either academic or behavioral development in children between the ages of 5 and 15. Like many other psychological studies today, this investigation worked with a large data set that had been collected for a wide range of purposes, rather than specifically for the study of the effects of family meals. These were longitudinal data from the Early Childhood Longitudinal Study–Kindergarten Cohort (ECLS-K). That study began in 1998–1999 with about 21,400 children then entering kindergarten, and data were collected at that time, and when the children were in first, third, fifth, and eighth grades. When children moved to new schools they were not followed, so that by the eighth-grade year only about 9,700 children were assessed. Reading and mathematics scores were evaluated at each measurement, and scores on science were taken from third grade on. Information about behavior problems came from parents, teachers, and the children's self-reports. There was no significant association between family meal frequency and academic or behavioral outcomes for either younger or older children.

Miller et al. (2012) discussed an important issue with respect to any research on the effect of everyday routines on children's development. This was the problem of *endogeneity*. This they described as a situation that occurs when "unobserved characteristics are correlated with both an independent and dependent variable of interest" (p. 2106). In the case of our present concern—the impact of shared family meals on academic and behavioral development—the independent variable is the frequency of family meals, and dependent variables are academic and behavioral characteristics of the children. On the face of it, this is straightforward enough, except that we must remember that meal frequency cannot truly be an independent variable because the researchers cannot actually control it. This means that it is possible that family meal frequency is associated with other variables omitted from the study, and that those omitted variables are the real causes of any differences (or lack of differences) between groups. If this is the case, family meal frequency is only a "proxy measure" for the factors that create outcomes. As Miller et al. (2012) point out, "parents who recognize the value of shared family mealtimes may also engage in other activities that they believe are good for children, such as promoting extracurricular activities, reading to children, or pursuing high-quality schooling, each of which might affect children's school performance. In such a case, the frequency that a family eats meals together may act as a marker for other such activities" (p. 2107) but may not actually be the cause of children's developmental outcomes. These authors also pointed out that frequent family meals may indicate that parents' and children's schedules work well together, so that good communication and parental monitoring can keep children's development on track, while infrequent family meals may mean that parents and children spend little time of any kind together.

The Miller et al. (2012) paper showed no evidence that frequent family meals improved children's development, but it is true that absence of evidence does not necessarily mean that no evidence can ever be found. In addition, their conclusions did not suggest that children did better when they had fewer shared family meals. It's an important point that Miller and his colleagues gave careful consideration to a wide range of variables that needed to be controlled, such as whether parents are single. They even noted that by the time the children reached eighth grade and their number had been considerably reduced by families moving away, those who remained were more likely to be of higher socioeconomic status, more likely to be white but non-Hispanic, and less likely to live in a single-parent home. These facts did not invalidate the conclusions of the research, but they did require special statistical treatment, and they serve to remind us of the many factors other than family meals that contribute to children's good or poor developmental outcomes.

Conclusion

Like most parents, Qwanisha wanted to do her best to ensure Michael's good behavior and success in school. Again, like most parents, she got worried about the idea that one single factor could completely determine how Michael would develop. Even if the evidence were very strong that frequent family meals are a powerful cause of good development (which it is not), it's clear that they are not the only important factor. The advantages to Michael of physical development and sports skills, as well as of social interaction with other kids on his team, outweigh the possible disadvantages of missing family meals even several times a week during the baseball season.

Critical Thinking

1. Compare the information and reasoning in the Gibbs (2006) article to those in a peer-reviewed journal article. What differences do you see?

2. What is an "operational definition"? What are two ways you could operationally define the frequency of shared family meals? (The article by Miller et al. [2012] can help you with this.)

3. If children do not have shared family meals, what other forms of meals can they have? Can these supply any of the benefits discussed by Larson et al. (2006)?

4. Were the children studied by Miller et al. (2012) the same ages as those studied by Eisenberg et al. (2008)? State three ways that age differences might affect the outcomes of these studies and lead to different conclusions.

5. What is "endogeneity"? Discuss how both family meals and spanking may be "proxy measures."

References

Eisenberg, M. E., Neumark-Sztainer, D., Fulkerson, J. A., & Story, M. (2008). Family meals and substance abuse: Is there a long-term protective association? *Journal of Adolescent Health, 43,* 151–156.

Gibbs, N. (2006). The magic of the family meal. *Time, 167,* 50–55.

Larson, R. W., Branscomb, K. R., & Wiley, A. R. (2006). Forms and functions of family mealtimes: Multidisciplinary perspectives. *New Directions for Child and Adolescent Development, 111,* 1–15.

Miller, D. P., Waldfogel, J., & Han, W.-J. (2012). Family meals and child academic and behavioral outcomes. *Child Development, 83,* 2104–2120.

Claim 47

Children are more likely to become delinquent if their fathers are absent or uninvolved.

Marta and Jack had struggled with each other throughout their marriage. Now, with their children, Sean and Kylie, 12 and 9 years old, Marta feels that divorce is inevitable. Jack is drinking heavily, and Marta sometimes joins him. Domestic violence between the parents is occurring more frequently, and the children were once so frightened that they called the police even though they knew they would be punished. One day, Marta told her mother that she was going to see a lawyer and start divorce proceedings. "Oh, honey, I wouldn't do that," her mother commented. "How are you going to control Sean by yourself when he's a teenager? Boys need a father in the house to keep them from getting in trouble."

Is Marta's mother right? Are the chances better for Sean's adolescent life if his father continues to live with the children?

Curiously, in the past, people expected widows' sons to do very well in life. For example, the unusual leadership and other abilities of George Washington are sometimes attributed to his mother's childrearing. Washington's mother was a widow who did not remarry but devoted herself to her son's interests. The belief that father involvement is essential to good development is a more modern attitude, but today, of course, the absence of a father is much more likely to be a result of divorce (or no marriage) rather than death.

A large number of U.S. children and adolescents rarely see their fathers, as a result of high divorce rates and the high rate of births to unmarried couples. In many cases, fathers never live with the children; after a legal custody decision, it is common for primary custody to go to the mother. The fathers in these cases may end up living some distance from their children, may marry and have other children, or for many other reasons may reduce their contact with their children.

Marriage of a father to a child's mother has been suggested as a way to ensure the child's good development and to prevent delinquent behavior. One reason given for this suggestion concerns the economic viability of the family unit: Two adults should be able to earn a living and care for children more effectively than one adult can. But the suggestion of marriage as a cure is also associated with the assumption that fathers can control children's behavior—especially that of boys—more successfully than mothers can. However, this may not be the case when mothers are authoritative (firm but reasonable) in their parenting style (Simons & Conger, 2007).

Research on large numbers of children concluded that the effect of fathers depends not just on their presence but also on who they are and how they behave. One study of fathers' parenting styles found that in intact families a father with an authoritarian parenting style is more likely than fathers with other parenting styles to have a son involved in delinquent activity and drug and alcohol use. If the father-son relationship is positive, however, the ill effects of authoritarian parenting are less than in families where the relationship is hostile and negative. These effects are stronger for boys than for girls (Jaffee, Moffit, Caspi, & Taylor, 2003).

The study just described emphasized the role of attitudes toward children and the quality of parent-child relationships. However, intensely negative attitudes may culminate in actual maltreatment, and when this occurs in adolescence, teenagers are more likely to be involved with antisocial behaviors, such as drug use, drinking, and violence. The presence of a maltreating father may thus be more harmful than his absence.

Many studies of father involvement and delinquency are correlational studies, in which a statistical connection between the two factors is calculated. In these cases, it can be difficult to interpret correlations and to conclude which factor caused the other—or, indeed, whether additional factors caused both of them. Most readers will assume that father involvement causes the level of child delinquency rather than the other way around, but is this necessarily the case?

One correlational study examined connections between adolescents' perceptions of their parents' antisocial behavior and reports of adolescents' own behavior. The authors discussed the possibility that the parents' behavior and parenting skills could be disrupted by the extremely challenging behaviors of their children. Anger and frustration with child behaviors might be "medicated" by drug and alcohol use or expressed through aggressive behavior toward the children. Resident or nonresident fathers might feel especially challenged or disrespected by child delinquency because the fathers accept popular beliefs about their powerful position and expectations that they can exert control over their children. The result might be maltreatment of a challenging child, either by the annoyed father or by a mother who does not want the father to be agitated (Smith, Ireland, & Thornberry, 2005).

To understand the effect of fathers on children's development, genetic factors as well as the children's experiences in the family need to be considered. Detailed analysis of the effects of antisocial fathers suggests that their children receive a "double whammy" of genetics and environmental pressures toward behavior problems—that is, the children may inherit their father's genetic makeup and experience his behavior. Researchers reported that these children do better with less contact with their antisocial fathers, whereas children of socially appropriate fathers benefit from father involvement. Children of socially appropriate fathers have a double advantage rather than a whammy because they carry genetic material associated with positive social behavior, and they experience good social interactions with their fathers. The separate roles of heredity and environment suggest that children of antisocial fathers may be positively influenced by socially appropriate stepfathers, but a child who is genetically directed toward appropriate social behavior can be negatively influenced by an antisocial stepfather.

Attempts to understand father influences are complicated by the possibility that families may function differently within different demographic groups. Groups with large numbers of single-mother households may respond in their own characteristic ways to father absence (Salem, Zimmerman, & Notaro, 1998). Thus, it may be unreasonable to compare effects of father involvement in intact families with events in divorced or never-married families, unless the family patterns of others in the neighborhood or demographic group are considered. Family experiences that are strikingly different from those of relatives, friends, or neighbors may have their own effects on children's behavior. Of course, the effects of father presence or absence can be different for different groups—for example, for boys versus girls, in large versus small sibling groups, or in extended families versus nuclear families. One study of the rare but growing phenomenon of the father-only family suggested that children in these families are more likely to become delinquent (Demuth & Brown, 2004).

Conclusion

Although an intact and well-functioning family provides many benefits for children, the simple presence of a father is not necessarily beneficial to children's social development, and the presence of an antisocial father actually may be harmful. Marta's mother is mistaken in advising her daughter to stay in a violent marriage as an alternative to having a delinquent son. If Sean's father is hostile to him, the continuation of the marriage is likely to encourage delinquency in adolescence. In addition, other factors, such as Marta's own drinking, will continue to have negative effects on Sean whether the parents stay together or not.

Critical Thinking

1. In a recent study, the authors analyzed data from the National Longitudinal Study of Youth 1997 (Bronte-Tinkew, Moore, & Carrano, 2006). Read the study and describe how the researchers chose the participants.

2. Read the article by Jaffee et al. (2003). According to the authors, what confounded variables confuse comparisons between intact and single-parent families? Do Salem et al. (1998) suggest different confounding variables?

3. Read a child development textbook to find out about girls' delinquent behavior. Explain why father involvement might influence girls differently than boys. (Hint: Is adjudication based on different reasons for girls than for boys?)

4. What genetic factors might make both fathers and children more antisocial than the average person? What evidence suggests the presence of these factors? Use information from a child development textbook to support your answer.

5. Demuth and Brown (2004) reported a greater tendency toward delinquent behavior in father-only families. Under what circumstances do you think such a family would come into existence? What variables may confound and confuse this conclusion? How would those confounded variables be associated with delinquent behavior? Is post hoc reasoning a potential problem for thinking about these questions?

References

Bronte-Tinkew, J., Moore, K. A., & Carrano, J. (2006). The father-child relationship, parenting styles, and adolescent risk factors in intact families. *Journal of Family Issues, 27*, 850–881.

Demuth, S., & Brown, S. L. (2004). Family structure, family processes, and adolescent delinquency: The significance of parental absence versus parental gender. *Journal of Research in Crime and Delinquency, 41,* 58–81.

Jaffee, S. R., Moffitt, T. E., Caspi, A., & Taylor, A. (2003). Life with (or without) father: The benefits of living with two biological parents depend on the father's antisocial behavior. *Child Development, 74*(1), 109–125.

Salem, D. A., Zimmerman, M. A., & Notaro, P. C. (1998). Effects of family structure, family process, and father involvement on psychosocial outcomes among African-American adolescents. *Family Relations, 47*(4), 331–341.

Simons, L. G., & Conger, R. D. (2007). Linking mother-father differences in parenting to a typology of family parenting styles and adolescent outcomes. *Journal of Family Issues, 28,* 212–241.

Smith, C. A., Ireland, T. O., & Thornberry, T. P. (2005). Adolescent maltreatment and its impact on young adult antisocial behavior. *Child Abuse and Neglect, 29,* 1099–1119.

Claim 48

Violent television programs and video games cause increased aggressive behavior.

Fourteen-year-old Jared and his younger brother Jimmy were "addicted" to violent TV programs. They had a television set in their bedroom, and it emitted a constant roar of bangs, booms, shrieks, shouts, and emergency sirens. Their parents often told them to switch programs or at least turn down the volume, but Jared and Jimmy begged, whined, and sulked until they were allowed to watch what they wanted, as loud as they wanted. But their mother was worried because the boys seemed so explosive in some ways, especially if their favorite teams lost a game. This problem became apparent when Jared reached his teen years. Their neighbor—who had to listen to the loud TV in the summertime—commented that a cause-and-effect phenomenon was at work. "Those violent shows make kids so angry and aggressive. If you didn't let them watch that stuff, there wouldn't be any problem." The boys' mother wasn't so sure. She remembered that her father had been in a lot of trouble for fighting as a kid, and that was before violent TV programming.

Who is right? Is aggressiveness caused by violent TV programs and games?

Aggressive behavior, aimed at hurting or distressing another person, is very much a part of human life, beginning in the toddler period. (It might begin earlier, but infants are not physically or cognitively able to organize aggressive acts.) People do not have to seek a cause of general aggressive tendencies because they are a part of normal human behavior. However, the amount of aggression displayed, its circumstances, and its targets are not necessarily the same for different individuals or for a single person at various times in his or her life. Although young children share characteristic modes and situations of aggression, older children and adults may have extensive individual differences. It is thought that previous experiences and present circumstances help to determine how often an individual behaves aggressively and the type of aggressive action the person displays (Loeber & Stouthamer-Loeber, 1998).

Most if not all human groups want to *regulate* aggressive behavior. They want to foster aggression used instrumentally and for the perceived benefit of the group, as in war or contact sports, but they want to limit harmful aggression that has no perceived benefit, such as attacks on other group members—although certain individuals may be permitted aggression against their own group as they carry out police or disciplinary functions. Parents are often permitted or even expected to use limited aggression toward their children for disciplinary purposes, and in traditional societies husbands are permitted this type of aggression against their wives.

Regulating aggression in teenagers and young men is a concern common to many societies and one that is evident in the United States today. Excessive aggression among these large, strong, quick members of the community can be frightening and even harmful to their targets. These facts have led to an examination of adolescents' preferred activities as potential causes of aggression, with the hope that controlling such possible causes might help to regulate aggression within the community.

Past studies of children and adolescents who watch many hours of violent television programs demonstrated that these individuals show unusually high levels of aggressive behavior, a fact that can be interpreted as evidence that viewing of violent programming causes aggressiveness. However, because these studies did not involve experimental designs that controlled confounding variables, it is important to consider alternative interpretations.

One alternative conclusion is that adolescents who behave aggressively also prefer violent television programs and choose to watch them frequently, just as teenagers who play baseball might choose to watch sports programs. The choice of television program in this case is caused by the existing general tendency toward aggressive behavior, not the other way around. A second alternative is that a third or fourth factor, such as family income or neighborhood characteristics, influences both aggression and television choices. Another possibility is that parental preferences for or against violent programs play a role in determining which television shows are seen in a home—the parents may provide role models for violence or an opposing system to be rejected by adolescents. These alternative explanations are less obvious than the original idea (that violent television causes violent actions), and their existence weakens the argument for the first interpretation.

An important and relevant question is whether inquiries should focus on violent television programs or on television viewing in general. Violent events are common even in programs that are not classed as violent. For example, an average prime-time hour of programming shows three to five violent events, and an average hour of children's programming includes 20 to 25 acts of violence, according to one study.

However, even completely nonviolent TV programs might be associated with aggressive behavior. What is known about the association between all television watching and aggressiveness? One study investigated this connection, collecting data about the amount of television watching by adolescents and young adults. The researchers found more aggressive behavior among those who spent more time watching television. Boys who watched more than three hours of television a day at 14 years of age were involved in five times as many assaults or fights as those who watched less than one hour a day. In addition, the behavior exhibited by the children in this study was specifically one of aggression against other people, not general antisocial behavior, such as theft or other property crimes (Johnson, Cohen, Smailes, Kasen, & Brook, 2002).

Of course, a statistical association does not allow people to conclude that an excessive amount of television viewing causes aggressive behavior. Once again, aggressive adolescents may choose to watch television rather than entertain themselves in other ways. Or factors such as childhood neglect may cause both aggressive behavior and high levels of television watching.

One problem in research on violent television and games is that much of the work has been retrospective in nature, as well as being correlational. Retrospective research looks at past events that may have influenced what is happening in the present—for example, whether delinquent youths report having watched violent programs or played violent games in the past. Retrospective studies may run into trouble with memories or reporting of past events that were not recorded in any systematic way. Prospective studies record information about the present or the recent past and return to it at later events to see how it relates to the established past history. Ferguson et al. (2011) did a prospective study on use of violent video games and serious aggressive behavior and found that the two were not associated; instead, past depressive and antisocial personality characteristics were followed by youth violence.

The issue of violent video games received national attention when the state of California created legislation that would have forbidden the sale of such games to minors, a plan based on the assumption that such games cause youth violence. A related lawsuit, *Brown v. Entertainment Merchants Association*, was considered by the United States Supreme Court in 2010 and resulted in the decision that the legislation was an interference with the rights of citizens under the First Amendment (http://www.supremecourt.gov/opinions/10pdf/08-1448).

The decision was in part a response to an amicus curiae brief of information about research on violent games by a group of social scientists and others.

Conclusion

Although some research has shown associations between television viewing and aggressive behavior, it is not clear whether violent television programs cause aggressiveness. Other work implicates depression and other personality problems as most responsible for youth violence. Jared and Jimmy's mother is right to be concerned if they are watching violent television to the exclusion of other social and physical activities, especially if their behavior is unacceptable, but simply removing the TV is not likely to solve the problem of explosive aggressiveness.

Critical Thinking

1. Read the article by Johnson et al. (2002). List the factors (other than television viewing) that the authors mention as possible causes of adolescent aggressiveness. Explain briefly the logical connections between these potential causal factors and the outcome of increased aggression. Is post hoc reasoning a potential problem for thinking about these issues?

2. Has youth violence become more common since violent screen games have been available? Use Childstats.gov (2014) or other sources to provide an answer.

3. If someone were to conduct a quasi-experimental study of aggression in teenagers who watch violent television programs, comparing them to those who do not, what possible confounding variables would need to be considered? Explain your answer.

4. In a paper by Ferguson (2007), a review examines some positive as well as some negative possible outcomes of playing violent video games. What positive outcomes does the paper discuss, and which ones were supported by this examination of previous research?

5. The article by Ferguson (2011) notes the difference between prospective and longitudinal studies. Use your textbook, a book on research methods, or Ferguson's paper to find and describe these two methods. Can a study be both prospective and longitudinal? What advantages would be offered by a longitudinal study of the effects of violent television programs and games? Look at the paper by Dumontheil, Apperly, and Blakemore (2010) to see whether teenagers might be expected still to be maturing in their cognitive responses to screen games. Would this factor make a difference to the research design?

References

Brown v. Entertainment Merchants Association, 131 U.S. 2729 (2011).

Childstats.gov. (2014). *America's children: Key national indicators of well-being, 2013.* Available at http://www.childstats.gov/.

Comstock, G. (2008). A sociological perspective on television violence and aggression. *American Behavioral Scientist, 51,* 1184–1213.

Dumontheil, I., Apperly, I. A., & Blakemore, S.-J. (2010). Online usage of theory of mind continues to develop in late adolescence. *Developmental Science, 13,* 331–338.

Ferguson, C. J. (2007). The good, the bad, and the ugly: A meta-analytic review of positive and negative effects of violent video games. *Psychiatric Quarterly, 78,* 309–316.

Ferguson, C. J. (2011). Video games and youth violence: A prospective analysis in adolescents. *Journal of Youth and Adolescence, 40,* 377–391.

Johnson, J. G., Cohen, P., Smailes, E. M., Kasen, S., & Brook, J. S. (2002). Television viewing and aggressive behavior during adolescence and adulthood. *Science, 295,* 2468–2471.

Loeber, R., & Stouthamer-Loeber, M. (1998). Development of juvenile aggression and violence. *American Psychologist, 53*(2), 242–259.

Claim 49

If parents are not strict enough, children will behave badly and may become criminals.

Fifteen-year-old Daniel's parents were recently divorced and still argued frequently about Daniel's upbringing. Daniel's mother, Christin, insisted that Daniel needed strict rules and heavy punishments if he broke them. If Daniel were even five minutes late in coming home from school, she grounded him for a week. Christin did not tolerate any excuses or even discussion of the rules and their consequences, and she secretly feared that she would lose control of Daniel if she did not insist that he toe the line. Daniel's father, Mike, was more relaxed about rules and somewhat pleased to think Daniel had more fun at his house than at Christin's. But Christin argued this point. "Daniel's the one who's going to suffer if he gets his own way all the time. He has to learn to tell right from wrong and to respect authority. You're too lazy to keep after him, but how are you going to feel if he ends up in jail because you're not strict enough? It'll be too late then!"

Was Christin right about this? Is parental strictness necessary to ensure children grow up to be respectable citizens?

The first step in understanding this common belief is to examine the meaning of *strictness*. A small number of people who deplore laxity in childrearing support treatment that most people consider abusive, such as locking children in dark closets or beating them with electrical cords. A larger number reject such extreme severity but advocate some level of physical punishment and consider parents "not strict enough" if they do not spank their children occasionally. Much existing research on strictness focused on the use of physical or other punishment, though researchers also studied parents' expectations and rules for their children. For example, one study asked parents whether they agreed or disagreed with statements such as "I expect my child to obey without questioning me" and "I don't let my child complain." Understanding strictness requires knowing what a child might be punished for, what the family rules are, and what kind of punishment is used. When examining strictness of parenting, the kind of control parents are aiming for must also be considered—for example, behavioral control achieved through attentive monitoring and discipline or psychological control achieved through guilt and other emotional influences on children.

Research on parenting strictness is difficult to conduct and interpret because family life involves many confounding variables. Parental strictness is associated with characteristics of children, such as their activity levels, and characteristics of their living situations. For instance, a family living in an upstairs apartment may be under more pressure than a family in a house to keep children quiet. If children from strict families behave better—or, possibly, worse—than children with laxer parents, it is hard to know whether the children's development was determined by the parenting behavior or by one or many related factors. Nevertheless, this issue is so important that ongoing research is exploring a variety of issues connected to strictness.

Past research on psychological control looked at a factor called *intrusiveness* as an important aspect of strict parenting. Intrusive parenting involves high levels of personal control by parents who can be described as both possessive and unusually protective of their children. This personal control is manifested in negative, critical remarks that use the parent-child relationship for leverage. One researcher (Barber, 1996) concluded that intrusive parenting "potentially inhibits or intrudes upon psychological development" (p. 3297) and is "a consistently negative and inhibiting experience for children" (p. 3314).

Other related research investigated the effect of parents' control on school-age children's *internalizing* problems (e.g., excessive worry, stomachaches with no physical cause) and *externalizing* problems (e.g., getting into fights). In addition to examining behavioral and psychological control by parents, these researchers also studied how much affection the parents showed their children. Surprisingly, the children with high levels of both internalizing and externalizing problems were those whose mothers showed much affection and exercised high psychological control. The smallest numbers of externalizing problems, such as fighting, were shown by children whose mothers used high levels of behavioral control and low levels of psychological control (Aunola & Nurmi, 2005).

An intriguing but confusing factor related to the effects of parental strictness is ethnicity, which seems to be important in determining outcomes. African American children whose parents are restrictive, and might even be classed as harsh disciplinarians, are reported to have good developmental outcomes, as measured by school success and low anxiety. This is not the case for European American children. What might cause this ethnic difference? Do genetic factors cause children of different ethnicities to respond differently to strict parenting practices? This may be a possibility, but it may also be that ethnic differences in living conditions play a powerful role.

Recent research tried to explore the effects of ethnicity by examining environmental confounding variables—experiences that may be different for most African Americans than they are for most European Americans. Ethnicity in the United States is strongly associated with living conditions, employment, education, and family income, although there is a good deal of overlap in the experiences of different ethnic groups. In the study discussed here, the researchers compared a group of African American families who were living in poverty with a group of European American families with similar life circumstances. The families were evaluated for the number of stressful events (e.g., a family member's death, homelessness) that they had experienced in the previous year. The restrictiveness of the parents' behavior toward their children was measured with a questionnaire and observations of parents playing a game with their children. The children of the *less* restrictive parents had more behavior problems as family stress levels increased. In families with more restrictive parents, the children had little stress-related change in problem behaviors. For these very poor families, parental restrictiveness seemed to protect the child from the impact of family stress, for both African American and European American families. It may be the case that apparent ethnic differences in the effects of restrictiveness are related to the effects of different living conditions rather than specific genetic or cultural differences (Bhandari & Barnett, 2007; Hill & Bush, 2001). Cultural differences in values may also make a good deal of difference in the ways children respond to various parenting styles (Dwairy et al., 2006).

Much of the past research on strictness focused on obvious, important influences, such as the frequency of delinquent behavior. However, the effect of strict or more relaxed parenting may be a more subtle factor that results in less obvious outcomes. For example, children familiar with different parenting styles may expect adults to use different reasoning about rules, some expecting that rules will be based on equality of social relations, others expecting rules to be associated with consequences of their actions for other people (Leman, 2005).

Conclusion

Strict parenting practices, in general, do not seem to support good development or behavior in children, but such practices may be positive when used by families living in poverty or experiencing other types of stress. Christin probably does not need to be so strict to keep Daniel on the right path, although she may feel the need to control her child as the family goes through the changes inherent in divorce.

Critical Thinking

1. Some of the work described in this section assessed parental strictness by means of a questionnaire, but one study (Bhandari & Barnett, 2007) used an observational approach. Read about the methods used in the observational approach and describe the advantages and disadvantages of each method.

2. Describe variables that may be confounded with parenting practices. Locate information that supports your answer in a child development textbook or in Hill and Bush (2001).

3. How does the idea of the post hoc fallacy apply to thinking about the effects of parenting? How about overgeneralization?

4. Consider the effect of homelessness on a family. What are some direct effects of homelessness on school-age and adolescent children? How might the effects of homelessness on parents indirectly affect the children?

5. It is not uncommon to hear people claim that the level of parental strictness they experienced as children is correct and suitable for all children. Explain whether changes in the social environment during a few decades determine the level of parental strictness of a generation. Refer to the conclusions of Bhandari and Barnett (2007) in your response.

References

Aunola, K., & Nurmi, J.-E. (2005). The role of parenting styles in children's problem behavior. *Child Development*, 76, 1144–1159.

Barber, B. K. (1996). Parental psychological control: Revisiting a neglected construct. *Child Development*, 67, 3296–3319.

Bhandari, K. P., & Barnett, D. (2007). Restrictive parenting buffers Head Start students from stress. *Infants and Young Children*, 20(1), 55–63.

Dwairy, M., Achoui, M., Abouserie, R., Farah, A., Sakhleh, A. A., Fayad, M., & Khan, H. K. (2006). Parenting styles in Arab societies: A first cross-regional research study. *Journal of Cross-Cultural Psychology, 37*, 230–247.

Hill, N. E., & Bush, K. R. (2001). Relationships between parenting environment and children's mental health among African American and European American mothers and children. *Journal of Marriage and the Family, 63*, 954–966.

Leman, P. J. (2005). Authority and moral reasons: Parenting style and children's perceptions of adult rule justifications. *International Journal of Behavioral Development, 29*, 265–270.

Claim 50

Marijuana use by adolescents causes long-term problems in brain and cognitive functioning.

Fifteen-year-old Elias Henderson confessed to his parents that he had been smoking marijuana regularly for a year. (Well, he didn't actually confess; his mother found his stash.) The Henderson parents were devastated and frightened by this revelation. Mrs. Henderson was in tears as she said to her husband, "I've just been reading about how marijuana permanently affects teenagers' brains. I had such great hopes for Elias! Does this mean he might not ever be able to go to college? His grades have been terrible the last few marking periods. Could it be that he's damaged his brain already?" Her husband didn't bring up the fact that he had smoked marijuana as a teenager himself, but he also thought it was probably a different situation because he had been 18 already at that time, and the marijuana available was not as potent as what can be bought today.

Were Elias's mother's fears justified? Does the evidence show that adolescent marijuana use causes permanent or at least long-lasting changes in mental ability?

Changes in social approval of marijuana use by adults can be expected to impact adolescent use as well as adult use. Significant changes in recent years are the legalization of marijuana sales in some states and decisions not to pursue charges against people holding small amounts in some cities. In addition, the approval and sale of marijuana for medical use has suggested not only that consumption is harmless but even that there are general health benefits to its use.

Although there are clinical studies of the usefulness of marijuana smoking for some conditions, these investigations have not included child or adolescent participants (Kazura, 2013). This means that there are no well-designed systematic studies of the effects of marijuana on adolescents, healthy or sick. Instead, current understanding of the results of adolescent marijuana use depends on two types of research. One type involves the use of animals, and although there may be interesting material to be found in this way, the well-known existence of species differences makes it difficult to know whether to generalize from a particular animal to human beings. In addition, although animals undergo puberty, they do not have a socially defined adolescence in the same sense that many human cultures do, and the development of their brains is limited in comparison to what humans experience.

A second type of research involves correlational or other nonrandomized studies, in which it is not possible to isolate factors that can cause outcomes. A factor like marijuana smoking tends to be confounded with other important factors that could cause good or bad cognitive changes. For example, adolescents who smoke marijuana are also more likely than others to use tobacco and alcohol. Because it's difficult to do the two things at the same time, adolescents who smoke marijuana may also study less and do less homework than others of their age. In addition, it's possible that adolescents who initiate marijuana use are already less competent cognitively or emotionally than those who do not, and their poor performance is the cause of the marijuana use, rather than the other way around. All this makes it difficult to know whether poor cognitive achievement following marijuana use was caused by the marijuana or came about for some other reason.

Because it's known that marijuana, like alcohol and other drugs, works by influencing the brain, an obvious question is how this influence works. Researchers who want to investigate this may use brain imaging techniques on human beings, but these do not answer questions about the chemical and functional changes in the brain that a drug may cause, or whether the changes were actually brought about by the drug. In one study with mice (Raver & Keller, 2014), the authors looked at cortical oscillations, patterns of neural network activity that are associated with cognitive processing. These oscillations are in the process of maturing during adolescence and mature around the time of puberty in mice. Exposure to cannabinoid compounds around puberty suppressed the development of the usual cortical oscillations, which were still absent in adulthood. Raver and Keller concluded that human adolescents might experience the same effect as a result of smoking marijuana.

What does research on human beings say about the permanence of brain and cognitive changes resulting from marijuana use during adolescence? One study (Jacobus et al., 2012) compared cerebral blood flow and cognitive abilities in a group of heavy marijuana users (adolescents with more than 200 marijuana use days) to a group of adolescents without marijuana use. There were differences between the groups at the beginning but not after 4 weeks of abstinence from marijuana confirmed by urine tests. In another study (Hooper, Woolley, & De Bellis, 2014), adolescent marijuana users who were abstaining from use were no different from comparison groups after 30 days of abstinence. They suggested that reports of long-term cognitive problems may have resulted from lingering drug effects, use of other drugs such as nicotine, cognitive problems that existed before marijuana use, or emotional disturbances.

Are there characteristics of adolescents that make them more likely to start marijuana use and also to show cognitive problems? These could have to do with culturally based beliefs and attitudes or with personal factors, including genetic makeup.

Keyes et al. (2011) published an analysis of attitudes about marijuana use in birth cohorts (groups born at about the same time) year by year, from 1976 to 2007. Members of each cohort were asked about their attitudes in 8th grade, in 10th grade, and in 12th grade. When a whole group was more disapproving of marijuana use, individuals were less likely to use it, even if their personal attitudes were approving. The important factor in encouraging or discouraging marijuana use seemed to be the attitudes of the birth cohort (i.e., peers of the adolescents surveyed) rather than the attitudes of the society as a whole. This study pointed to the effect on individual marijuana use of a subculture's attitudes.

However, individual characteristics have also been shown to help determine adolescents' marijuana use. Vaske (2013) examined a genetic factor that has been considered the "risky" genotype for some problem behaviors. She reported that adolescents who were homozygous for the genotype of concern *and* whose parents did not set a curfew for them were more likely than others to start marijuana use.

Most work on individual characteristics that are related to marijuana use has focused on events or experiences that seem to cause changes in use. But could there be individuals who are "preprogrammed" from an early age to be likely to begin marijuana use in adolescence? Sibley et al. (2014) followed a group of children diagnosed with ADHD in early childhood to age 18 and compared them with a matched non-ADHD group. The ADHD group smoked tobacco earlier, drank alcohol earlier, and used marijuana more frequently than the non-ADHD group; in addition, the ADHD individuals who initiated marijuana use were more likely to go on to heavy use. This longitudinal study indicated that differences between the heavy marijuana users and others in the study existed before marijuana use began.

Conclusion

Heavy marijuana use does not foster academic achievement in adolescents any more than heavy alcohol use would do. However, although a study of mice indicates long-term brain problems associated with marijuana use in adolescence, cognitive effects of marijuana use in human adolescents appear to disappear after a month of abstinence from the drug. When adolescents show cognitive problems after marijuana use, it's possible that those problems already existed and have simply become more obvious as schoolwork becomes more challenging. If Elias's parents can help him cut down or stop marijuana use, and if he can be helped to catch up with the academic work left undone over the previous months, it should be possible for him to recover cognitively and academically. However, if he has problems that predispose him to marijuana use, he will need treatment for those, too.

Critical Thinking

1. In the Raver and Keller (2014) paper, brain development of mice was studied, but they were not tested for their cognitive abilities. Use the Internet or other sources to find how such testing might have been done. Would cognitive testing of the mice strengthen the claim that the mouse results could be generalized to human beings? Why or why not?

2. Look at the paper by Vaske (2013). What was the source of Vaske's data? Use the Internet or other sources to describe the large study from which the data were drawn.

3. The Sibley et al. (2014) paper used a longitudinal design. What are the advantages of that design over other research designs, for studies seeking causes of behavior like marijuana use?

4. Use a child development textbook or other sources to find characteristics of ADHD. What connections may exist between those characteristics and marijuana or alcohol use?

5. If adolescents have a "risky" genotype, as described by Vaske (2013), what does this suggest about the genotypes of their parents and therefore about the probable behavior of some of the parents?

References

Hooper, S. R., Woolley, D., & De Bellis, M. D. (2014). Intellectual, neurocognitive, and academic achievement in abstinent adolescents with cannabis use disorder. *Psychopharmacology, 231,* 1467–1477.

Jacobus, J., Goldenberg, D., Wierenga, C. E., Tolentino, N. J., Liu, T. T., & Tapert, S. F. (2012). Altered cerebral blood flow and neurocognitive correlates in adolescent cannabis users. *Psychopharmacology, 222,* 675–684.

Kazura, A. (2013). Medical marijuana laws and teens. *Brown University Child and Adolescent Behavior Letter, 29*(4), 8.

Keyes, K. M., Schulenberg, J. E., O'Malley, P. M., Johnston, L. D., Bachman, J. G., Li, G., & Hasin, D. (2011). The social norms of birth cohorts and adolescent marijuana use in the United States, 1976–2007. *Addiction, 106,* 1790–1800.

Raver, S. M., & Keller, A. (2014). Permanent suppression of cortical oscillations in mice after adolescent exposure to cannabinoids: Receptor mechanisms. *Neuropharmacology, 86,* 161–173.

Sibley, M. H., Pelham, W. E., Molina, B. S. G., Coxe, S., Kipp, H., Gnagy, E., . . . Lahey, B. B. (2014). The role of early childhood ADHD and subsequent CD in the initiation and escalation of adolescent cigarette, alcohol, and marijuana use. *Journal of Abnormal Psychology, 123,* 362–374.

Vaske, J. (2013). Interaction of the TaqIA polymorphism and poor parental socialization on changes in adolescent marijuana use. *Substance Use & Misuse, 48,* 258–264.

Claim 51

High self-esteem makes children perform better in school.

Fourteen-year-old Eric was not doing very well in his ninth-grade algebra class. Eric's mother met with his teacher to discuss how to encourage him to do better work. "He seems so depressed and withdrawn sometimes," his mother told the teacher. "I don't think he has much self-esteem, and that's probably the problem with his schoolwork." Eric's teacher agreed, and they planned a program to help increase Eric's self-esteem. The teacher had "try again" stickers to place on work that Eric failed and "congratulations" stickers on work that showed effort. Eric's mother said that she would take Eric somewhere he would like to go every weekend and tell him what a special person he was. They discussed the possibility of hiring a math tutor for Eric but decided extra work on the subject would just lower his self-esteem even further because it would call attention to his poor school performance.

Were Eric's mother and teacher right to assume that low self-esteem caused his poor schoolwork and that their plans will raise both self-esteem and algebra grades?

Gold stars, Student of the Month awards, and the oft-repeated refrain "good job!" are outgrowths of a national concern with self-esteem and the belief that raising self-esteem raises performance. Research reports have contradicted this view (Baumeister, Campbell, Krueger, & Vohs, 2005), although some authors maintain that raising self-esteem is important in itself.

Despite research evidence to the contrary, the conviction that raising children's self-esteem raises their academic and extracurricular performance has created a self-esteem industry focused on methods and materials for increasing the sense of self-worth (Humphrey, 2004). Why, after all, should teachers and parents drill children on multiplication tables if making the children feel better about themselves will provide the motivation to work? Although this approach to solving children's problems has some logic, the possibility of finding supportive research evidence depends on researchers' ability to measure both performance and self-esteem.

In considering the effects of self-esteem on academic performance or sports or social activity, the first problem is to decide how to measure an individual's assessment of himself or herself. As is the problem for so many aspects of psychology, researchers cannot get inside people's heads and directly examine their experiences, nor can researchers necessarily estimate from observed behavior what is felt about the self because people, even school-age children, have learned to behave in socially approved ways.

Measures of self-esteem are indirect and usually involve asking individuals to agree or disagree with statements about the self. For example, in one self-esteem scale for children (Battle, 2003), individuals are asked to say whether they agree with certain statements, such as "Most boys and girls are better at doing things than I am"; "My parents make me feel that I am not good enough"; and "Boys and girls like to play with me." These statements seem to be related to self-esteem as people usually think of it. Unfortunately, this kind of measurement is problematic: Both children and adults might shape their answers in the direction of social desirability. Rather than respond in a way that reveals their true feelings, participants may provide answers expected of a "good" person. In fact, children with low self-esteem are probably more likely to bolster their reported thoughts about themselves and to try to claim that they are "better" than they think they are. However, measures of self-esteem have consistent associations with some objective measures (e.g., school grades), so the self-esteem measures seem to be assessing something, although it might not be self-esteem.

There appears to be a correlation between high school academic achievement and measures of self-esteem, with higher self-esteem accompanying higher marks. But, as is usual with correlational studies, readers need to ask the following questions: Which factor causes, and which is caused? Do teenagers feel highly motivated to study and achieve because they think well of themselves? Or, alternatively, do they think well of themselves because of a long history of high achievement? Or do other additional factors, such as parents' education, ability to model confidence, and support for school success, influence both self-esteem and academic work?

The belief that high self-esteem causes high academic performance has been associated with practices such as social promotion and grading policies that focus more on effort or social cooperation than on objective achievement. These well-intentioned efforts may help some children through the occasional period of academic difficulty, but they probably do not have positive effects on self-esteem or later school performance. After the first school years, children are aware of their own performance and accurately assess whether it is better, worse, or about the same as that of their classmates. To the extent that self-esteem is influenced by school, children's feelings of self-worth are likely to alter with their actual sense of achievement. Undeserved passing grades may be a relief but will probably not communicate to most children that they have done well and can feed into the belief that a good grade is given "because the teacher likes me." This type of grading may communicate to children that adults are unpredictable and also poor judges of performance or that grading is concerned with personal charm rather than ability combined with effort. Unearned grades, promotion, and excessive rewards or praise also can make children feel that they are worse in school than they previously thought; otherwise, they would not be receiving unusual treatment.

Can a reward system of the type planned by Eric's mother and teacher affect his school achievement? Behavior can be changed by rewards, whether self-esteem is affected or not. However, with this approach, behavior change occurs only through effective planning and management of the plan. The individual must want the reward, and it is doubtful that Eric, a ninth-grader, wants stickers on a paper. Rewards must be reserved for desirable behaviors, such as completing a homework problem, not distributed in ways unrelated to the behavior changes that can help school performance. To give rewards appropriately, adults must be attentive to the child's behavior and observe carefully whether desirable actions are occurring. Paradoxically, minimum rewards are most effective, and over time more performance should be required before a reward is given—perhaps two homework problems rather than one, then three, and so on. This use of reward, or *operant conditioning*, assumes that the adults know which behaviors need to be increased in frequency to improve school performance and that the child can do what is wanted. If it is not clear what the child needs to do to improve, or if the child is not capable of the action, reward is not an effective way to improve academic achievement. It seems unlikely that the reward in Eric's case will make a difference: His mother and teacher do not know what he can do and what he cannot—nor are they planning to reward actual achievement.

Another consideration about Eric involves his mood. His mother said he was sad and depressed often, but rather than considering those problems alone, she moved quickly to what they meant for his self-esteem. Children and teenagers can be depressed, just as adults can, and it is possible Eric's depression is linked to his present lack of academic achievement (Grimm, 2007).

Finally, the "positive psychology" movement has led to some work focusing on self-esteem and its relationship to academic success. Froh et al. (2010) reported correlations among positive views of the self, absorption in tasks, concern with the needs of others, and academic achievement of adolescents. However, it may be no simple matter for adults to manipulate teenagers' beliefs about themselves or their ability to become engaged with work; in one study (Wood, Perunovic, & Lee, 2009), being told to make positive statements about oneself had positive outcomes for some people, but for those who were depressed or pessimistic, the practice worsened their moods.

Conclusion

Although self-esteem measures and academic achievement are positively correlated, it is not clear that one causes the other. Neither is it clear that reward programs, including unearned high grades, cause an increase in self-esteem, although appropriate use of reward may cause improved academic work. Eric's mother and teacher mean well, but their plan will probably not improve either Eric's mood or his schoolwork. Tutoring for his academic weakness and consideration of a possible mood disorder might be more effective ways to help him.

Critical Thinking

1. Discuss factors that can influence measures of self-esteem and also affect school performance. Explain your answer, using evidence from a child development textbook for support.

2. Search the Internet to find a program that claims to raise children's self-esteem. What does the program recommend as a way to raise self-esteem? What evidence is given to support this claim? What is the cost of the program and materials, such as books and videotapes?

3. If you were designing a quasi-experimental study to compare school performance of children with high self-esteem scores versus children with low self-esteem scores, what confounded variables would you consider? Keep in mind characteristics of home and school environments as well

(Continued)

(Continued)

as characteristics of the children. What does Battle (2003) say about cultural issues in the measurement of self-esteem? (If you cannot find Battle's book, you may be able to find a useful summary or review of the work.)

4. Read the article by Baumeister et al. (2005). What evidence in the article suggests that there might be advantages to lower self-esteem rather than to higher? Explain your answer.

5. In a child development textbook, read about activities during the high school years. Explain whether school performance is an important factor in determining self-esteem in most adolescents. Does your textbook discuss this issue in terms of "positive psychology"?

References

Battle, J. (2003). *Culture-free self-esteem inventories: Manual.* Austin, TX: Pro-Ed.

Baumeister, R. F., Campbell, J. D., Krueger, J. I., & Vohs, K. D. (2005). Exploding the self-esteem myth. *Scientific American Mind, 16*(4), 50–57.

Froh, J. V., Kashdan, T. B., Yurkewicz, C., Fan, J., Allan, J., & Glowacki, J. (2010). The benefits of passion and absorption in activities: Engaged living in adolescents and its role in psychological well-being. *Journal of Positive Psychology, 5,* 311–332.

Grimm, K. J. (2007). Multivariate longitudinal methods for studying developmental relationships between depression and academic achievement. *International Journal of Behavioral Development, 31,* 328–339.

Humphrey, N. (2004). The death of the feel-good factor? Self-esteem in the educational context. *School Psychology International, 25,* 347–360.

Wood, J. V., Perunovic, W. Q. E., & Lee, J. W. (2009). Positive self-statements: Power for some, peril for others. *Psychological Science, 20,* 860–866.

Claim 52

Single-sex schools give better outcomes of academic achievement than do coeducational schools.

Annie was complaining to her mother about her high school chemistry class. "It's just awful," she said. " The teacher never calls on girls because the boys just shout out all the time. I used to think I wanted to be a scientist, but I give up—it's just so boring when you never get called on, and I just stop paying attention after a while. That's why my grades haven't been so good." When Annie's mother passed these remarks on to their next-door neighbor, the neighbor burst out laughing. "Ha! You should hear what my Sean says about that class! He says the girls are all the teacher's pets, and they stay so quiet it gets on his nerves to have them there. That's why *he* isn't doing so well!" The mothers thought their kids' excuses were funny, but they also wondered whether there was a serious concern here. Annie's mother had read that single-sex schools might have real advantages for both boys and girls, letting each gender learn in the way that worked best. It seemed like too much to ask for a whole boys' school or girls' school, but they wondered whether some classes might be taught best to a single-sex group.

Is single-sex education the best approach for teenagers?

Teenage boys and girls are very different from each other in more than the obvious way. The timing of their arrival at puberty averages about two years earlier for girls than for boys. The earlier-maturing girls remain shorter and lighter than the later-maturing boys, and their differences make for diverse experiences of social attitudes, sports, and family life. But whether they have different academic needs and basic abilities remains so difficult to document that one review article has referred to much of the work on this subject as "pseudoscience" (Halpern et al., 2011).

Single-sex education was a tradition for centuries, in part because girls rarely received much in the way of schooling. Mandatory elementary education, beginning in the 19th century, provided for girls and boys both, together or separately. Meanwhile, elite private schools and colleges in the United States, like the British "public school," retained the single-sex approach until the 1970s, when most of them moved to the coeducational plan preferred by their students. In the 1990s, documents like a report by the American Association of University Women, called attention to difficulties girls experienced in negotiating the coeducational system; a few years later, the focus shifted to boys with *Why Gender Matters* (Sax, 2005).

What does the research evidence tell us about the effects of single-sex education in modern times? The answer to this depends on the topic under investigation. A large proportion of published articles about single-sex education stress issues like sex-role stereotyping or the satisfaction of teachers and of students with their experiences, not academic achievement Allan, 2009; Williams, 2010). A review by the United States Department of Education (2005) found that a comparison of achievement in single-sex and coeducational schools was "equivocal."

Research on academic outcomes of single-sex schooling is often plagued with confounded variables. Generally, students at single-sex schools or in single-sex classes within a coeducational school have chosen that form of education because they or their parents think it is preferable. Students in coeducational settings are more likely to have taken the default option simply by failing to apply to single-sex programs. Teachers, although probably less likely to be able to choose their program, may in some cases have actively sought to teach in a single-sex setting. This suggests that students in self-chosen single-sex programs may be more aware of schooling issues and more concerned with their own academic success than other students who have remained in coeducational programs because they made no choice. These self-placed students would be more likely than others to do well academically—but the reason would have to do with their own motivation and existing academic skills, not with the effects of single-sex or coeducational schooling.

Although it would be possible to randomly assign students (and teachers) to single-sex or to coeducational settings, and such a design would remove some confounding factors, there are both ethical and practical barriers to doing this. Students in public schools are recipients of educational services provided by the community, and are not required to participate in research projects. If asked to participate in research, students and their parents would have to provide documentation of their informed consent before they could be enrolled in a project. Those who did not give consent could not ethically be included in a randomization procedure, nor could their academic achievement be included in the analysis of data from the project. There are similar problems from a practical point of view. Because families must send their children to their local district schools, or pay a hefty tuition to a private school or another public school district, families who relocate will usually remove their children from the school in which they may have been participating in a research program, thus changing the makeup of a treatment or comparison group. Charter schools or magnet schools may require children to meet admissions standards and may encourage them to transfer out if they do not do well—again altering the composition of the group.

As a result of the confounded variables just mentioned, it is often difficult to draw conclusions from studies of single-sex schooling and its effect on academic achievement. This problem is worsened by the frequent failure of educational researchers to clarify whether single-sex and coeducational groups were established by their own choices, randomized by the researchers, or chosen in some other way (for example, see Hoffman, Badgett, & Parker, 2008). No amount of advanced statistical analysis can remove the problems created when groups are different in some way before the intervention—in this case, the schooling plan—has even begun.

Arguments in favor of single-sex schooling have tended to focus on the belief that boys and girls learn differently (i.e., require different kinds of schooling experiences) because their brains and other parts of the nervous system function differently in academic and other tasks. To come to this conclusion legitimately would require research to show *both* (1) that there are substantial differences between male and female brains, and (2) that boys and girls reach their highest academic achievements when each is instructed in a gender-oriented way, and each gender does much less well when instructed in the way that works best for the other gender. Unfortunately, single-sex schooling proponents like Sax (2005) have concentrated on sex-related brain differences, but have neglected to establish evidence that boys and girls each do their best when their instruction follows gender-determined lines. It is known that boys have a larger brain volume than girls and that girls complete brain development on a different schedule from boys, but these differences are not clearly related to learning or instructional issues. Even if there were clear and relevant differences in male and female brain structure and function, this in itself would not explain learning or indicate instructional needs, any more than the differences between left-handed and right-handed individuals indicate that they need to be taught in different ways.

Conclusion

Single-sex education has not been demonstrated to lead to better academic achievement than coeducation. The research on this topic has been weak, and studies of sex differences in brain structure and function have not been acceptable substitutes for high-quality work on outcomes of schooling arrangements.

Critical Thinking

1. The comments on single-sex schooling by Halpern et al. (2011) attribute some apparent successes of single-sex education to the "Hawthorne effect." What is this effect, and what has the psychologist Scott Lilienfeld pointed out about it? How does this information affect the conclusions of the Halpern article?

2. Use the Internet or other sources to locate 10 articles discussing single-sex education. What proportion of the articles is concerned with academic achievement? What other concerns are presented?

3. Which problems discussed with respect to comparing single-sex and coeducational schooling are also relevant to comparisons of religious schools with public schools, or charter schools with ordinary public schools? Explain.

4. Some arguments in favor of single-sex schools seem to be similar to the idea of "learning styles." Use the Internet and other sources to find what instructional methods are claimed to be suitable for boys, for girls, and for students with different "learning styles." What kind of evidence would be needed to support the claim that different people need different forms of instruction?

5. What is the "genetic fallacy"? How does it apply to claims made about single-sex education, particularly about the use of information from brain research to support single-sex or coeducational education?

References

Allan, A .J. (2009). The importance of being a "lady": Hyper-femininity and heterosexuality in the private, single-sex primary school. *Gender & Education, 21*, 145–158.

Halpern, D. F., Eliot, L., Bigler, R. S., Fabes, R. A., Hanish, L. D., Hyde, J., Liben, L. S., & Martin, C. L. (2011). The pseudoscience of single-sex schooling. *Science, 333*, 1706–1707.

Hoffman, B. H., Badgett, B. A., & Parker, R. P. (2008). The effect of single-sex instruction in a large, urban, at-risk high school. *Journal of Educational Research, 102*, 15–36.

Sax, L. (2005). *Why gender matters.* New York: Doubleday.

United States Department of Education (2005). Single-sex versus coeducation schooling: A systematic review. Retrieved from www2.ed.gov/rschstat/eval/other/single-sex/index.html

Williams, J. A. (2010). Learning differences: Sex-role stereotyping in single-sex public education. *Harvard Journal of Law and Gender, 33*, 555–579.

Claim 53

The DARE program is an effective way to prevent children and adolescents from dealing or using drugs.

The Riverside town council and the town's high school principal were discussing the problem of drug dealing and use among teenagers. Although drug use was not blatant in Riverside, many people worried enough about it to try to prevent any increase. "We need to think of the future," commented the principal. "It makes no sense to try to fix a problem after it's started. Preventive measures are the way to go, and there are good antidrug programs out there. I think it would be worth the money to buy one." The Riverside chief of police, who was on the council, agreed. "Let's get the DARE program," he suggested. "I think it's great the way they have police officers go to the schools. The men enjoy it, and they get to know the kids. What's more, I saw on the DARE website that the program really works." The other members of the group agreed. They liked the idea of a positive interaction between police officers and teenagers.

What does the evidence say, though? Was the council right in thinking that DARE is an effective program?

DARE (Drug Abuse Resistance Education) is a program conducted in schools by police officers for the purpose of preventing children's use of recreational drugs and other harmful behaviors associated with drugs.

The program is widely advertised through bumper stickers and other public announcements. An extensive website (www.dare.com) includes claims that "DARE works." Yet some research provided no more than weak support for the DARE program, and some studies indicated worse outcomes for children who participated in the DARE program than for children who didn't.

It appears that the claim that DARE effectively reduces drug use is not only a myth but a myth supported and advertised by governmental and private organizations. Analysis of the DARE myth provides a valuable example for understanding the rare but important phenomenon of publicly advocated erroneous beliefs about child development.

An analysis of the program should begin with some of DARE's own claims. An assessment on the DARE website as evidence for the effectiveness of DARE shows a serious conceptual difficulty. The DARE site includes two stated goals: to provide children with information that will change their belief that "everyone is doing drugs" and to provide them with social skills that will help them refuse to use or sell drugs. Achievement of these goals can be measured by comparing information gathered from children who have completed the program and children who have not participated in the program. The evaluation DARE offers as "proof," however, involved a survey of parents, teachers, and principals, with their ratings of the DARE program and the extent to which it effectively prevents drug use. Tests of students' attitudes were also performed before and after DARE exposure, but the website does not report whether attitude changes occurred. Actual drug use was not measured, although of course there are many reasons why this would be difficult to do.

Pre- and post-testing (testing before and after a treatment or lesson) is usually a poor way to collect information about children and adolescents because an important variable, *maturation,* becomes confounded with the treatment. Children age, and as they become older, they change. The longer the time period involved in the research, the more natural maturational change is expected; consequently, researchers cannot easily determine whether a change was caused by maturation or by an intervention such as DARE. The only way to understand the effect of the intervention is to use a comparison (control) group of students who did not experience the intervention. The amount of change seen in the comparison group is compared to the amount of change in the treatment group (i.e., those who attended DARE presentations). Any difference between the two measured changes may have been caused by the treatment, provided that the two groups are similar in other characteristics.

One difficulty in evaluating a program like DARE, which is taught in many different schools by hundreds or thousands of police officers, is the possibility that the program alters over time or that different versions are used by different instructors. Such possible changes or variations in the program are unidentified confounding variables that can interfere with interpretation of evidence about effectiveness.

Even if an intervention program were clearly shown to be effective in one study, repeated assessments would be wise because the program—or the children participating in it—might change in meaningful ways. According to the DARE website, a new assessment program is in progress. This program employs random assignment of schools either to the DARE program or to a drug education program already in use at a school. This design is much better than the pre- and post-test design mentioned earlier, but some of schools in the evaluation used existing curricula that were very similar to the DARE program, making it difficult to interpret any differences in outcome.

A difficult design issue involves *blinding* problems. For an objective assessment of the effects of a program, it would be best that children, parents, and teachers did not know which program was used. If they know, their attitudes and expectations can affect the outcome of the treatment. But of course it is impossible to prevent everyone in the school from identifying the program in use. In fact, the whole community may know, if the well-known DARE bumper stickers begin to appear on local cars. (Other drug prevention programs do not seem to use this ploy as often.)

In a progress report on the DARE website, the researchers carrying out this new evaluation noted two factors that may be challenges to their interpretation of the data: Police officers were reported to use the appropriate instructional method considerably less than 100% of the time, introducing an additional confounding variable, and several New Orleans schools participating in the study were so badly affected by Hurricane Katrina in 2005 that they had to drop out of the study after having participated for four years, making a complete data analysis impossible.

Studies comparing DARE and other drug education programs have used a technique called *meta-analysis*, a statistical procedure that takes many small studies and combines them in a way that allows better identification of causes and effects. One meta-analysis found that the DARE program's lecture format was significantly less effective than other programs' use of interactive, peer-oriented discussion techniques (Tobler & Stratton, 1997). The DARE program currently being evaluated includes discussion groups and role-play methods that add an interactive component; thus, this new version of DARE may be more effective than the earlier one.

Programs like DARE were originally put together in ways that agreed with the assumptions and convenience of police officers and other sponsors. In recent years, however, these programs have been evaluated by the standards of *evidence-based treatment* (EBT). EBT criteria are stringent requirements for detailed analysis of data and for research designs, including factors such as randomization and comparison to standard treatment (Gandhi, Murphy-Graham, Petrosino, Chrismer, & Weiss, 2007; Petrosino,

2003). It is not surprising that high-powered assessments are sometimes in disagreement with the views of police officers who are involved with the DARE program and feel the experience is positive.

Conclusion

As of 2007, published research on the DARE program did not demonstrate that DARE effectively prevented child and adolescent drug use. However, the new program, still in the process of evaluation, includes new methods that have been shown to have good results. The Riverside town council should consider a variety of programs and review the independent research evidence about them, rather than accepting what program advocates advertise.

Critical Thinking

1. Examine the DARE website, particularly the posted research reports. How do the methods and conclusions of those reports compare with the comments in this section? Have there been changes over time?

2. In a child development textbook, find information about cognitive and social development in adolescence. List the reasons why an interactive, peer-oriented program might be more effective than a lecture program. What do Tobler and Stratton (1997) say about this issue?

3. What might be the effect of a drug prevention program on children's responsiveness if they and their families frequently see program advertising, such as the DARE bumper stickers? Is advertising a potential confounding variable? Explain your answer, using the concept of *confirmation bias* (which you can find defined in Internet or other sources).

4. Read in a child development textbook about adolescent cognitive and emotional development. Explain the advantages and disadvantages of asking adolescents to indicate the frequency and extent of their drug use on a survey form. What factors might make this information less than accurate?

5. Read about cognitive and social development in a child development textbook. Describe the amount of change expected of children between 7th and 12th grade, even in the absence of a program such as DARE. Be specific about the kinds of changes that occur and how they might affect attitudes toward drugs. How can these changes be considered and kept from interfering with the assessment of DARE or similar programs? List any relevant research design issues.

References

Gandhi, A. G., Murphy-Graham, E., Petrosino, A., Chrismer, S. S., & Weiss, C. H. (2007). The devil is in the details: Examining the evidence for "proven" school-based drug abuse prevention programs. *Evaluation Review, 31*, 43–74.

Petrosino, A. (2003). Standards for evidence and evidence for standards: The case of school-based drug prevention. *Annals of the American Academy of Political and Social Science, 587*, 180–207.

Tobler, N., & Stratton, H. (1997). Effectiveness of school-based drug prevention programs: A meta-analysis of the research. *Journal of Primary Prevention, 18*(1), 71–128.

Claim 54

Children and adolescents learn bad behavior from their peers.

Sixteen-year-old Wanda used the "F word" in front of her grandmother and grandfather and didn't apologize or even look embarrassed. When her mother, Lisa, reprimanded her, Wanda just rolled her eyes and muttered, "Get a life!" Later, Lisa tried to smooth over the incident that had offended her parents. "She's really a good girl," Lisa explained. "She never used to talk like that, but when we moved here she started running with some bad kids, almost delinquents, I guess you'd call them. They apply a lot of peer pressure and get Wanda to misbehave. She stays out too late, and I think she's even skipped school some days. I just wish she'd make some nicer friends and get a better attitude."

Was Lisa right? If Wanda decided to befriend classmates who were not antiso-cial, would the result be more appropriate behavior from Wanda?

Most children and adolescents manage to learn from their friends some behaviors that adults don't like. For preschoolers, these behaviors might include spitting and calling people "poopy face"; for older children and adolescents, the behaviors might be gross jokes, swearing (or saying words close to swear words), and efforts to go to R-rated movies. But what about really bad behavior, such as stealing, drug and alcohol use, and extended school truancy? Are these learned from bad companions?

School-age children and adolescents who commit crimes (or status offenses that bring them into the juvenile justice system) often have friends who show similar behaviors; they are less often associated with well-behaved peers. It seems reasonable to assume that a child who is in trouble "fell in with" undesirable companions by chance, then copied their behavior, becoming delinquent as a result of exposure to delinquent society. Some might also assume that if the same child had made friends with a socially appropriate group, the child would not have become delinquent.

Obviously, a child who associates with delinquent friends can learn from them some new techniques of robbery, fighting, or drug use. Delinquent peers may also encourage antisocial behavior in members of their group by threatening to exclude them if they do not participate. Younger group members may be required to commit antisocial acts that benefit older ones, with the argument that the younger children will not receive serious penalties if caught, but the older ones will. Delinquent groups can also be rewarding to their members, admiring them for daring acts and emphasizing their contempt for conventional behavior, although some research suggested that members are only indirectly rewarded for their actions (Rebellon, 2006). Such groups offer role models and acceptance to adolescents who are struggling to find an identity and who fail to find one in school or other conventional activities.

However, the idea that learning from a delinquent group is the main factor in becoming antisocial assumes that the individual was equally ready to go in either a "good" or a "bad" direction. According to this view, the child was pushed toward delinquent attitudes and behavior by a chance association with delinquent peers. Is this a possibility? Can any child who enters a delinquent group adopt and commit to the views and actions typical of delinquents?

It appears that children who become delinquents had some undesirable characteristics before they began to associate with delinquent peers. Their impulsive, aggressive, antisocial behavior causes them to be rejected by nondelinquent children. Delinquent children and adolescents, on the other hand, may have no objection to antisocial acts and may in fact admire bold, aggressive, unconventional behavior. For this reason, an alternative interpretation of the association of delinquents with other delinquents is that an antisocial person seeks out similar peers, rather than learning bad behavior through an accidental association.

Why is it that antisocial children leave the rejecting group rather than try to fit in with well-behaved peers? Most school-age children and adolescents receive some criticism and rejection from peers (who may not be very subtle) as well as from teachers (who may use sarcasm and public ridicule in their efforts to change child behavior). Most of these children stay with the conventional group and try to comply, rather than approach and enter a delinquent group. Those children and teenagers who are effectively driven away by rejection may receive an unusually high level of criticism. However, they also may be *rejection-sensitive* people who interpret even ambiguous responses as evidence of intentional rejection. These individuals feel rejected as a result of behavior or speech that would be dismissed as unimportant by most people. Rejection-sensitive adolescents become increasingly disruptive in school and have more absences and suspensions than other teenagers. Their lack of school involvement, or even attendance, frees them from supervision, making it easier for them to engage in antisocial acts (Downey, Lebolt, Rincon, & Freitas, 1998). Experimental work with preadolescents reported a predictable connection between the experience of rejection and the tendency toward antisocial behavior (Nesdale & Lambert, 2007).

A complex outcome such as delinquency is not likely to be caused by a single factor, so it is wise to look beyond peer relationships for causes of antisocial behavior. One such cause appears to be the children's beliefs about their parents' antisocial behavior, such as substance abuse or reckless driving. Children who are not aware of a parent's actions are not in a position to model the parent's behavior, so the children's perceptions of the parent are more important than the parent's actual behavior, at least in research on two-parent families. Children who believe their parents behave antisocially are more likely to do so themselves. As a result, they are more likely to be rejected by conventionally behaved children and accepted by antisocial groups (Dogan, Conger, Kim, & Masyn, 2007).

The similarities between antisocial parents and antisocial children suggest a genetic factor and a learning factor as causes of delinquency. A study of behavior genetics did not report a specific gene or genes that determine delinquency, but a more general tendency toward impulsiveness and irritability may have a genetic cause. Familial tendencies toward alcoholism and antisocial behavior seem to involve some genetic factors (Harden et al., 2007). A biological parent who has a genetic makeup that causes impulsiveness and aggressive behavior (e.g., fragile X syndrome) may pass this genetic material to a child, who will then have an underlying tendency toward antisocial behavior, whether or not the child remains in the custody of that parent. Of course, the impact on the child may be increased if both parents are genetically inclined toward antisocial behavior and if the child lives with them or with other antisocial adults.

Conclusion

Although children may learn undesirable behavior from a delinquent peer group, this learning is only one of many factors that lead to delinquency. Rejection by conventional social groups is an important issue. Lisa should not assume that Wanda can choose to make well-behaved friends because that group may have rejected her previously. It is likely that Wanda has some characteristics that make her acceptable to a delinquent group, and those characteristics may include her family experiences and her genetic makeup.

Critical Thinking

1. In the research reported by Nesdale and Lambert (2007), 8- and 10-year-old children were unhappy and felt impulses toward antisocial behavior when they experienced apparent rejection in a controlled experimental setting. Discuss how these children might be cognitively different from teenagers and whether you would expect teenagers to respond similarly in an experiment. Use information from the article and from a child development textbook as support for your answer.

2. Consider the use of school suspension to change children's behavior. Would you expect suspension to make undesirable behavior more or less likely? Use information from this section and from a child development textbook to form your answer.

3. Read the article by Dogan et al. (2007). What were the characteristics of the families they studied? Did these characteristics limit the extent of the parents' antisocial behavior? Explain your answer.

4. After reading the Downey et al. (1998) article, describe a possible ambiguous situation that a rejection-sensitive child might incorrectly interpret as intentional rejection. Explain your answer.

5. Use information from this section and Downey et al. (1998) to describe methods teachers might use to help an adolescent avoid a sense of rejection.

References

Dogan, S. J., Conger, R. D., Kim, K. J., & Masyn, K. E. (2007). Cognitive and parenting pathways in the transmission of antisocial behavior from parents to adolescents. *Child Development, 78*(1), 335–349.

Downey, G., Lebolt, A., Rincon, C., & Freitas, A. L. (1998). Rejection sensitivity and children's interpersonal difficulties. *Child Development, 69,* 1072–1089.

Harden, K. P., Turkheimer, E., Emory, R. E., D'Onofrio, B. M., Slutske, W. S., Heath, A. C., & Martin, N. G. (2007). Marital conflict and conduct problems in children of twins. *Child Development, 78*(1), 1–18.

Nesdale, D., & Lambert, A. (2007). Effects of experimentally manipulated peer rejection on children's negative affect, self-esteem, and maladaptive social behavior. *International Journal of Behavioral Development, 31,* 115–122.

Rebellon, C. J. (2006). Do adolescents engage in delinquency to attract the social attention of peers? An extension and longitudinal test of the social reinforcement hypothesis. *Journal of Research in Crime and Delinquency, 43,* 387–411.

Claim 55

Young teenagers should be tried and sentenced as adults if they commit serious crimes.

Seventeen-year-old Ali and his parents were discussing at the dinner table a news story about a 13-year-old who had stomped a younger child to death during a "game." Ali felt the boy should be tried as an adult, not adjudicated in juvenile court. "Thirteen is plenty old enough to know right from wrong," he commented. "Besides, if other kids see that he gets off easy after doing this, they'll figure they can do the same thing if they feel like it." Ali's parents were not so sure. His mother felt that people might make the decision to try the boy as an adult simply because they were upset and angry and felt that someone ought to be punished, rather than for any better reason. Ali's father thought that juvenile courts served a good function: Because young teenagers' thinking is not fully developed, the boy who had killed should not be treated as an adult.

Who is right?

The question of the right reaction to serious juvenile crime is not just theoretical. At the time of this writing, it is estimated that 73 people are serving life sentences without possibility of parole for crimes committed in early adolescence. What is the right action to take in these cases? Can child development research answer this question?

One consideration is whether all the needed, relevant research exists. Of course there are many studies of thought patterns and emotional responsiveness in adolescence and the early adult years. However, there are still limits on empirical knowledge of the results of different actions taken against juvenile offenders. How are the outcomes different if young people are treated as adults rather than juveniles? Surprisingly—considering how ready people are to draw conclusions on this subject—there is relatively little empirical work on the effects of different treatments (Redding, 2003).

When trying to deal with this difficult, conflicted question, the first step must be to try to understand what is being asked. The most important word involving juvenile offenders is *should*. There are many kinds of *should*, and not all of them can be dealt with through information about child development. Which *should* is being considered here? One possibility is that this is a moral *should*, one that considers how justice can be done. For example, a person focusing on justice might argue that justice demands that anyone who takes a human life must have his or her own life taken in retribution. Or, alternatively, a moral view might state that people older than a specific age are properly treated in one way, people under that age in another. Although psychology and the study of child development can provide information on the ways people think about justice, research studies have nothing to say about moral truths.

Some kinds of moral *should* involve the idea that justice treats some people differently from others. Mentally retarded adults, and, more rarely, mentally ill adults may correctly receive different treatment from others, according to this belief. For questions involving this kind of *should*, the issue about the young teenager may be whether the person's abilities are similar to those of an older person who receives special treatment or whether they are more like those of an adult who receives the full punishment allowed by the law. The study of child development can provide information relevant to the second part of this idea—not the moral issue of how justice is done but the question about similarities between young teenagers and specific others. These similarities can be identified through empirical research.

Another type of *should* involves the best outcome for the community. What type of treatment of the young killer would yield the greatest safety and comfort for other community members? If the young person were adjudicated in the juvenile court, would his later behavior be better or worse than if he were tried and sentenced as an adult? Does one of these treatments make this individual less likely to kill again? And does the example set by the treatment make other young teenagers more or less likely to kill? Are the others deterred from violent acts or encouraged to follow their aggressive impulses? In theory, it is possible for empirical research to provide answers to these questions, but in practice it is quite difficult, in part because there are so few events to study (Redding, 2003).

Finally, *should* statements may involve consideration of the best outcome for the young killer. What if we want to provide the best opportunity for this person to recover from what has happened and regain a healthy developmental trajectory, growing into an adult who can develop his best talents? Is this outcome more likely to occur if the young person goes to juvenile court and receives the intervention considered appropriate there, or is it more likely to occur if adult treatment is meted out? Again, these questions have the potential for empirical answers, but because the events are infrequent the practical aspects of such research are challenging (Liptak, 2007). Questions involving types of moral *should* cannot be answered through research. Even questions about the effects of different treatments on the individual and the community are extremely difficult to deal with for a variety of practical reasons, such as frequency of events. (There is some work that looks at the effects of treatments, however; see Eddy, Whaley, & Chamberlain, 2004.) Can the study of child development offer anything of use to this issue? The most valuable information available is probably that pertaining to comparisons between young teenagers and adults. This information can at least tell whether there are substantial differences between the mental lives of teenagers and those of the older people, whom the law considers completely responsible for their own actions.

One important contribution of child development work is information about adolescents' cognitive abilities as they compare to those of adults. This comparison is not as simple as it appears to be, however, because stages of cognitive development are not perfectly linked to chronological age. Although it is possible to describe cognitive characteristics that are typical of a particular age group (Packard, 2007), there are large individual differences, and an individual may not display exactly the same cognitive patterns as his or her age-mates.

Generally, people in their early teens show some of the performance characteristics of *formal operational thought*, but they do not necessarily have abilities equivalent to those of well-developed adults. They are able to hypothesize possible outcomes of an action, but they are more likely than adults to expect the "ideal" outcome out of all the possibilities. Teenagers usually have less experience than adults and may not be able to bring as much information into their decision making. The adolescent criminal might be expected to have a good deal of ability to predict the outcome of an act, but the individual's lack of knowledge and other cognitive immaturity may foster a decision to carry out a serious crime.

The teenager's cognitive ability, although of much interest for this topic, may not be as important as emotional and behavioral factors. Although an adolescent, like an adult, might make a reasoned decision about committing a robbery, murders and rapes are more likely to occur without planning and as circumstances arise. Whether these crimes occur might depend more on emotional characteristics than on the ability to use formal operational thought. The young perpetrator may be drawn into a crime by emotional reactions to the behavior of other people, which the adolescent feels must be addressed—for example, behavior that the individual perceives as disrespectful (Lewis, 1992).

An important cognitive issue has to do with the adolescent's ability to understand police and legal procedures, including the *Miranda* warning that assures individuals of the right to legal counsel and the availability of free legal assistance. Many defendants of all ages misunderstand these rights and believe that they simply have a choice between talking and not talking or think that if they fail to talk this fact will be held against them at their trial. Others believe that there are limits to evidence the police can bring—for example, that the police cannot accuse them of fictitious crimes. In one study, it was calculated that 58% of persons between 11 and 13 years of age misunderstand the Miranda warning, as do 33% of 14- and 15-year-olds, but less than 10% of people aged 16 or 17. Rogers (2011) estimated that out of one and a half million juvenile arrests per year, at least 311,000 adolescents are impaired in their ability to understand the Miranda warning they were given and to decide how to act on it. This estimate omitted other factors like educational or intellectual deficits that might further interfere with a defendant's ability to understand his or her legal situation.

Conclusion

The evidence shows that adolescents' cognitive and emotional characteristics are different from those of the adults for whom the criminal justice system is designed. There has been little research on the outcomes for the individual or the community of treating delinquent teenagers as adult offenders compared with treating them less harshly. This important moral question is one that empirical research cannot answer. Ali's parents are somewhat more in line with what is known about child development, but it is not clear whether they and their son are trying to answer different questions. Neither has considered the difficulties teenagers may experience in understanding police and legal procedures.

Critical Thinking

1. In a child development textbook, or in the book by Lewis (1992), find information about the development of the social emotions. Would a sense of guilt or a sense of shame make adolescents more likely to commit a serious crime? Explain your answer.

2. Describe formal operational thought. How would formal operational abilities make a teenager *more* vulnerable than a younger child to social anxiety? Use information from a child development textbook to support your answer.

3. Read the article by Packard (2007). Describe three cognitive or emotional differences between adults and adolescents as described in the article.

4. Discuss the possible relationship between the experience of social anxiety and the tendency to yield to peer pressure, especially in risky or potentially criminal situations.

5. Rogers (2011) uses the term *metaignorance*. What does he mean by this, and how would this cognitive characteristic influence adolescents' decisions about committing crimes or about dealing with the courts after being arrested? Is metaignorance related to formal operational thinking? Explain your answer.

References

Eddy, J. M., Whaley, R. B., & Chamberlain, P. (2004). The prevention of violent behavior by chronic and serious male juvenile offenders: A 2-year follow-up of a randomized clinical trial. *Journal of Emotional and Behavioral Disorders, 12*, 2–8.

Lewis, M. (1992). *Shame: The exposed self.* New York: Free Press.

Liptak, A. (2007, October 17). Lifers as teenagers, now seeking second chance. *New York Times*, pp. A1, A24.

Packard, E. (2007). That teenage feeling. *Monitor on Psychology, 38*(4), 20–22.

Redding, R. E. (2003). The effects of adjudicating and sentencing juveniles as adults. *Youth Violence and Juvenile Justice, 1*, 128–155.

Rogers, R. (2011). Getting it wrong about *Miranda* rights: False beliefs, impaired reasoning, and professional neglect. *American Psychologist, 66*, 728–736.

Claim 56

Adolescence is an emotionally dangerous time when teenagers are likely to attempt or commit suicide.

Fifteen-year-old Elena and her parents were very disturbed by a series of events at Elena's school. A student in the senior class had been found hanged, and the conclusion was that he had committed suicide. The school called in professional grief counselors and had several meetings for students and parents, in which they discussed some symptoms of depression and suicidal thinking and cautioned parents that some imitations of the suicidal act might occur. When Elena's parents discussed the situation later that night, her mother said, "I'm so scared about this. We've always done everything to protect Elena, now we can't do anything about this. I feel so sorry that she's upset about this boy, but I'm even more worried that there might be more deaths—that even Elena might start to think about suicide now that it's been put in her mind. It seems so unfair that teenagers have to be so vulnerable to suicide when they've hardly started to live."

Of course Elena's mother is worried about her daughter, but is she right in thinking that Elena's age group is especially suicidal?

Disturbing as the idea of adolescent suicide is, and important as preventive efforts are, suicide among adolescents is not as common as it is among older people. The National Institutes of Mental Health reported in 2004 that the suicide rate among adolescents 15 to 19 years of age was

8.2 per 100,000 people in the age group. For individuals 20 to 24 years of age, the rate was 12.5 per 100,000. With increasing age, suicide rates increase: The rate for people 65 years and older is 14.3 per 100,000. The highest suicide rate is among non-Hispanic white men 85 years and older, whose rate of 17.8 per 100,000 is more than twice the rate for teenagers (National Institute of Mental Health, n.d.).

The greatest danger of adolescence is accidental injury or death, especially due to motor vehicle accidents. Alcohol consumption before or while driving and failure to use seatbelts are important factors in teenage motor vehicle accidents. In 2002 alone, 5,000 deaths of adolescents 16 to 19 years old were caused by motor vehicle accidents in the United States. Permanent injuries and disabilities may result from nonfatal accidents, too, and many thousands of U.S. teenagers suffer that fate.

The second leading cause of child and adolescent deaths in the United States is not suicide but homicide. However, much discussion has taken place about the possibility of counting some of these deaths as a form of suicide—*victim-precipitated homicide*—in which individuals carry out actions, such as attacks on others, that are in ways almost guaranteed to bring a fatal response from police. An important issue of adolescent suicide is the role played by depression in triggering suicidal thinking and actions (Liang & Eley, 2005). Girls appear to experience more depression after they enter their teens. That girls are much more likely than boys to attempt suicide without actually dying makes it more difficult to understand the connections between depression and suicide. That drug use and eating disorders are also associated with depression complicates the question even further. In addition, both genetic factors and negative life experiences play a part in depression and therefore may also influence suicidal behavior.

About 7% of high school students in the United States attempt suicide per year. Some of those attempts pose little threat to the person's life, but of course they should not be dismissed as meaningless. Suicide attempts can be predictors of later "successful" efforts, and of course even a weak attempt may accidentally cause death, especially among adolescents who self-mutilate by cutting themselves. The understanding that adolescent suicide attempts are somewhat predictable has led to a variety of antisuicide efforts by high schools and parent groups. These interventions often involve grief counseling for students distressed by the death of a classmate and educational efforts to emphasize to teenagers that they should not promise to keep secret a friend's suicidal preoccupation. However, antisuicide work may be more effective when it focuses on individual characteristics that are associated with suicidal thinking and actions.

The most difficult issue in adolescent suicide studies has been whether the use of antidepressant drugs increases the risk of suicide among teenagers. Warnings of such a risk were first published soon after the year 2000, and the

United States Food and Drug Administration (FDA) in 2004 ordered antidepressant drugs to be packaged with cautions about a possible associated risk of suicide. However, some researchers did not agree with the FDA position. They carried out a meta-analysis, a statistical examination combining a large number of separate studies. The result of the meta-analysis showed a statistically significant increase in suicidal thinking related to antidepressant use, but it was a very small increase. It may be that treatment with antidepressants combines a very small detrimental effect with a bigger beneficial effect.

Some researchers are concerned about the effects of the FDA warning. Parents and mental health professionals have become concerned about the effects of antidepressants on teenagers and have hesitated to use the drugs. Meanwhile, suicide rates for teenagers increased in 2004, the year when the FDA warning began. A 14% increase was reported in the United States, and a 49% increase in the Netherlands (Couzin, 2007). However, two points should be kept in mind when considering the importance of these increases. One is that every natural event, including suicidal behavior, shows spontaneous variations that are caused by multiple factors. Even if drug use and other important factors were held constant, there would still be increases in the suicide rate in some years and decreases in others, so it is not possible to conclude that a change in the suicide rate was caused by a single factor, such as the FDA warning. A second important point is that the percentage of variation has different meanings depending on the frequencies of the events. For example, if only one person commits suicide in a year and two do so the next year, the increase in suicide is 100%—but only one additional death. Infrequent events such as adolescent suicide are easily described in confusing ways when percentage increases or decreases are the measure used.

It is important to realize that not every adolescent has an equal probability of suicide. Certain risk factors allow people to identify individuals with a higher probability of suicidal thoughts and actions. In addition to depression, these risk factors include a history of suicidal thinking, previous suicidal acts, and a history of fighting, especially with threats of or the actual use of weapons (Evans, Marte, Betts, & Silliman, 2001; Perkins & Hartless, 2002). Young people with minority sexual orientations (e.g., homosexual, bisexual, or transgendered) have reported more suicidal thinking, planning, and attempts than occur among heterosexual adolescents. One report that looked at a number of studies found that 28% of sexual minority youth had histories of suicidal thinking and actions (Marshal et al., 2011), possibly because of negative social experiences, but only 12% of heterosexual adolescents reported similar histories. In addition, teenagers who perform nonsuicidal self-injury like cutting themselves are a good deal more likely to attempt suicide than those who do not (Wilkinson, Kelvin, Roberts, Dubicka, & Goodyer, 2011).

However, to look at adolescent suicide in a balanced way is not to deny the presence of mental illness in teenagers' lives. Adolescence and early adulthood are times when mental illness is likely to emerge, if an individual is at risk for emotional disturbance. Half of all mental illnesses that will ever be experienced begin before age 14, and 75% before age 24 (Fritz, 2014). These may have devastating effects on lives, whether or not they are associated with suicide.

Conclusion

Suicide rates among teenagers in general are not high compared with rates of other age groups or teenage death rates from other causes. Elena's mother would actually do better to think about other possible dangers to her daughter and to encourage the high school to work on education about accidental deaths. However, if Elena were to become distressed, to come out as having a minority sexual orientation, or to begin to injure herself, chances that she might become suicidal would be a good deal higher.

Critical Thinking

1. How are statistics about suicides and accidental deaths collected? Explain why the most recent reports are from several years in the past.

2. Read the article by Couzin (2007). Describe the drawbacks of the meta-analysis discussed in this section. What are the advantages and disadvantages of using the results of a meta-analysis to make decisions about treating teenagers with antidepressants?

3. What is the meaning in actual numbers of a 14% increase in teenage suicides? What is the meaning in actual numbers of a similar increase in suicides by non-Hispanic white men older than 85 years of age? To answer these questions, you need to know both suicide rates and the number of each group in the U.S. population.

4. What death rate is represented by 5,000 motor vehicle deaths of adolescents 16 to 19 years old? How does this compare with the suicide rate for this age group (or as near an age group as you can find)?

5. Search the Internet to find media productions, such as films and TV programs, that refer to suicide. What age groups do they focus on and how realistic are they about suicide rates in those groups? Is their view of suicide rates any more or less realistic than views of rape or murder rates? Should high school educational programs take into account the beliefs about suicide that students may have acquired from the media? Explain your answer.

References

Couzin, J. (2007). Study questions antidepressant risks. *Science, 316*, 354.

Evans, W. P., Marte, R. M., Betts, S., & Silliman, B. (2001). Adolescent suicide risk and peer-related violent behaviors and victimization. *Journal of Interpersonal Violence, 16*, 1330–1348.

Fritz, G. K. (2014). The financing of integrated care. *Brown University Child and Adolescent Behavior Letter, 30*(7), 8.

Liang, H., & Eley, T. C. (2005). A monozygotic twin differences study of non-shared environmental influence on adolescent depressive symptoms. *Child Development, 76*, 1247–1260.

Marshal, M. P., Dietz, L. J., Friedman, M. S., Stall, R., Smith, H. A., McGinley, J., et al. (2011). Suicidality and depression disparities between sexual minority and heterosexual youth: A meta-analytic review. *Journal of Adolescent Health, 49*, 115–123.

National Institute of Mental Healtrh (n.d.). 1999-2007 trends in suicide rate. Retrieved from www.nimh.nih.gov/health/statistics/suicide/index.shtml

Perkins, D. F., & Hartless, G. (2002). An ecological risk-factor examination of suicide ideation and behavior of adolescents. *Journal of Adolescent Research, 17*, 3–26.

Wilkinson, P., Kelvin, R., Roberts, C., Dubicka, B., & Goodyer, I. (2011). Clinical and psychosocial predictors of suicide attempts and nonsuicidal self-injury in the Adolescent Depression Antidepressants and Psychotherapy Trial (ADAPT). *American Journal of Psychiatry, 168*, 495–501.

Claim 57

Punishment is an effective way to change children's and adolescents' undesirable behaviors.

Fifteen-year-old Lance was a high school freshman and thought a book assigned for his English class was boring. He decided to not read the book and not do any of the related assignments. When his mother asked about his English homework, he told her he had already done it—but she went to a parent-teacher conference and found out differently. When Lance's father came home from a business trip, he soon heard the story and decided that Lance must be punished. His father yelled at Lance for quite a long time, and then grounded him for a week, so he missed his favorite cousin's big birthday party. What's more, when the report cards came out, Lance had a D in English, which did not please him. During the next marking period, another book was assigned that bored Lance, and he did exactly the same as before. His father decided that because the punishment Lance had received had not worked, a more severe punishment would need to be given.

Was Lance's father right in thinking that a more intense punishment would work when a milder one had not?

The use of punishment has been the subject of years of argument among parents, teachers, and mental health professionals. As is the case for many ongoing disagreements, part of the problem is the definition of the term *punishment*. When this word is used in an unspecified way, neither physical discomfort nor any disagreeable nonphysical experience is particularly implied. The term *punishment* simply refers to the infliction of an experience that the recipient will find undesirable, simultaneous with or following an action of the punished person, and with the intention on the part of the punisher to prevent the unwanted behavior from occurring again. (Note that there is a difference between punishment and the negative reinforcement described by B. F. Skinner. *Negative reinforcement* refers to the removal of an unpleasant stimulus when a desired behavior occurs, to reinforce the desired behavior; it has no direct effect on unwanted behaviors.)

Punishments can range from severe physical pain or even death to social disapproval or deprivation of treats, such as dessert or permission to go to the movies. Some experiences that are intended as punishment—for example, physical pain—may occur in different circumstances, such as sports or medical treatment, and when they occur in those cases they are not considered to be punishment. The essence of punishment lies in the intention with which it is given, as well as in its timing with or following an unwanted action.

Human beings have used punishment for many centuries in efforts to change adult behavior, but little evidence supports its effectiveness. Research on children and adolescents suggests that punishment immediately after an undesirable behavior can stop the behavior in the short term, but physical punishment is associated with, at least, later aggressive behavior by the punished child. Nevertheless, the use of physical punishment remains common (McClure & May, 2008).

Of course, studies of punishment's effects on children or adolescents cannot ethically or practically be conducted as experiments. Instead, researchers depend on quasi-experimental studies that compare outcomes when children are punished to those when they are not. As a result, outcomes of research are difficult to interpret and may be affected by confounding variables. These factors accompany the use of punishment and may cause other events that influence a child's later behavior. For example, parental attitudes might determine both decisions about punishment and other child-rearing decisions, such as those about education. The extensive body of research on child and adolescent punishment has not managed to solve the problem of confounding variables.

Some suggestions about punishment's effect on children may be derived from studies on whether animals learn from punishment. Animal studies can be conducted according to the rules about experiments, so they are much less affected by confounding variables. Although it may not be completely reasonable to try to generalize from animal studies to young human beings, it is possible to implement animal studies that seem to parallel events in human lives. One study focused on a rather practical problem that closely resembles some situations in the correction of children's behavior: how to teach puppies not to eat forbidden objects. The researcher compared two groups of puppies. The puppies in each group received a smack with a rolled-up newspaper if they ate a food they really liked, but they did not receive a smack if they ate a less-preferred food. The difference between the two groups was that puppies in one group were smacked after eating the food, according to the conventional punishment pattern. The other puppies were smacked as they approached the food and prepared to eat it but had not actually chewed or swallowed any food. Later, all of the puppies were tested for their resistance to temptation by being left alone in a room with the favorite food. The puppies that had been punished after eating had poor resistance to temptation and often ate the favorite food but displayed guilt and cringed or hid afterward. Those who had been smacked as they approached the food displayed good resistance to temptation on the whole and did not usually eat even when alone with their favorite food; however, if they gave in and ate, they showed little guilt or fear afterward (research discussed by Walters & Demkow, 1962).

In generalizing from puppies to humans, this study suggests that the most effective punishment is a type that begins when a child or adolescent is starting to do something undesirable. Actually, parents of very young children often use exactly this approach to train their children to stay away from dangers such as a hot stove or an electrical outlet. Later, when older children do things that are annoying or rude but not dangerous, parents are more likely to save punishment until after the act has occurred. Observing these events in everyday life, people can note that most careful parents have no trouble teaching a child not to touch the electrical outlet, but jumping up and down on the sofa is much more difficult to stop, no matter how often it is followed by slightly delayed punishment.

It seems that timing is of the essence in making punishment effective. But timing is hard to control if the punishment used is not a physical one. Being grounded for a week is a punishment that does not begin until the child wants to go out, and much of the punishment is delayed until days after the offense. Parents in the United States use less physical punishment as children become older (in fact, it is considered abusive to use physical punishment with adolescents), so it becomes increasingly difficult for parents to control the timing of the punishment and keep it effective.

Consistency of punishment is also known to be an important factor in effectiveness. As parents turn to nonphysical punishments, such as deprivation of privileges, they also become less likely to follow through on the punishment they decreed. A couple of swats on the bottom are quickly administered and may, or may not, be quickly forgotten by both parties. A week's grounding of a resentful adolescent can take a great deal of determination for a parent to carry out, and after a day or so the offense may be forgiven or even forgotten. These punishments can become empty threats because they are rarely or never completely carried out and cannot be expected to be effective in changing behavior.

Finally, the punishable offenses of older children and adolescents are usually fairly complex. Not doing homework over a period of time involves many instances of failing to do what is required and doing something less appropriate instead. It would be very difficult for a parent to observe a child so closely that a punishment began whenever an act of not doing homework was about to commence. If the punishment were to be given after the whole chain of events is complete, it would be difficult to know which action is being punished. It is not nearly as easy to use punishment effectively as some people may think. It appears, too, that some types of punishment can backfire; for example, in one study of punishment and reinforcement of juvenile offenders, those who were punished had an increase in self-esteem; those who were not punished did not show an increase in self-esteem (Tsytsarev, Manger, & Lodrini, 2000).

Conclusion

Punishment is not an effective way to change behavior unless it is handled with great care, and this is by no means easy to do, especially with respect to the complex behaviors of adolescents. Lance's father will probably find that increasing the severity of the punishment does not have much effect, except to make everyone in the family angrier than they already are.

Critical Thinking

1. Does this section argue for physical punishment as a good choice for parents of children and adolescents? Explain your answer.

2. In a child development textbook, find definitions of *child abuse*. How are these definitions relevant to the use of physical punishment for adolescents? Explain your answer. How may thinking about this issue involve overgeneralization?

3. Read the article by Walters and Demkow (1962). Is it reasonable to generalize from the puppy study described in this section to the use of punishment with school-age children? In what significant ways are

(Continued)

(Continued)

children and adolescents different from puppies? Be sure to comment on differences in cognitive abilities, such as theory of mind.

4. Why do you think the puppies that were punished after eating showed poor resistance to temptation? Did they experience positive reinforcement as well as punishment for their actions? Are there similar situations experienced by adolescents? Explain your answer.

5. Name two reasons that might cause parents to continue to use punishment even though it has proved ineffective in changing adolescents' behavior. Consider a problem of critical thinking as one of your explanations.

References

McClure, T. E., & May, D. C. (2008). Dealing with misbehavior at schools in Kentucky: Theoretical and contextual predictors of use of corporal punishment. *Youth and Society, 39*, 406–429.

Tsytsarev, S., Manger, J., & Lodrini, D. (2000). The use of reinforcement and punishment on incarcerated and probated substance-abusing juvenile offenders. *International Journal of Offender Therapy and Comparative Criminology, 44*, 22–32.

Walters, R. H., & Demkow, L. (1962). Timing of punishment as a determinant of response inhibition. *Child Development, 34*, 207–214.

Claim 58

Children are reaching puberty earlier with each generation.

Becca and Rich were the parents of 7-year-old Megan, who was one of the tallest children in her second-grade class. Even though Becca and Rich were tall, they worried because Megan's height seemed so far above the average. Becca had read that rapid growth in height could mean that a child was approaching puberty, and she was concerned that her child might soon be sexually mature. Their next-door neighbor sympathized with Becca's worries but said, "Yes, she might be getting close to puberty. I read that every generation is becoming sexually mature at an earlier age. It's happening 5 or 6 years earlier than it did 150 years ago. What's going to happen—are we going to have 2-year-olds who need to shave?"

Was Becca right to think that Megan's height meant early puberty? And was the neighbor right in thinking that puberty would continue to be earlier with each succeeding generation?

Changes in physical growth and development patterns over time are referred to as the *secular trend*—*secular* meaning something that occurs over a period of time, not something that opposes religious belief. The secular trend in growth and maturation is a well-established phenomenon of childhood and adolescent growth. During the last 150 years, children in Europe and North America have been taller and heavier at specific ages than their parents' generation was at the same ages. They have also reached sexual maturity at earlier ages than the immediately previous generations.

The idea of children growing more rapidly is a rather scary one. The novelist H. G. Wells wrote a science fiction story about a baby food that caused gigantic growth and the awful consequences of great size and strength governed only by infantile minds. The secular trend worries people, who wonder whether there will be any end to the "progress." Of course, it is also concerning to think about sexually mature bodies with very childish minds.

Some facts about the secular trend can put these anxieties into perspective. The first fact is that changes in growth rates are flattening, with smaller changes during at least the last 20 years. Although there are large differences between the present average height of 5-year-olds in the United States and the average height of 5-year-olds in 1900, the height difference between 5-year-olds in 1970 and 5-year-olds in 2000 was small.

A second fact has to do with historical information about growth, especially about puberty. Although keeping statistics about growth rates is a modern practice, historical material tells something about the timing of sexual maturation. For example, the Old Testament set the minimum marriage age at 14 years for boys and 12 years for girls, figures very similar to present average ages at puberty. It does not seem likely that the Old Testament authorities would have wanted marriages to take place 3 or 4 years before sexual relations were possible. To look at a more recent time, Shakespeare depicted Juliet as wanting to marry Romeo when she was not yet 14 years old—and her father said, "Younger than she are happy mothers made" (although her mother did not approve of this view). Shakespeare may have been wrong, but he obviously felt it was not unusual for a 13-year-old girl to have reached puberty.

Do these historical facts contradict the evidence for the recent secular trend? No, that evidence is well established. In the 19th and early 20th centuries in Europe and North America, children grew more slowly and reached puberty later than they do presently—and, apparently, than they had in previous centuries. Growth rates were lower during the 19th century compared to what they were at other times. A number of factors may have been responsible for the reduction. The Industrial Revolution, with long hours of hard work for children as well as adults, is one factor. Another is 19th-century life in cities and industrial centers, with little access to healthy food or clean water. City life at that time also involved high rates of contagious disease because people lived in crowded conditions that made disease communication easy. These risk factors are better controlled in modern times, so general health has improved and growth rates have returned to the human average.

Sexual maturation is considered to occur when a girl experiences *menarche* (the first menstruation of her life) or when a boy begins to produce viable sperm. Obviously, a girl's menarche is much easier to confirm than a boy's maturation. But both boys and girls experience detectable maturational changes before any final step occurs, so it is possible to predict maturation and to collect relevant information before puberty. These maturational changes are on a timetable similar to that of sexual maturation itself, so they provide some important information about the secular trend. A system for measurement of breast and testicle development was developed years ago by J. M. Tanner and is used for research on sexual development.

Surprisingly, the secular trend in these early maturational steps does not seem to be exactly the same as that for menarche. This fact was revealed in studies of *precocious puberty*, the abnormally early occurrence of sexual maturation. Until recently, precocious puberty was defined as involving the onset of early stages (previous to menarche or sperm viability) before 8 years of age for girls and before 9 years of age for boys.

Recent research shows that although the average age at menarche has not changed for some years, some of the preliminary maturational steps occur earlier than they did in the known past. The cut-off points—ages that mark the divide between precocious puberty and normal development—are now considered to be 7.7 years for girls and about the same for boys. These cut-off points are established by finding the 3rd percentile for the chronological age when development occurs for a large sample of children. Thus, only 3% of children show a particular level of sexual development at an earlier age than 7.7 years, and 97% do not show that level until they are older (Parent et al., 2005). Precocious puberty—very early sexual maturation—should be considered as more than a socially awkward event because it is possible for endocrine or neurological problems to cause this developmental event (Nield, Cakan, & Kamat, 2007).

Although growth in height is a predictor of a child's puberty schedule, an increase in fat and relative fat levels are also useful predictors for girls. Girls with higher fat levels are likely to experience menarche earlier (Lin-Su, Vogiatzi, & New, 2002).

Conclusion

Although growth in height is quicker and puberty is considerably earlier today than it was 150 years ago, major changes in the pattern of development seem to have come to a stop, and it seems that the 19th century was a time of slowed growth and sexual maturation caused by poor health conditions rather than the present time being a period of unusually fast growth. However, some of the early steps in sexual maturation seem to be occurring a bit earlier than they did 40 or 50 years ago. In Megan's case, her unusual height for her age may be inherited from her tall parents and not evidence of unusually early development, but if her parents are concerned, they can ask for a medical examination. Measurements of her skeletal development can show whether her development is in the normal range for her chronological age.

Critical Thinking

1. Describe the secular trend for girls' sexual maturation. When did the biggest changes in timing occur? Use information from a child development textbook to support your answer.

2. Read about the onset of puberty in a child development textbook. Explain why girls who grow more rapidly also reach menarche earlier. (The explanation for boys is similar but more complicated.)

3. Look at the work of J. M. Tanner (1989), who developed a system for evaluating the early stages of sexual maturation. What might be some practical and ethical problems of conducting research on this topic? Is it possible that such problems have caused inaccurate measurements of the developmental steps used in defining precocious puberty? Explain your answer.

4. A graph in the article by Parent et al. (2005) shows a comparison of ages at menarche for girls born in the United States and Europe, girls adopted from their own countries to the United States and Europe, and girls growing up in the countries where the adoptees were born. What differences between these groups do you see? What factors might explain the differences? (The article offers one explanation.)

5. The cut-off point for abnormal precocious puberty is the 3rd percentile. Of two children who are very similar in development, can one be considered developmentally normal and the other developmentally abnormal? Explain your answer.

References

Lin-Su, K., Vogiatzi, M. G., & New, M. I. (2002). Body mass index and age at menarche in an adolescent clinic population. *Clinical Pediatrics, 41*, 501–507.

Nield, L. S., Cakan, N., & Kamat, D. (2007). A practical approach to precocious puberty. *Clinical Pediatrics, 46*, 299–306.

Parent, A. S., Rasier, G., Gerard, A., Heger, S., Roth, C., Mastronardi, C. . . . Bourguignon, J.-P. (2005). Early onset of puberty: Tracking genetic and environmental factors. *Hormone Research, 64*(Suppl. 2), 41–47.

Tanner, J. M. (1989). *Fetus into man*. Cambridge, MA: Harvard University Press.

Claim 59

Psychological treatments like "conversion therapy" can change a person's same-sex orientation to a heterosexual orientation.

Alan was concerned about his 14-year-old son, Aaron. Aaron's interests had always been what his father thought of as "girly," and now that he was in his teens he was attracting the attention of older boys who seemed to identify as gay. Alan was very uncomfortable with this situation. He was genuinely worried about the prospect of a homosexual life for his son. He felt that such a life would be dangerous in terms of sexually transmitted disease as well as because of possible "gay-bashing" attackers. He also felt that people in same-sex relationships were likely to miss some aspects of community and family life that he thought very valuable. In addition, Alan's religious beliefs clearly categorized same-sex attraction and sexual activity as sinful, which gave him real concerns for his son's spiritual future. When a friend told Alan about the practice of "conversion" or "reparative" therapy, he began to think that such treatment might be the best thing he could do for Aaron.

Was Alan right in thinking that Aaron's sexual orientation could be altered by a psychological treatment like conversion therapy?

Before discussing this claim, some background needs to be provided. First, you need to understand that homosexuality was at one time "officially" considered to be a mental illness, as described in the American Psychiatric Association's *Diagnostic and Statistical Manual of Mental Disorders*. By 1980, however, sexual orientation was listed as a psychiatric concern only when it was "ego-dystonic" or uncomfortable with respect to an individual's perception of himself. In reports from task forces, the American Psychological Association has stated that sexual orientation, in itself, is not a mental health problem and that it is unethical for psychologists to treat it as if it were (APA Task Force, 2009).

Most recently, the American Psychological Association has asserted that there is "no research demonstrating that providing SOCE [sexual orientation change efforts] to children or adolescents has an impact on adult sexual orientation. The few studies of children with gender identity disorder found no evidence that psychotherapy provided to those children had an impact on adult sexual orientation. There is currently no evidence that teaching or reinforcing stereotyped gender-normative behavior in childhood or adolescence can alter sexual orientation. We have concerns that such interventions may increase self-stigma and minority stress and ultimately increase the stress of children and adolescents" (APA Task Force, 2009, p. 4).

An additional background fact is that calling a treatment a "therapy" does not, in itself, mean that it is beneficial. Lilienfeld (2007) pointed to the possible harm done by some well-intentioned treatment methods and referred to these as "potentially harmful treatments" (PHTs). The idea of the PHT reminds us that it is not enough to ask whether a treatment like conversion therapy is or is not effective; we also need to ask whether it may be harmful. This is a concern about psychotherapies for people of any age, but it is especially important when we are talking about children and adolescents. Young therapy clients are vulnerable because of their need for continuing healthy development and also because they usually are not allowed to make their own decisions about their treatment. Attempts to alter sexual orientation have included the use of electric shock and other less dangerous but painful and frightening physical intrusions (Clair, 2013; Cohen, 2007).

There is little systematic research on the effect of conversion therapy on sexual orientation; certainly, there are none of the randomized controlled trials that are considered the "gold standard" for evidence-based therapies. There are many anecdotal reports of distress caused by the treatment. One study (Flentje, Heck, & Cochran, 2014) interviewed 38 "ex-ex-gay" people—individuals who had considered themselves "cured" of their same-sex orientation but then had realized that they continued to feel attracted to people of the same sex. These adult participants were asked about both short- and long-term helpful and harmful effects of conversion therapy. Some reported that the therapy was helpful in terms of their understanding that their same-sex orientation was not something to be "overcome." A few stated that they met a first gay partner or lover as a result of the treatment. Others reported harmful effects: "It was fear-inducing—horrible. Almost like an exorcism performed on me. I had panic attacks and anxiety." "It . . . led me to start blaming my parents for things they were not responsible for." "In spite of the therapist's efforts, my depression grew worse under his care rather than growing better. I began cutting, secured a gun license in my state, and almost killed myself" (Flentje et al., 2014, pp. 1258–1259).

In the absence of systematic evidence of benefits or harm from conversion therapy, it can be helpful to consider whether the treatment is plausible—that is, does it make sense in terms of other things we know about the development of sexuality? Treatment efforts that use reward or punishment to try to change sexual orientation are implausible with respect to the evidence that sexual orientation is probably primarily genetically determined rather than strongly influenced by experience (Dawood, Bailey, & Martin, 2009). Some authors, like Cohen (2007), attribute same-sex attractions to "hetero-emotional wounds" stemming from experiences with dominating mothers and disengaged fathers, which leave boys seeking other males who will supply the missing paternal love. To remedy these problems, Cohen advises a method that he believes intensifies the attachment relationship with the father; this treatment involves "holding therapy" as formulated by the psychiatrist Martha Welch (1989), in which the father embraces the son face-to-face and will not release him for an hour or more. There is no evidence that homosexuality is related to attachment, or that holding affects attachment, or that holding influences same-sex orientations.

Conversion therapy is almost unique among psychotherapies in that mental health professionals have been prohibited by law from using it for minors in two states, California and New Jersey (see Clair, 2013). The treatment is not prohibited for adults, and members of the clergy can legally do it.

When these legislative prohibitions were under consideration and hearings were held to discuss evidence for and against allowing the treatment, it was notable that most of the testimony turned on two kinds of personal experiences and beliefs. One kind came from witnesses with same-sex orientations, who told of their distress as they underwent conversion therapy and their concern that their families could not accept them as they were. The other type of testimony came from members of religious bodies that regard homosexuality as a sinful condition that needs to be corrected by any means possible. Only a few witnesses testified about the lack of evidence to support the effectiveness of conversion therapy, about its potential for harm to clients, or about its implausibility with respect to established understanding of child development. The legal prohibition of conversion therapy probably has more to do with the political power of persons with same-sex orientations and their friends and families than it does with systematic research evidence.

Conclusion

If Alan and Aaron live in California or New Jersey, it is illegal for Aaron to be given conversion therapy by a mental health professional as long as he is a minor. It would be possible for Alan to seek a member of the clergy to do this treatment, but it seems likely that the therapy would be frightening and uncomfortable for Aaron and would not culminate in any change in his adult sexual orientation. If either Alan or Aaron is unhappy with the situation, it is possible for them to seek affirmative treatment that will help them come to terms with each other and with the reality of Aaron's apparent sexual orientation (APA Task Force, 2009).

Critical Thinking

1. Is it valid to assume that every person who has undergone conversion therapy had harmful effects like those described in the Flentje et al. (2014) study? Why or why not?

2. As of the writing of this book, New York and Maryland were also considering legislation to ban conversion therapy for minors. Use the Internet to find whether those and other states have now passed such legislation and what arguments were used for or against it. The paper by Clair (2013) will give some idea of the kinds of reasoning that may be used.

3. What penalties did the California "conversion therapy" legislation prescribe for mental health professionals who break the law?

4. Which of the problems of critical thinking discussed in the Introduction to this book seem to be involved in the assumption that sexual orientation is influenced by attachment? Explain your answer.

5. Given all the resources you would need, how would you test the hypothesis that dominating fathers and disengaged mothers cause same-sex orientation? Would this hypothesis predict the same outcomes for males and for females?

References

American Psychiatric Association. (1980). *Diagnostic and statistical manual of mental disorders* (3rd ed.). Washington, DC: Author.

APA Task Force on Appropriate Therapeutic Responses to Sexual Orientation. (2009). *Report of the Task Force on Appropriate Therapeutic Responses to Sexual Orientation.* Washington, DC: Author. Available at www.apa.org/pi/lgbt/resources/therapeutic-response.pdf.

Clair, N. (2013). Chapter 835: "Gay conversion therapy" ban: Protecting children or infringing rights? *McGeorge Law Review, 44*(3), 550–558.

Cohen, R. (2007). *Coming out straight.* Winchester, VA: Oak Hill Press.

Dawood, K., Bailey, J. M., & Martin, N. G. (2009). Genetic and environmental influences on sexual orientation. In Y.-K. Kim (Ed.), *Handbook of behavior genetics* (pp. 269–279). New York: Springer.

Flentje, A., Heck, N. C., & Cochran, B. N. (2014). Experiences of ex-ex-gay individuals in sexual reorientation therapy: Reasons for seeking treatment, perceived helpfulness and harmfulness of treatment, and post-treatment identification. *Journal of Homosexuality, 61*(9), 1242–1268.

Lilienfeld, S. O. (2007). Psychological treatments that cause harm. *Perspectives on Psychological Science, 2,* 53–70.

Welch, M. (1989). *Holding time.* New York: Fireside.

Afterthoughts

Some Ideas to Take
Into Your Future

Are you now thoroughly prepared to assess all claims about child development? Even if you have carefully worked through every question and example in this book, the answer, of course, is no. There are a number of reasons why such assessments are difficult and will remain difficult throughout your life. One important issue is that the study of child development is full of unanswered questions; the more professionals learn about it through research, the more new questions arise. The existence of unanswered questions explains why you are likely to find some poorly supported claims in any child development textbook, even though its author has struggled to report the best evidence about the topics. In fact, child development has been a topic of scientific study for a rather short time (Cahan, 2007).

Another reason for the difficulty is that claims can have personal meaning for readers. Many claims involve emotional experiences and personal memories. Most of them are in some way related to moral obligations—how you or others ought to behave toward children and how children should behave toward others. Quite a few claims have a combination of these factors, and they resonate with readers about how their parents treated them (and how they treat their own children, if they have any). The most difficult claims to assess may be those that have to do with what one might call *righteousness*. Many claims about parenting, education, and criminal justice fall into this category.

Assessment of claims about child development also share some problems with analysis of other scientific claims. Readers cannot directly know or evaluate much of the evidence for any of these claims, so they fall back on other approaches in which critical thinking is difficult. One discussion of this issue made the following point:

> Few of us are qualified to assess claims about the merits of string theory, the role of mercury in the etiology of autism, or the existence of repressed memories. So rather than evaluating the asserted claim itself, we instead evaluate the claim's source. If the source is deemed trustworthy, people will believe the claim, often without really understanding it. . . . Their belief is not necessarily rooted in an appreciation of the evidence and arguments. Rather . . . [they accept] this information because they trust the people who say it is true. (Bloom & Weisberg, 2007, p. 997)

This tendency can create problems both for your own critical thinking and your ability to change other people's beliefs.

Changing Assumptions and Future Possibilities

Earlier parts of this book mentioned certain assumptions made in the study of child development—for example, that developmentally appropriate practice is an important consideration and that transactional processes are important to development. Though most of these assumptions are still present, professionals need to realize that new assumptions are likely to be added in the future. For example, research and theory in child development are increasingly oriented toward *dynamic systems theory*, a way of thinking that emphasizes the importance of many variables that work together to produce an outcome. An essential aspect of dynamic systems theory is the assumption that in some cases, small changes in relevant variables can produce a major outcome change, and in other cases, large variations in causal factors may create little or no change in outcome. Dynamic systems theory, like the transactional process approach, emphasizes the idea that development may be based on small changes that accumulate gradually over time (Spencer, Clearfield, Corbetta, Ulrich, Buchanan, & Schöner, 2006).

Using Critical Thinking About Child Development Claims: Personal and Professional Issues

There are real personal advantages for those who have learned to assess claims about child development. Critical thinking about child development can be helpful in life decisions, enabling people to make some appropriate choices for themselves and their families. The ability to assess claims can protect people against confused or even fraudulent persons who want to "sell" their practices or ideas. It can be very gratifying to learn how to assess claims and to practice what one has learned. Unfortunately, this achievement may not mean that one will win more arguments! On the contrary, using critical thinking about common beliefs can be very offensive to opponents who are committed to their unexamined beliefs. Those people can become even more entrenched in their belief system as they hear it assessed critically. This may be the case particularly when there is a connection between religious or political ideology and the claim in question—then the proponent of the belief feels that analysis of the claim attacks him or her at a serious level. Few people are actually objective about popular child development claims, and it is possible that no one is totally objective about all of them.

In addition to the personal advantages of thinking critically about child development beliefs, some related issues are of importance to the entire community, such as those dealing with the concept of *evidence-based practice*. In the mid-1990s, the medical profession began to emphasize the idea of an evidence basis for medicine. Physicians and surgeons felt it was time to reject the traditional reliance on authority and accepted methods and to seek empirical evidence that showed whether or not a practice was both safe and effective. Psychologists and other members of the helping professions soon followed this path and began to demand that interventions be chosen on the basis of research that supported their appropriateness.

The concept of evidence-based practice is now commonly used in education, parent training, and child and family mental health work. Members of these disciplines agree that methods should be chosen on the basis of evidence of their safety and effectiveness. However, this agreement is not as simple or as complete as it might appear to be. Some educators and mental health professionals reject the idea of evidence based on research. Others believe that choices of evidence-based practices should include not only empirical research evidence but also the clinical experience of the professional and the values of the child's family. These factors—experience and values—need to be assessed through critical thinking. The implication that evidence-based practice is objective and "scientific" cannot be accepted unquestioningly when these subjective factors are included.

There is still another problem that demands critical thinking about evidence-based practices. There is really no good general definition of the evidence needed to make a practice legitimately evidence based. What research evidence shows an intervention to be safe? What shows it to be effective? How are these two terms defined? None of these questions has received an adequate answer, so it remains the task of teachers, principals, child care providers, parents, social workers, and mental health professionals to apply their critical thinking abilities when they choose educational programs, discipline techniques, or mental health interventions.

The Problem of Woozles

As Linda Nielsen (2014) and others have pointed out, it's very possible for what appears to be a valid claim about child development to be a "woozle." Woozles are ideas that are based on little evidence, but they owe their acceptance simply to repeated statements about them. They are like their namesakes, the woozles identified by Winnie-the-Pooh and his friends, who see their own footprints and follow them around and around, creating more footprints and believing that they are tracking an ever-larger group of strange animals. When people read about the advantages of high self-esteem or the dangers of overnight visits to an estranged parent often enough, they tend to believe these things are true for no real reason except that the ideas have become familiar and recognizable. They identify the "tracks" of the ideas as indicating the presence of important woozles—who may or may not exist.

Many child development woozles are related to mental health and delinquent or criminal behavior. For example, some Internet sources stress the idea of a "Primal Wound" suffered by all adopted children when they are separated from their biological mothers that is a cause of life-long distress, depression, and anxiety (Verrier, 1993, 2014). The Primal Wound idea has no support in empirical evidence and seems to have achieved its woozle position through repeated claims and references. (This is, of course, not to deny that adopted individuals may have various reasons for emotional distress, just as nonadopted people do.) Nevertheless, in at least one recent case, a threatened lawsuit has included references to the Primal Wound as a reason for allowing a biological mother access to a child adopted years ago by another family.

Similarly, Internet and other sources—including print and TV journalists—have referred to a woozle version of Reactive Attachment Disorder. This is a genuine diagnosis described in DSM-5, but it has become "woozled" in the sense that sources provide a completely different list of symptoms from the conventional version, including scary symptoms like "fascination with blood and gore" that have nothing to do with the actual disorder ("Parenting Children & Teens with Reactive Attachment Disorder," n.d.). These sources also predict that children with Reactive Attachment Disorder will grow up to be serial killers unless they are treated in special ways. Like the Primal Wound, the Reactive Attachment Disorder woozle has appeared in the legal arena in the form of a "RAD defense," arguing that a parent may have been forced to harm or kill a child because Reactive Attachment Disorder made the child so dangerous.

There are many other woozles, but I will mention just one more. This is the belief that "psychomotor patterning," or specific movements of a child's body and limbs by various methods, can cure the effects of traumatic brain injuries, cerebral palsy, or even autism. This form of treatment has given rise to similar methods like *qi gong* (the Chinese exercise method) for children, horseback-riding therapy, and "sensory rooms" in which flashing lights and repeated sounds and movements are expected to treat serious disorders. Although some of these techniques can stretch muscles and improve physical movement control, there is no evidence that they can treat mental, behavioral, or emotional problems. However, because some of these techniques, especially "equine therapy," have been mentioned so often, it's common for them to be accepted and approved by the public.

Critical thinking, and careful reading for evidence, is the key to avoiding the "woozle trap" of accepting ideas just because you've heard of them often.

The End for Now—But Don't Get Uncritical!

In conclusion, you may want to keep in practice by pursuing two more questions with your critical thinking skills. First, consider the child development textbook you have been using. What were some topics that were presented with little or no research evidence for the claims made? And, second, what kind of research evidence would you want to require as support for the effectiveness of, say, a child care program or a suicide-prevention plan for adolescents? You may not feel prepared to answer these questions right now, but keep them in mind as you pursue your studies and work at higher levels—you will find these matters simpler with more practice and more information.

Critical thinking about child development issues like these is hard work. But don't forget that your critical thinking skills can make a difference in your life—and in what you can give to your community. Thinking critically is worth the trouble.

References

Bloom, P., & Weisberg, D. S. (2007). Childhood origins of adult resistance to science. *Science, 316,* 996–997.

Cahan, E. D. (2007). The child as scientific object. *Science, 316,* 835.

Nielsen, L. (2014). Woozles: Their role in custody law reform, parenting plans, and family court. *Psychology, Public Policy, and Law, 20*(2), 164–180.

"Parenting children & teens with Reactive Attachment Disorder." (n.d.). Available at www.reactiveattachment-disorder.com.

Spencer, J. P., Clearfield, M., Corbetta, D., Ulrich, B., Buchanan, P., & Schöner, G. (2006). Moving toward a grand theory of development: In memory of Esther Thelen. *Child Development, 77,* 1521–1538.

Verrier, N. (1993). *The primal wound.* Lafayette, CA: Author.

Verrier, N. (2014). *The primal wound.* Available at www.nancyverrier.com/the-primal-wound/.

Index